COMPARATIVE RELIGIOUS ETHICS

COMPARATIVE
RELIGIOUS ETHICS

David Little

Sumner B. Twiss

1817

Published in San Francisco by

HARPER & ROW, PUBLISHERS

New York, Hagerstown, San Francisco, London

Acknowledgment is made for permission to quote from the following books: H.L.A. Hart, *The Concept of Law*, © Oxford University Press 1961, used by permission of Oxford University Press; *Dialogues of the Buddha*, vol. 3, Pali Text Society: 1920; *Book of Discipline*, vol. 1, Pali Text Society: 1970; *Sutta-Nipata*, vol. 10 in Sacred Books of the East, Motilal Banarsidass: 1965.

Portions of this book originally appeared in somewhat different form as "Basic Terms in the Study of Religious Ethics," Copyright © 1973 by David Little and Sumner B. Twiss, Jr., from *Religion and Morality*, Gene Outka and John P. Reeder, Jr., eds., Garden City, N.Y.: Doubleday & Co., Anchor Books.

FIRST EDITION

Designed by Jim Mennick

Library of Congress Cataloging in Publication Data

Little, David.
  COMPARATIVE RELIGIOUS ETHICS.

  Bibliography
  Includes index.
  1. Religious ethics—Comparative studies.
I. Twiss, Sumner B., joint author. II Title.
BJ1188.L57 1978   291.5   76-10003
ISBN 0-06-065254-3

78 79 80 81 82 10 9 8 7 6 5 4 3 2 1

Contents

Preface

Over the years, scholars with four different objectives have contributed to the comparative study of religious ethics. Because of these disparate concerns, it would be hard to speak of a unified field of study. Some scholars have been apologists, arguing for the superiority of one or another religious or philosophical position. Some have been grand theorists, like Edward Westermarck or L. T. Hobhouse, who, along with recommending a particular normative position, have tried to provide a comprehensive account of "the origin and development" of practical beliefs. Still others, like Max Weber, Emile Durkheim, and Bronislaw Malinowski, along with more contemporary anthropologists, have offered social scientific accounts of religious and moral phenomena in a comparative mode. Finally, certain philosophers, like Alexander MacBeath and John Ladd, have attended to the processes of practical reasoning in different cultural settings.

Our study ought to be seen in relation to the third, and especially to the fourth, approaches. To the extent we are indebted to the social scientific tradition, it is with Max Weber, and with his way of trying to understand the "logical relations or the internal structure of cultural values," that we identify ourselves. We have found contemporary philosophical work useful in increasing our capacity to understand and compare religious and moral beliefs in different cultures.

This book has been a long time in gestation. The ideas began to develop when the two authors were associated at Yale in the late 1960s. David Little formulated a preliminary approach to the comparative study of religious ethics (1970), and S. B. Twiss carried some of the notions forward in seminar papers, and in his dissertation (1974). The two authors collaborated on a trial article (1973), parts of which have been retained here. The chapters of the final version have been worked over by both authors, even though primary responsibility for original drafting was divided between them.

Certain people have supplied invaluable assistance in reading portions of the book at various stages, and in providing criticism and encouragement. Professors Wendell S. Dietrich, John P. Reeder, Jr., and Jacob Neusner, of the Department of Religious Studies at Brown University, were particularly helpful. We also acknowledge the interest and comments of Professors Alan Fuchs of the Department of Philosophy at the College of William and Mary, Donald Evans of the Department of Philosophy at the University of Toronto, and John H. Whittaker of the Department of Religious Studies at the University of Virginia. In addition, certain students in the graduate programs at the University of Virginia and at Brown University have, in the past several years, made stimulating contributions to the ideas developed in this book: Robert Brewbaker, Michael Duffey, John Feldman, Barbara Hall, and Edmund Santurri. We also wish to thank Thomas Kennedy of the University of Virginia for compiling the index.

Professors George and Jane Webb of the Departments of Physics and Humanities at Christopher Newport College have been singularly helpful and supportive, not only in responding to portions of the manuscript, but in putting the general approach to work in their own imaginative ways.

Professor Harvey B. Aronson of the Department of Religious Studies at the University of Virginia was conscientious in providing help and criticism on the chapter on Theravada Buddhism. An expert in the Theravadin tradition, he drew up extensive and painstaking assessments of early drafts of the chapter, and took hours of his time to discuss central points. We also acknowledge the influence of his dissertation (1975) on our conclusions about the Theravadin tradition.

We wish to thank especially our editor, John Shopp, for the care, wisdom, and patience with which he goaded and guided us in bringing this volume, at long last, to publication.

The authors bear full responsibility for all use made of the generous suggestions given to them by these and other people.

DAVID LITTLE
S. B. TWISS

Charlottesville, Virginia
Providence, Rhode Island

REFERENCES

LITTLE, DAVID

1970   "Comparative Religious Ethics." In *The Study of Religion in Colleges and Universities*. Paul Ramsey and John F. Wilson, eds. Princeton: Princeton University Press.

LITTLE, DAVID AND TWISS, S. B.

1973   "Basic Terms in the Study of Religious Ethics." In *Religion and Morality*. Gene Outka and John P. Reeder, Jr., eds. Garden City, N.Y.: Doubleday & Co., Anchor Books.

TWISS, S. B.

1974   *The Dialectic of Moral Communication: A Conceptual Inquiry*. Unpublished Ph.D. dissertation, Yale University. Ann Arbor, Mich.: University Microfilms.

I | METHOD

I | The Study of Religious Ethics

1. INTRODUCTION

The study of religious ethics stands in need of conceptual and methodological clarification. This book is an attempt to meet the need by proposing definitions for such basic terms as *ethics* and *religion,* and by indicating a method of study that is, we hope, more rigorous and consistent than some other approaches. The book is intended to be a systematic introduction to the comparative study of religious ethics. Three lengthy case studies illustrate the nature of this field of inquiry. The method by which the case studies are analyzed is original in important respects and is explained in the first part of the book.

"Comparative religious ethics" is an expression used to refer to the study of religious ethics when the study is not confined to a single religious tradition. It could be argued that all students of religious ethics should be concerned with comparative religious ethics simply because the consideration of cross-traditional data may contribute to their understanding of the principal tradition in which they are interested. Moreover, any general view or theory of religious ethics must take into account the similarities and dissimilarities between specific religious ethical traditions, and hence is dependent on comparative inquiry.

We cannot now happily sail away into our comparative case studies, however, without paying attention to serious theoretical problems. Indeed, problems are raised by the very use of such terms as *ethics* (and *morality*), *religious,* and *comparative.* The material and the method that properly make up the study of comparative religious ethics are by no means self-evident. At the present time the field lacks systematic rigor and direction. Many scholars from many points of view do make comparative statements about religious ethics, but few stop to reflect critically on basic concepts and methodological issues. This critical task requires immediate attention at the outset of our inquiry.

1.1. Definitional and Methodological Confusion

Although definitions are difficult to formulate, especially for the notions of morality and religion, much of the literature has been unnecessarily misleading. Max Weber, who made an enormous contribution to the investigation of religious ethics, was uncharacteristically confusing when he wrote: "To define 'religion,' to say what it *is,* is not possible at the start of a presentation. . . . Definitions can be attempted, if at all, only at the conclusion of the study" (Weber 1963: 1). Unless one is prepared to offer *some* definition of the term *religion,* it is impossible to see how one can begin to conduct a study of comparative religious behavior (which is, of course, what Weber undertakes to do in his comparative study of religion). In fact, though, Weber does assume certain defining characteristics for distinguishing religious from legal, customary, and other sorts of behavior.[1] But for some reason he is less explicit about this definition than he is for the definitions of no less complex terms such as *ethics* and *law* (Weber 1947: 127–30; Weber 1954: 17; cf. Rheinstein 1954: lv).

In a recent comparative anthropological study, *Morals and Merit,* Christoph von Fürer-Haimendorf is similarly unclear with respect to the concept of morality.

Philosophers are not agreed on the definition of morality, and no sensible anthropologist will want to intrude into a debate in which the best brains of the past fifty or sixty generations have been engaged without reaching a definite conclusion. Yet, no one can live in a primitive or any other society without realizing that certain activities seem to be regarded as morally neutral while the exercise of an individual's choice in other activities is subject to moral assessments (Fürer-Haimendorf 1967: 9).

Again, the matter of defining basic terms is not optional. Because he uses the word *moral* throughout his study, as he does throughout this passage, to differentiate "certain activities" from others, Fürer-Haimendorf is responsible for explaining and defending his definition. His failure to attend to definitions, not only with respect to "morality," but also to "religion" and "law," produces some confusions that mar an otherwise useful work. He often distinguishes religion from morality, and gives much evidence that the peoples he is studying make such a distinction. Nevertheless, one is never sure what the differentia of each concept are for him.

There are many other examples of the inexact use of basic terms in social scientific literature. John Milton Yinger, in *The Scientific Study of Religion*, contends that it is "possible and desirable to define [religion and morality] in independent terms and separate them analytically" (Yinger 1971: 51). But though he discusses the relationship of religion and morality, he supplies only the vaguest definition for morality, and his use of the term *religion* shifts. "Morality," he says, "is concerned with the relationship of man to man," though that is too inclusive to be of much help (Yinger 1971: 51). Religion, on the other hand, "is concerned with the relationship of man to some higher power or idea" (Yinger 1971: 51). That attribute is not only rather inexact in itself, but it is also not part of the "operational definition of religion" he supplies earlier (Yinger 1971: 33). Yinger makes another passing attempt to clarify his concepts when he asserts that "the distinction [between religion and morality] is in terms of the authority and the sanctions that are attached to the codes [of each]" (Yinger 1971: 51). This sentence is too cryptic, however, without explanation and defense.

Alexander MacBeath has demonstrated difficulties with Bronislaw Malinowski's understanding and application of the concepts of religion and morality (MacBeath 1952: 308–21). At one point Malinowski tells us that "all the morality of primitives is derived from religious belief," but elsewhere he contends that the ordinary rules of individual and social morality among primitive peoples "in no way have the character of religious commandments . . . but [are] provided with a purely binding social force" (Malinowski 1954: 64, 58). Such inconsistent usage can be traced to insufficient precision in defining terms as well as to careless argumentation. Malinowski is given to oversimplifying other basic terms, as, for example, his definition of law (Malinowski 1959: 58–59; cf. Pospisil 1974: 29–30).

Social scientists are not the only culprits. Philosophers who undertake to write about the relation of religion and morality, and who ought to be able, if anyone is, to clarify basic concepts for

descriptive and comparative study, often produce the most disap-
pointing results. This is true of William Warren Bartley's recent
book *Morality and Religion*. In his opening paragraph, Bartley
states:

I propose to begin by assuming, as others have done, that there is some such
thing as morality and some such thing as religion, and I shall take as my
first task the clarification of what would be involved in the inter-dependence
of these two things (Bartley 1971: 1).

It is hard to see how one can trace relationships between two
concepts, particularly concepts as complex as religion and morality,
without first specifying what the concepts mean. Given the diversity
of understanding of these terms, we are hardly at the point where we
can assume definitions!

Aside from conceptual shortcomings, there are substantial methodological confusions in much of the literature. In the first place,
social scientists, particularly those of the functionalist school, often
muddle the study of comparative ethics by failing to indicate when
they are offering sociological or psychological explanations for the
existence of a code of conduct, and when they are examining the
beliefs and reasons the practitioners themselves aver for behaving as
they do. Fürer-Haimendorf's account of the moral practices of a
group of Polynesian food-gatherers is a good example. On the one
hand, the islanders, according to Fürer-Haimendorf, believe that
violations of the moral code will evoke supernatural retribution as
well as public condemnation. On the other hand, he informs us,
infringements are likely to be disapproved of because they will
"disturb the harmony of the group" (Fürer-Haimendorf 1967: 33).

It is impossible to tell from the context whether the second
proposition is something the islanders themselves affirm—something they would offer as a reason for opposing violations of their
code—or whether it is Fürer-Haimendorf's own explanation as to
the "real," though unconscious, reason the islanders hold the beliefs
they do. Though the two possible readings are not mutually exclusive, it is important to clarify whether a belief is being reported or
an explanation advanced. This equivocation is not peculiar to Fürer-
Haimendorf (for a discussion of other examples, see Ladd 1957:
46–47).

A second methodological difficulty is the lack of clarity about the distinction between "descriptive" and "normative" ethics. Broadly, the former is an empirical and analytical account of a given person's or group's moral code; the latter is the advocacy and defense of a particular moral position (cf. Frankena 1973: 4–11; Taylor 1975: 4–9). Fürer-Haimendorf is an example of one who does not always keep firmly in mind the difference between these two tasks. Having asserted that the anthropologist "must confine himself to describing" different systems of morality, Fürer-Haimendorf goes on to claim that:

any value-assessment he may be tempted to make will ultimately depend on his own ideological background and personal predilections. For it seems that we cannot measure and judge morals by absolute, scientifically determined standards but can only evaluate the moral norms of one society by comparing them with the moral system of another. In this process of comparison the essential features of the individual systems may be exposed and clarified, but an element of subjectivity in the value judgements appears to be an inescapable feature of all our thinking about morality (Fürer-Haimendorf 1967: 228).

Though Fürer-Haimendorf shows no sign he is aware of the point, it is obvious that his claim about the subjectivity of moral evaluations is a normative claim, as is his statement that comparative study is inherently evaluative. These contentions require independent defense, and in no way follow from the nature of the descriptive tasks he recommends. Presumably, one may engage in useful descriptive work, whether sharing Fürer-Haimendorf's subjective relativism or not. The literature manifests too many examples of a similar carelessness in jumbling descriptive and normative arguments (for discussion of, and objections to, such carelessness, see Taylor 1958: 32–44; Ladd 1957: 322–28).

1.2. Conceptual and Methodological Orientation

From this cursory review of work in the fields touching on comparative religious ethics, it is clear that we shall not be able to make much headway until we begin to straighten out some fundamental difficulties. Fortunately, we are not without help. Some moral philosophers and social anthropologists have started to examine critically the problems we have mentioned—the analysis of basic concepts like religion and ethics (and morality), the relation between descriptive and normative inquiry, and the bearing of ethical theory on the field of comparative ethics (see, for examples, Mac-Beath 1952; Brandt 1954: chaps. 5 and 11; Ladd 1957; Edel and Edel 1959; Taylor 1961; Emmet 1966; Barnsley 1972).

In our view, John Ladd's study *The Structure of a Moral Code,* while not without defects and limitations, provides an admirable starting point for rectifying some of the conceptual and methodological confusions we have noted (Ladd 1957). As we shall make clear, however, we depart from Ladd at several critical points. Also, we develop further than he does some of his suggestions for the study of descriptive and comparative religious ethics.

To begin with, Ladd is aware that in order to engage in the study of descriptive and comparative ethics, "we must decide upon some reasonably exact criterion of what is to taken as ethical" (Ladd 1957: 42).[2] His approach to formulating definitions is, in keeping with trends in analytic philosophy, to focus upon the language of ethics, or ethics as a form of discourse. "Ethical ideas and thoughts are always in principle communicable because they are formulated in the language of the society concerned" (Ladd 1957: 19). The question, then, that Ladd asks, is what defining characteristics distinguish an ethical utterance or statement from other statements. His conclusion is as follows: "A moral statement . . . will be defined as 'A statement expressing the acceptance of a prescription for conduct which claims superiority and which is regarded as legitimate' " (Ladd 1957: 85). An ethical statement, by contrast, "is either a moral statement or a statement made in connection with one; for example, in justification of it" (Ladd 1957: 85). For Ladd and for many other moral philosophers, ethical statements are generally *reflective* responses to moral statements, usually in defense of them.[3]

In the next chapter we shall advance our own definition of morality, a definition that is, in certain respects, similar to Ladd's. In elaborating on and defending it we shall go over in detail some of the same ground Ladd goes over in discussing his proposal. We may, therefore, defer comment on the substance of our definition, though a few remarks about the general task of defining—particularly in regard to open-textured words like *morality* and *religion*—are in order.

The sort of definitions we seek are equivalent to Rudolf Carnap's and Carl Hempel's notion of *explication* or *rational reconstruction*

(Hempel 1952: 11–12). Such definitions provide, as theoretical and analytical devices, clear and precise concepts of morality, religion, and law, reinterpreted from ordinary usage, for use within comparative religious ethics (Ladd 1957: 44–45; Pospisil 1974: 19). The general canons for a well-formed and properly asserted definition, including "formal" and "literary" requirements are obviously applicable, and need not be stated: These are usually collocated, formulated, and denoted as "rules for complete definition" (see Leonard 1967: 608–16). Those canons peculiar to reconstructive definition within a comparative context include the following: (1) that the definition permit reformulation of a large part of what is customarily expressed by the terms in ordinary usage (the proposed definition, when used within the natural language community, must not be counterintuitive to the members of that community); (2) that the definition permit the formulation of testable hypotheses that may, if possible, have explanatory and predictive force; (3) that the definition have the capacity-in-principle to permit the development of a comprehensive and rigorous theory; and (4) that the definition possess cross-cultural applicability and thereby avoid the "fallacy of ethnocentricity" (cf. Spiro 1966: 86–87).

We are naturally aware of the standard objections that are raised regarding the quest for precise definitions of apparently imprecise terms. First, it is sometimes argued that vagueness and inconsistency are intrinsic to the customary usage of many natural language terms, and, therefore, the search for "true" analytic definitions is hopeless (Hempel 1952: 9–10). Second, and related to the first objection, is the point of view regarding the generalized application to ordinary language of Ludwig Wittgenstein's notion of family resemblances. This view holds that any search for "if and only if" definitions is often misguided since such an approach too easily assumes that there are distinctive generic properties for concepts like morality and religion. It recommends instead that we "look and see" whether there are any such generic properties by observing the use of the term in different contexts, and it goes on to suggest that rather than generic properties, one is likely to find vaguer "family resemblances" among uses—now one set of common properties linking two uses, now another, but no one necessary, ever-present set of defining characteristics (Wittgenstein 1964: 17–18; Wittgenstein 1967: 66–71; Bambrough 1966: 186–204; Kovesi 1967: 22–23).

Third, it is sometimes contended that terms like *moral* have been used indiscriminately in a persuasive manner by the natural language community, that is, without responsible presentation and justification (Stevenson 1963: 33–54). Such usage has led both to inescapable confusion over the meaning of the term, and to a predominantly emotive use of the term. Given this state of affairs, controversy about definitions is not fruitful.

Our basic response to all three objections is to advocate following Wittgenstein's counsel that we first of all "look and see" the use to which concepts like morality, religion, and law are put, and come to our own conclusions as to whether they have "core meanings" or not. While we remain skeptical that any "true" or "if and only if" definitions can be found, we are confident we can identify some common attributes of the concepts of morality, religion, and law that, for purposes of comparative work, are more determinate than the second objection would lead us to expect and less exclusively emotive in content than the third objection suggests. Incidentally, the family resemblance approach may itself be inadequate in that it fails to specify where one "family" (for example, morality) begins and another (for example, law) ends. Overlaps and similarities ad infinitum seem to result in a large "family" indeed, making specific discourse about a particular phenomenon difficult if not impossible (for a convincing attack on the "family resemblances" approach, see Kovesi 1967: 22–23; cf. Lange 1970: 35–37).

It is interesting that in a field bordering closely on our own, the comparative study of law, much creative attention is being given to the definition of "an analytical concept of law that can be applied cross-culturally" (Pospisil 1974: 40). According to Leopold Pospisil, anthropologists have gradually come to realize, much as we have, that comparative analysis of social phenomena cannot proceed without clear conceptualization. Moreover, despite opinions to the contrary, it appears possible to formulate a relatively determinate set of attributes of the concept of law that can "serve as criteria for a more exact delimitation of the law's boundaries and for separating legal phenomena from other, non-legal social categories" (Pospisil 1974: 40; cf. Bohannan 1965). We will propose our own reconstructive definition of "law" later, in Chapter 4.

Having helped to specify what constitutes a moral code in the first place, Ladd makes two methodological advances in studying such codes. First, he clearly separates the task of causal investigation from the task of analyzing the mode(s) of moral reasoning or justification employed by a given group. Second, he carefully identifies the latter task as the primary activity of descriptive ethics, and brackets off from the descriptive analysis of moral reasoning all normative considerations. As Ladd and we understand it, descriptive ethics is "a scientific meta-theoretical inquiry into the ethical discourse of a specified informant or group" (Ladd 1957: 30). Thus, to engage in *comparative descriptive ethics* is to describe and compare the patterns of moral reasoning employed by the members of two or more designated groups to justify the respective moral codes of those groups.

Ladd's procedure, as applied to the moral code of the Navajo, provides an instructive model of analysis, but we are compelled, for our own purposes, to depart from it somewhat. (As will be seen in Chapter 6, we also dissent from Ladd's substantive analysis of the Navajo code.) Ladd's method, which he labels "the method of hypothetical reconstruction," is particularly well adapted to the analysis of the moral codes of groups presently in existence. The method aims at proposing hypotheses about the content and form of moral reasoning prevalent in a given group, and then, on the basis of those hypotheses, predicting what sort of moral judgments members of that group will make. Finally, it aims at testing those predictions by means of interviewing an informant, who may be taken as representative of the group. In this way, it is possible to verify scientifically the "hypothetical reconstruction" of the code that the analyst advances. Obviously, such a procedure requires the presence of a living informant to whom one may apply the appropriate tests.

There are two reasons why, in the study of religious ethics, we do not restrict ourselves to Ladd's interview technique. First we are concerned with analyzing moral and religious codes for which there are no longer any available "informants," such as the code of the early Christians (see Chapter 7). Second, while it is perhaps true that in the case of contemporary religious and moral codes the most reliable scientific method is Ladd's direct interview procedure as conducted by a sophisticated investigator, it is also true that the student of comparative ethics can perform an indispensable preliminary activity by learning how to both utilize secondary literature and develop his own secondhand intuitions so as to formulate significant hypotheses regarding the structure and content of a particular code. As a matter of fact, given time and resources, sometimes the most a comparativist may hope for is the generation of plausible hypotheses. (This statement characterizes, for the most part, the status of our case studies in Chapters 6 through 8.) He therefore ought to know how to do the job well.

Since we wish to include historical materials in our analysis, over and above Ladd's interview technique, we are thrown back on something like the *verstehende* or "interpretive" method, associated with Weber and many other scholars of religion. Despite Ladd's disparaging comments about the method, it does account for his basic distinctions between, to use Weber's terminology, explaining social action causally, and investigating the "meaning system" or the "internal structure of cultural values" by which a given group justifies its action (Ladd 1957: 40–41). This sort of investigation involves, much as for Ladd, developing a "reconstruction" or "ideal type" of a hypothetical pattern of "intended meaning" according to which a group understood its behavior, and then attempting to verify the reconstruction against the relevant literature produced by the group, and/or by the relevant secondhand accounts of what the group believed. We are aware that the results of such a procedure are hard to verify rigorously; that is an unavoidable impediment in this type of inquiry, as in most intellectual historical inquiry.

2. CONCEPTUAL ANALYSIS AS A METHOD OF INQUIRY

It seems clear that if we are going to undertake a reasonably sophisticated inquiry in comparative religious ethics, we shall have to clarify our use of such notions as morality, religion, and law. The question naturally arises as to what is our procedure for clarification. How are we going to go about offering reasonable and acceptable criteria for our uses of these rather open-textured notions? In framing our answer we shall, for convenience, refer to the concept of moral (morality).

Recently there has been much discussion among moral philosophers and other scholars about the definitions of "moral" and "morality" (see, for example, Wallace and Walker 1970). The central issue posed is what are the essential defining characteristics of morality and related concepts, what are the features that distinguish these notions from, say, law and legal notions, or custom and matters of etiquette. Though the issue is often raised and talked about in the abstract, it acquires a real point when inquiries of a specific nature are undertaken—for example, sociological inquiry into a group's moral views, or, more to the point, cross-cultural investigation in comparative ethics. The issue is not a bogus one in such investigations, for their conceptual and methodological clarity often hangs upon the precision with which basic terms are used.[4] Why and in what way does "moral" ("morality") pose problems? The answer is not hard to find.

First, it should be observed that "moral" and "morality" are used in a variety of contexts. It is a virtual commonplace that "moral" is used both as a term of approval (first-order use) as opposed to "immoral" and as a classificatory term (second-order use) as opposed to "nonmoral." Moreover, even as a second-order term, "moral" is used in a variety of ways. We speak of a specific person's moral convictions and views, as contrasted with his religious beliefs and aesthetic tastes. We also speak of the moral point of view, the moral forms of life, moral rules and principles, and moral reasons.

By itself, then, this first observation raises the possibility that "moral" ("morality") may not have a single unified sense. That is, even the classifactory use of the term may be systematically ambiguous or context-variant. This point suggests that the following condition must be met by any adequate account of "moral" ("morality") in the second-order, classificatory sense: Insofar as the term is used in a variety of contexts, any adequate account (definition) of the term in one context should be capable of extension to cover the uses of the term in other contexts in which it has the same sense. For example, what the account says of "moral" as applied to "point of view" should shed some light on and make good sense of moral rules and principles, moral reasons, moral forms of life, and so forth. These notations, of course, relate to the term as it is employed in ordinary language. Therefore, the adequacy of any account is settled at least in part by an appeal to ordinary language. As we indicated in section 1.2, this appeal is built into the canons for reconstructive definition.

2.1. Definitions and Criteria of Meaning

We characterize our subsequent investigations into the notions of morality, religion, and law as "conceptual." Although we agree that the aim of the investigations in the next three chapters is to elucidate the meaning of these notions, this remark by itself does not sufficiently refine what is meant by "conceptual analysis." The question is: What is the nature of a conceptual inquiry? As a first step toward answering this question, let us explain our intention in engaging in conceptual analysis in this present context.

The intention, quite simply, is to clear up some bewilderment concerning the meaning of certain terms (concepts). We are in one sense familiar with the concepts in question: We know how and when to use them. But sometimes we find ourselves at a loss as to whether a certain phenomenon should be called, for example, "moral." We find ourselves in this quandary because we often do not know what features of this phenomenon count as grounds for or against calling it "moral." And we are put into such a quandary when we are challenged to reflect on these grounds and to produce the relevant criteria. In other words, by being challenged in this way we are encouraged to reflect on the meaning of "moral" and requested to produce adequate criteria to help specify its meaning. Reflection on such criteria of meaning constitutes a type of conceptual inquiry.

Now the question arises as to how such an inquiry is to be conducted. At this point a caveat must be introduced. The aim of such an inquiry is prompted by a challenge to reflect on the meaning, for example, of "moral," and to produce adequate criteria governing this meaning. If this challenge should be interpreted as a claim to the effect that lacking such criteria we do not (cannot) understand the term "moral" and that our concept of morality is defective in some sense, then this claim must be rejected on a number of grounds. First, note what the claim entails: (1) since we lack analysis and criteria for the concept, we do not (cannot) properly understand the concept; and (2) until we can provide adequate analysis and criteria for the concept, it is defective in some respects. Let us examine this claim.

It will not do to say simply that we lack criteria for the concept of moral (morality), for the definitions that we could give for uses of this term would provide criteria of some sort; for example, x is a moral judgment "if and only if" it is a judgment that claims superiority (for example, over matters of taste) and that is considered legitimate, in that its grounds for justification seriously take into consideration the welfare of others from their point of view. This sort of definition is precisely the sort we would give to someone who was seriously ignorant of what this term meant and wanted to know. No doubt the definition would need to be explicated further and would need to be supplemented with examples, but a criterion would have been provided. If such definitions are rejected as not good because they rely on other notions, such as judgment, legitimacy, and welfare, then it appears that what is wanted is a criterion or set of criteria of a different sort—perhaps "behavioral." But then it must be observed that this latter objection rests on certain mistaken assumptions about the relations between our understanding of a concept and our ability to provide criteria of a certain kind for its application.

The principal point here is that even if other criteria are proposed for the concept, we have to assess the adequacy of such criteria in terms of our prior knowledge of what "moral" means. In some sense we already know what it means by virtue of our ability to use the term correctly; that ability constitutes an understanding of "moral" (cf. Searle 1969: 4-15). Indeed, this ability is *presupposed* by any search for more rigorous criteria for the explication of the concept. In short, that form of argument that takes a concept about which there is some general agreement regarding its application and then says it is somehow defective because there are no criteria of a certain kind, is itself a defective argument. For it is self-defeating. How can one assess the adequacy of the more rigorous criteria without already having some conception of the notion in the first place? To have that conception and to possess the ability to assess is, in general, to understand the concept.

This caveat is important, but it should not be taken to imply that the search for rigorous criteria of a concept is an illegitimate enterprise. Properly construed, attempts to lay out criteria for our concepts are attempts to explain them by getting behind the sometimes bewildering complexities of common usage. Moreover, sometimes the grounds or criteria for some of our concepts are not entirely fixed. We have already indicated that this may to some extent be true of the classificatory uses of "moral" ("morality"). This fact suggests that philosophical reflection concerning the grounds or criteria for calling something x when there is no settled and fixed opinion as to what those criteria are, may well require the creative molding or reconstruction of certain vague, indeterminate, and loose aspects of those concepts. That is, within the context of a certain inquiry, it may be the case that certain key concepts need to be molded and their logical relationships established, particularly if that inquiry aims to be both precise and illuminative. It can be said that because of their indeterminate criteria such concepts are in search of a meaning, to put it metaphorically.

In their attempt to explicate criteria for certain concepts, certain conceptual inquiries may be forced to mold, as judiciously as possible, unmolded meanings—that is, to explicate concepts by proposing criteria left undetermined by ordinary usage (cf. Black 1970: 1–13). Does this necessity for sometimes shaping concepts in order to achieve explications and to aid an investigation—for example, an investigation into comparative religious ethics—imply that such conceptual activities aim at providing *arbitrary stipulative definitions?* Our answer to that question is no. Let us, however, put a cutting edge on this answer.

It has often been contended that under the aegis of such neutral sounding banners as "linguistic analysis" and "logical investigation," conceptual inquiries actually aim at producing stipulative and persuasive definitions of terms. This charge is false. Conceptual analyses aim to explicate concepts by educing and formulating their criteria. But in working with concepts for which there are only indeterminate and vague criteria, conceptual inquiry may also have to shape or reconstruct these criteria according to certain accepted or at least publicly available and justified canons in order to perform its explicative task. So the charge is also misleading. In the latter instance, to say that conceptual inquiries sometimes at least result in stipulative definitions is very misleading, for a peculiar sense of "stipulative definition" is being used in making the charge. First, the notion of "stipulative" does not capture the sense of "reconstruction" introduced in the previous section. Second, conceptual inquiries in general deal with fields of concepts, not isolated notions. So explications involve making logical distinctions and connections between a number of related concepts, rather than simply producing dictionary definitions. These two points require some refinement. We will first describe briefly the field orientation of our conceptual inquiry. Then, we will reiterate what is involved in shaping or reconstructing criteria for concepts.

In the conceptual inquiry we undertake in this book, we search for grounds or criteria that help, for example, to explicate the concepts of morality, moral forms of life, moral agency, and the like. To possess such notions in a precisely defined form is important for achieving a sophisticated orientation to the field of comparative religious ethics. These notions establish in part the conceptual framework for engaging in descriptive and comparative inquiry in religious ethics. The point of elucidating these notions is to illuminate a significant field of concepts logically associated with, indeed partially constitutive of, comparative religious ethics. The moral concepts relevant to this enterprise—value concepts, such as human welfare; action-guiding concepts, such as principle, rule, and duty; dispositional concepts, such as motive, virtue, and character trait—form a network of fundamental notions that needs to be explicated.

How are we going to explicate these and other concepts? The answer is simple, though the task is difficult. We intend to advance accounts of these concepts that attempt to specify their respective criteria in terms of necessary and sufficient conditions. Furthermore, we intend to draw out significant logical connections between these concepts. Broadly speaking, then, we offer, elaborate, and defend definitions of these concepts. So far as possible, we try to articulate definitions that are analytically true. But, since we have a healthy skepticism regarding our ability to provide analytic definitions, we at least attempt to provide definitions that meet the canons of rational reconstruction introduced in the previous section.

3. ON THE NOTION OF *COMPARATIVE*

At this point it is important to clarify our understanding of the *comparative* nature of the study of religious ethics. In recent years comparative work in the field of religion has been much criticized for three principal reasons. First, the attempt to typify "whole religious traditions," like Christianity, Buddhism, and Islam, and then to compare them with each other in broad terms, is liable to gross oversimplification. Such an approach ignores and obscures the complex and intricate variations and divergences within each tradition and thus distorts, rather than clarifies, religious phenomena. Second, the comparative study of religions has often been undertaken for apologetic purposes, either overt or covert, and that calls into question the objectivity of the results. Third, attempts have been made, on the basis of comparative study, to derive theories which purport to explain the origin and development of religion. According to critics, these theories, again because of the breadth of phenomena they encompass, are difficult to test. Comprehensive theories of religion, like those of Freud or Durkheim, are frequently regarded as more speculative than scientific.

These three objections to the comparative study of religion have also been directed against the comparative study of religious ethics. There has been a tendency to generalize broadly regarding the "type of ethic" to be found in Christianity, Buddhism, Judaism, or whatever. Hendrik Kraemer, the Dutch student of world religions, provides an example of such sweeping generalizations: "All ethics in the world, except the Christian ethic, are some form of eudaemonism" (Kraemer 1956: 86–88).

Another such example can be found in P. H. Nowell-Smith, who categorizes the entire Christian tradition as deontological (in the authoritarian sense), in distinction from "secular" (or teleological) ethics (Nowell-Smith 1966: 99). Claims like these patently distort the variations in ethical outlook among different religious and ethical traditions, not to mention those within the Christian tradition itself. And to compound the problem, comparative works in ethics often have an apologetic temper, as can be seen in the writings of both Kraemer and Nowell-Smith. Finally, there is the problem presented by the so-called grand theorists of comparative ethics. For example, L. T. Hobhouse, an early twentieth century student of ethical traditions, advances an evolutionary theory according to which he attempts to explain what he believes are the patterns of ethical development in the history of mankind. These sweeping theories have not survived very well (see, for example, Kemp 1964: 144–47).

We try to avoid these three difficulties. First of all, we are somewhat more specific about the object of our comparison than many students have been, and are, we hope, slightly more disciplined in our approach. *We seek to compare kinds or types of practical reasoning in different religious settings.* Once we have laid out our analytical apparatus—that is, defined our terms—and elaborated several types and levels of practical justification, we then examine selected materials from nonliterate and literate traditions, from Western and non-Western traditions, according to our apparatus. By employing this scheme we hope to demonstrate some of the different ways in which practitioners have undertaken to give reasons in support of their respective codes of conduct.

We are sensitive to the variations in practical reasoning within different religious and ethical traditions, and, for that reason, have restricted our analysis, particularly in the case of literate traditions, to selected materials. Therefore, we make no attempt to typify the whole religious tradition. Moreover, since we find several types of reasoning at work within these materials, we are not inclined to classify even the segments of the respective traditions we examine into one all-encompassing type. While our method may still not be delicate enough to do full justice to the range of variation within Christianity and Buddhism, for example, it does make a start in the right direction.

We have also attempted to remain descriptive, rather than apologetic, in our approach. We have attempted to refrain from evaluating the various kinds of practical reasoning that we elaborate. While we may have our own evaluative commitments from among the options, it seems to us that the issues involved in choosing among them are far from being closed to further discussion and argument. If hidden biases have distorted our interpretations, we assume that critics will help smoke out these biases by exhibiting whatever distortions there may be in our work, and by suggesting how certain evaluative assumptions have produced them.

Finally, we have no theory to advance as to why people think religiously and morally about practical life in the way they appear to do, nor as to what explains the range of patterns that we have discerned. These are interesting and important questions, but those who seek answers to them must, in our view, wait until the task of classification and internal clarification has been completed. Precisely because we are not concerned here with propounding any premature theortetical explanations, we avoid altogether the third difficulty which afflicts comparative studies: the advocacy of a pretentious theory of ethical development. Some may feel that this restriction lessens the interest of our undertaking. That may be. But our conviction is that we already have enough to do.

NOTES

1. Talcott Parsons comes close to an adequate summary of Weber's assumptions about the meaning of religion when he writes: "A crucial point in Weber's theory is that there is no known human society without something which modern social scientists would classify as religion. Every society possesses some conceptions of a super-natural order, of spirits, gods or impersonal forces which are different from and in some sense superior to those forces conceived as governing ordinary 'natural' events, and whose nature and activities somehow give meaning to the unusual, the frustrating and the rationally impenetrable aspects of experience" (Parsons 1963: xxviii).
2. A recent book by John H. Barnsley, *Social Reality of Ethics,* is one of the few studies in this field that takes Ladd's approach seriously in proposing a definition of morality. Barnsley's sensitivity to recent philosophical discussions, together with a useful survey of sociological and anthropological work in the field, makes this a valuable book. Nevertheless, we are not satisfied with Barnsley's proposal for a "formal definition of morality." Also, he gives a rather confusing and incomplete account of the "elements of a moral code" (Barnsley 1972: chaps. 2 and 3).
3. In ordinary English usage there is no clear distinction between the terms *morals* and *ethics*. Both terms and their cognates appear in this book more or less synonymously, though we tend to hold to Ladd's working distinction: "moral statements" make specific prescriptive or evaluative judgements; "ethical statements" reflect on and justify moral statements (Ladd 1957: 82–83). Actually, our use of the expression "moral action-guide" undercuts the need to make much capital out of this distinction.
4. Some philosophers think that the issue of defining "moral" and "morality" is not at all viable. Peter Singer, for example, takes this position in an article revealingly entitled "The Triviality of the Debate over 'Is-Ought' and the Definition of 'Moral' " (Singer 1973: 51–56). In a subsequent discussion with Professor Singer in 1974, however, we found that he now does consider the matter to be important, at least for the kind of enterprise in which we are engaged in this book.

REFERENCES

BAMBROUGH, RENFORD.
     1966 "Universals and Family Resemblances." Reprinted in *Wittgenstein: The Philosophical Investigations*. George Pitcher, ed. Garden City, N.Y.: Doubleday & Co., Anchor Books.
BARNSLEY, JOHN H.
     1972 *Social Reality of Ethics: The Comparative Analysis of Moral Codes*. London: Routledge & Kegan Paul.

BARTLEY, WILLIAM WARREN.
   1971   *Morality and Religion.* London: Macmillan & Co.
BLACK, MAX.
   1970   "Reasoning with Loose Concepts." Reprinted in Max Black, *Margins of Precision: Essays in Logic and Language.* Ithaca, N.Y.: Cornell University Press.
BOHANNAN, PAUL.
   1965   "The Differing Realms of Law." In *American Anthropologist* 67: 33–42.
BRANDT, RICHARD.
   1954   *Hopi Ethics.* Chicago: University of Chicago Press.
EDEL, ABRAHAM, AND EDEL, MAY.
   1959   *Anthropology and Ethics.* Springfield, Ill.: Charles C. Thomas.
EMMET, DOROTHY.
   1966   *Rules, Roles and Relations.* London: Macmillan & Co.
FRANKENA, WILLIAM.
   1973   *Ethics.* Second edition. Englewood Cliffs, N.J.: Prentice-Hall.
FÜRER-HAIMENDORF, CHRISTOPH VON.
   1967   *Morals and Merit: A Study of Values and Social Controls in South Asian Societies.* London: Weidenfeld & Nicolson.
HEMPEL, CARL G.
   1952   *Fundamentals of Concept Formation in Empirical Science.* Chicago: University of Chicago Press.
KEMP, JOHN.
   1964   *Reason, Action and Morality.* London: Routledge and Kegan Paul.
KOVESI, JULIUS.
   1967   *Moral Notions.* London: Routledge & Kegan Paul.
KRAEMER, HENDRIK.
   1956   *Christian Message in a Non-Christian World.* Grand Rapids: Kregel Publications.
LADD, JOHN.
   1957   *The Structure of a Moral Code: A Philosophical Analysis of Ethical Discourse Applied to the Ethics of the Navaho Indians.* Cambridge, Mass.: Harvard University Press.
LANGE, JOHN.
   1970   *The Cognitivity Paradox: An Inquiry Concerning the Claims of Philosophy.* Princeton: Princeton University Press.
LITTLE, DAVID.
   1970   "Comparative Religious Ethics." In *The Study of Religion in Colleges and Universities,* Paul Ramsey and John F. Wilson, eds. Princeton: Princeton University Press.
LEONARD, HENRY S.
   1967   *Principles of Reasoning: An Introduction to Logic, Methodolo-*

gy, and the Theory of Signs. Revised edition. New York: Dover Publications.

MacBEATH, ALEXANDER.

1952   *Experiments in Living: A Study of the Nature and Foundation of Ethics or Morals in the Light of Recent Work in Social Anthropology.* London: Macmillan & Co.

MALINOWSKI, BRONISLAW.

1954   *Magic, Science and Religion.* Second edition. Garden City, N.Y.: Doubleday & Co., Anchor Books.

1959   *Crime and Custom in Savage Society.* Second edition. Totowa, N.J.: Littlefield, Adams & Co.

PARSONS, TALCOTT.

1963   "Introduction." In Max Weber, *The Sociology of Religion.* Revised fourth edition. Ephraim Fischoff, trans. Boston: Beacon Press.

POSPISIL, LEOPOLD.

1974   *Anthropology of Law: A Comparative Theory.* Second edition. New Haven: HRAF Press.

RHEINSTEIN, MAX.

1954   "Introduction." In Max Weber, *On Law in Economy and Society.* Edward Shils & Max Rheinstein, trans. Cambridge, Mass.: Harvard University Press.

SEARLE, JOHN R.

1969   *Speech Acts: An Essay in the Philosophy of Language.* Cambridge: Cambridge University Press.

SINGER, PETER.

1973   "The Triviality of the Debate over 'Is-Ought' and the Definition of 'Moral.' " In *American Philosophical Quarterly* 10, 1 (Jan., 1973), 51–56.

SPIRO, MELFORD E.

1966   "Religion: Problems of Definition and Explanation." In *Anthropological Approaches to the Study of Religion.* Michael Banton, ed. London: Tavistock Publications.

STEVENSON, CHARLES L.

1963   "Persuasive Definitions." Reprinted in Charles L. Stevenson, *Facts and Values: Studies in Ethical Analysis.* New Haven: Yale University Press.

TAYLOR, PAUL W.

1958   "Social Science and Ethical Relativism." In *Journal of Philosophy* 55: 32–44.

1961   *Normative Discourse.* Englewood Cliffs, N.J.: Prentice-Hall.

1975   *Principles of Ethics: An Introduction.* Encino, Calif.: Dickenson Publishing Co.

WALLACE, G., AND WALKER, A.D.M., EDS.
1970   *The Definition of Morality.* London: Methuen & Co.

WEBER, MAX.
1947   *The Theory of Social and Economic Organization.* A. M. Henderson & Talcott Parsons, trans. New York: Oxford University Press.
1954   *On Law in Economy and Society.* Edward Shils & Max Rheinstein, trans. Cambridge, Mass.: Harvard University Press.
1963   *The Sociology of Religion.* Revised fourth edition. Ephraim Fischoff, trans. Boston: Beacon Press.

WITTGENSTEIN, LUDWIG.
1964   *The Blue and Brown Books.* Second edition. New York: Harper & Row.
1967   *Philosophical Investigations.* Second edition. G. E. M. Anscombe, trans. New York: Macmillan Co.

YINGER, JOHN MILTON.
1971   *The Scientific Study of Religion.* New York: Macmillan Co.

2 | The Concepts of Morality and Moral Action-Guide

1. INTRODUCTION

There have been many efforts on the part of scholars, especially moral philosophers, to provide adequate accounts of "moral," "morality," "moral judgment," and related cognate expressions. These accounts can be classified into two principal genres. One genre typically attempts to analyze or characterize moral concepts and judgments in a highly formal manner, avoiding the mention of substantive aspects of moral concepts and grounds for moral judgment. Although on the contemporary scene this sort of analysis was provoked by G. E. Moore's notion of the naturalistic fallacy—that is, the presumed error of defining moral concepts in terms of "natural" concepts—it is a pre-twentieth-century philosophical approach (Moore 1903: chap. 1).[1] For an early eighteenth-century example, consider Immanuel Kant's analysis of the categorical imperative (Kant 1959: 39, 47, 50, 57; cf. Paton 1963: bk. 3). This mode of characterizing the concept of moral (morality) involves analytic attempts to be wholly noncommittal as to what morality is about. It offers contentless characterizations of morality and moral concepts.

The other genre, by contrast, does not rule out the possibility of providing accounts of morality that attempt to identify and characterize its distinctive subject matter in terms of substantive content (see, for example, Warnock 1967: chap. 5). This approach takes the position that if one is properly to understand morality, it is essential to try to see the point behind this human phenomenon, to see what interests lie behind morality, the development of moral concepts, and the making of moral judgments. In general, it asks the following questions: If morality has to do with practical matters and is supposed to make a practical difference in human life and relationships, then just what sort of difference is it supposed to make? And why is there a need for this sort of difference to be made? Answers to these questions are assumed to lie in features of people and in the circumstances in which they live, that is, in broad generalizations about persons and what is called "the human condition."

Questions naturally arise about the status of these generalizations. Do they represent empirical generalizations about man and society, ontological claims about human nature, or, more loosely, "truisms" about people and their environment? As they are formulated, such questions are somewhat disquieting from a hard-nosed philosophical perspective. Since we align our account of morality with this second genre, such questions pertain to our endeavor also. But we refuse to be drawn into this rather sterile sort of philosophical debate. We contend simply that in seeking to present a reasonably adequate account of what morality is, and what it is about, one is compelled to invoke some bald facts about people that do not, on the face of things, appear particularly problematic. The point of our account is to explicate as best we can the concept of morality, and we rest content with the view that our proposal is plausible and remains open to public scrutiny.

1.1. Diversity, Change, and Stability in Morality

In light of our earlier discussion about the possible variant uses of "moral" ("morality") in the classificatory sense and the problems inherent in defining open-textured terms, the question now arises as to how the subject matter of morality is supposed to be identified (see Chapter 1, section 2). We have already admitted that there may well be some difficulty here; hence, our introduction to and subsequent reliance on the notion of reconstruction in the enterprise of conceptual analysis. We think it would be an error to become paralyzed by this sort of difficulty so early in the game. Morality does appear to shade off into other things (such as custom, law), so that border disputes are, to some extent, unavoidable. But it should be noted that this feature is not uncommon with regard to many of our concepts, nor is it necessarily fatal to conceptual explication (as we have already suggested). What matters is that there is some general agreement about certain important features of morality, so that it is not wholly implausible to hold that some issues and concerns are clearly and properly those of morality.

We grant that certain forms of behavior and evaluations about conduct—indeed "moral" forms of life and "moral" perceptions— change and that there is no single fixed moral landscape. But it does not follow from this admission that morality is merely a matter of opinion and that everything about morality is excessively relative. While acknowledging the phenomena of diversity and change in morals, should not one also pause and give some thought to the matter of *what* changes? In other words, does the basic meaning or concept of morality change? This rhetorical question is intended to elicit the recognition that there is no reason to suppose that the *basis* of moral conduct and perception changes also.

Consequently, in keeping with our methodological remarks regarding the canons for producing a reconstructive definition of morality, we begin by systematically "reformulating a large part of what is customarily expressed by the term in ordinary usage." Here and there we suggest how our proposed definition can be put to work in cross-cultural and cross-traditional analysis.

1.2. General Object of Morality

Before specifying and elaborating our proposed definition, it is necessary to draw attention, in a preliminary way, to certain minimal and intuitively obvious features of what we commonly understand by the concept moral. First, we assume that morality "functions" to guide the conduct of persons and human groups in such a way that it constitutes an institution or a shared system of expectations for regulating behavior.[2] Second, we take morality to be an action-guiding institution having to do, in an important sense, with *relational action,* that is, with the mutually interacting and impinging conduct of persons and groups. Though there may be exceptions, something counts as a "moral notion," generally speaking, when it fulfills the "restrictive condition . . . that it can be adopted as a means of initiating or preserving or extending some kind of cooperation or social activity between human beings"

(Kemp 1964: 196). In other words, morality, among other things, provides a way of responding to what we call the "problem of cooperation" among self-interested, competing, and conflicting persons and groups.

Obviously, these two general and minimal conditions, while important to our common understanding of morality, are, as they stand, neither sufficiently refined in themselves, nor satisfactory in distinguishing morality from other sorts of action-guiding institutions, such as law, etiquette, and religious ritual. With regard to the problem of refinement, two notions need to be discussed: action-guiding institutions and the problem of cooperation.

By the expression "action-guiding institution" we mean that morality has to do with a certain kind of evaluation of human actions and related notions, such as intentions, attitudes, motives, practices, and characters. We mean to suggest that morality has some more or less direct reference to the fundamental notion of action. Moreover, we mean to suggest that such evaluation is never just pointless or idle, but that its point, its rationale, its intrinsic aim, is practical in character, concerned more or less with influencing (in some way) how human beings and groups think, feel, and act. With these qualifications, "action-guiding institution" is a good name for what morality in general has to do with.

Our conception of the problem of cooperation simply deepens this understanding. By this notion we are suggesting that, having some general practical end in view, morality contributes in certain respects, by way of human thought, attitude, and action, to the amelioration of aspects of the human condition. Those aspects that we have in mind include limited human knowledge and intelligence, limited resources for satisfying human needs and wants, limited rationality, and limited sympathy for others. It is not necessary to describe in detail these aspects of the human condition; this has been done well enough by others (Hart 1961: chap. 9; Warnock 1971: 17–26). The meaning and implications of these limitations appear obvious: resources for life are limited; knowledge and intelligence are limited; people are often not rational in managing their affairs; people are vulnerable to interference by others; people are inevitably in competition with others; and, consequently, they often fail to cooperate in the pursuit of common ends.

These are facts, albeit contingent facts, about the human condition. They state truisms about man in his natural and social environments. And taken conjunctively they constitute the problem of cooperation for persons and social groups. This description of the human condition strongly suggests that the point or the general object of morality is to contribute to the amelioration of the human condition by resolving the problem of cooperation. An appreciation of this point helps us to understand both the conception of morality as an action-guiding institution and the common view that there is something peculiarly important about morality. Although adducing these conditions helps to illuminate the concept of morality, however, they are still too vague to be of much use. We therefore turn to our specific definition of "moral" ("morality").

2. DEFINITION OF MORALITY

For clarity and convenience we propose our definition in terms of a noun phrase that appears particularly apt following the discussion in the preceding section—namely, *moral action-guide*. Since classificatory (second-order) uses of "moral" rarely stand alone and are generally used to qualify a variety of phenomena—for example, moral rules and principles, moral duties and obligations, moral reasons and considerations, moral virtues and character traits—it seems natural to analyze the concept of morality in the logical form "moral *x*." And by using the phrase "action-guide" in this regard, rather than a more usual expression such as rule, principle, judgment, or prescription, we are attempting to employ the most inclusive term we can find consistent with the previous account of the general object of morality. "Action-guide," therefore, may be replaced by any number of noun phrases used in classificatory contexts: rule, principle, imperative, prescription, command, counsel, advice, fable, parable, duty, obligation, motive, reason, virtue, character trait, and so forth, as these are used to specify and guide behavior and attitudes within the moral life.

The definition may be briefly formulated as follows: A moral action-guide aims to resolve the problem of cooperation by claiming a distinctive sort of superiority based on a characteristic type of legitimacy that satisfies certain general conditions for justifiability and certain special conditions of other-regardingness. In other words, we take a *moral statement* to be a *statement expressing the acceptance of an action-guide that claims superiority, and that is considered legitimate, in that it is justifiable and other-regarding.* This reconstructive definition is schematized in Figure 1, a heuristic conceptual diagram of a moral action-guide; the diagram helps structure and clarify our elaboration and defense of this definition or conceptual explication.

First, we distinguish two primary features, the practical and the authoritative. The *practical or prescriptive component* is singled out to emphasize not only that a moral action-guide has a distinctive end in view, namely responding to the problem of cooperation, but also that in attempting to achieve this end, a moral action-guide is both constraining and directive in regard to courses of action. It "constrains" in the sense that it requires that a certain action be done or a certain attitude be held, whether or not the agent at first desires to do that action or take that attitude. Moreover, in some cases the moral action-guide indicates to the agent what to do, how to act, to whom, in what circumstances (the "variables" in the diagram) and in this sense "directs" him in the performance of a certain action or the taking of a stance.

The *authoritative component* of a moral action-guide, or what is sometimes called "the special authority of morality," has often been identified as a distinctive characteristic of a moral action-guide by philosophers and social scientists alike (see Durkheim 1953: chap. 2; Ladd 1957: 101–07; Barnsley 1972: 37–41).[3] We do not depart from this tradition, except perhaps in our particular analysis of the authoritative component. Following Ladd's analysis, this aspect may be broken down into two broad logical features: *superiority* and *legitimacy,* each of which is in itself an internally complex category (Ladd 1957: 102–07).

In general, "superiority" refers to the *autonomy* and *priority* of a moral action-guide, two features that identify the prerogative that moral action-guides are often thought to have over nonmoral action-guides. The "autonomy" of moral action-guides marks the recognition that moral action-guides can only be properly and sufficiently justified for independent, moral reasons (the apparent circularity here will disappear when we examine the feature of legitimacy). The autonomy of a moral action-guide rests on the logical requirement that no moral conclusions can be derived from premises that do not themselves contain a moral element. In brief, the autonomy of a

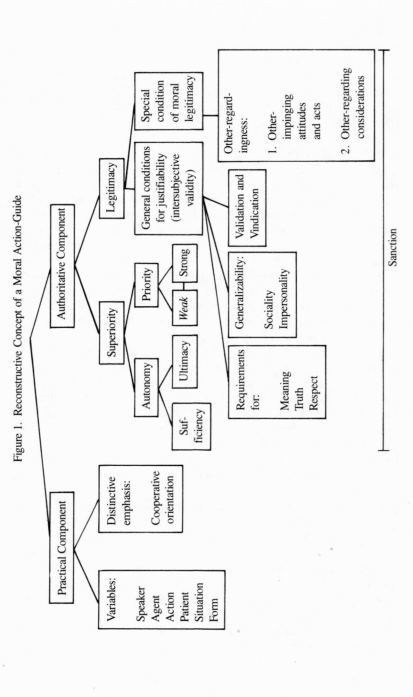

Figure 1. Reconstructive Concept of a Moral Action-Guide

moral action-guide can be specified by the conjunctive features of its sufficiency—that is, once a moral action-guide is accepted for moral reasons, no further, nonmoral, justification is needed—and its ultimacy—that is, a moral action-guide cannot in principle be justified on nonmoral grounds.

The other aspect of a moral action-guide's superiority, its "priority," indicates that moral action-guides tend to take precedence over other nonmoral action-guides. This recognition of a tendency to take precedence indicates that in various contexts priority may be asserted with varying degrees of strength, on a "strong/weak" continuum, so to speak. That is, there may be "strong" and "weak" priority. Strong priority means that moral action-guides always take precedence over any conflicting nonmoral action-guides. Weak priority signals something more limited. It means that a moral action-guide may, under special conditions, yield its position of preeminence to nonmoral action-guides, such as religious ones. But even though priority may be weak in this sense, an action-guide may not altogether lose its priority, by always being ignored or subordinated, without losing its status as a moral action-guide.

This reference to variations in degrees of priority identifies an issue in the study of comparative religious ethics of the utmost importance. Although many philosophers assume the truth of a view in favor of priority in the strong sense for all moral action-guides, such an assumption seems doubtful when looked at from the viewpoint of those religious positions that describe a tension, if not a direct conflict, between "moral duty" and "religious duty" (Kierkegaard 1941; Phillips 1967; Leiser 1969: 95–96; Outka 1973).[4] On such positions, it is by no means obvious that the moral always overrides the religious, for in such cases it is not merely a tension or conflict between two action-guides, but also a conflict between two sorts of justification, for example, between an ultimate "other-worldly" commitment and a human "this-worldly" obligation. Insofar as they tend to conceive of all nonmoral action-guides as necessarily subordinate to the "supremacy," "ultimacy," "finality," and so forth of moral action-guides, many philosophers overlook the "supremacy," "ultimacy," "finality," and so on of some of the nonmoral action-guides accepted by religious people (cf. Christian 1964: 60–77, 210–37). In order to do justice to the apparent tension between two different sorts of authoritative action-guides, we suggest that taking account of the priority continuum and of the weak sense of priority represents the more appropriate understanding, particularly for the comparative study of moral *and* religious codes. (cf. Leiser 1969: 85–98).

2.1. *General Conditions of Moral Legitimacy*

The second main feature of the authoritative component of moral action guides—*legitimacy*—is a crucial part of our reconstructive definition. This feature explicates the notion of the special authority of moral action-guides, and it provides the rationale for why moral action-guides have a superior claim in relation to nonmoral action-guides. Our elaboration of this feature is tied to certain assumptions implicit in the minimal functional account of the object of morality, namely, that morality aims to guide human conduct so that cooperative living is possible. It seems obvious that such guidance is achieved mainly by means of discursive, or otherwise symbolic, communication that permits action-guides to become formulated, promulgated, and effective. In short, the development and use of language, along with other forms of communication, is a necessary condition for social life and its patterned regulation.

Further, it seems clear that to engage in practical discourse, or discourse over recommended courses of conduct, is not only to utter and to adopt action-guides, but also to be prepared to give reasons in justification or legitimation of a recommended action-guide. We suggest that moral action-guides are like other action-guides in entailing legitimation, but that, in addition, they involve special conditions of legitimacy which distinguish moral justification from other sorts of justification. At this point, our task is: (1) to elucidate the general presuppositions underlying the activity of practical justification (the "general conditions for justifiability"); and (2) to adduce the criteria that specify the distinctiveness of moral justification (the "special conditions for moral legitimacy"). The first set of criteria is presupposed by any sort of practical justification and establishes necessary, though not sufficient, conditions for moral legitimacy. Together with the first set, the second set of criteria supplies necessary and sufficient conditions for moral legitimacy (Kemp 1964: 194–97; Frankena 1970: 156–59).

The general conditions of justifiability can be elucidated by analyzing the way in which people give reasons to justify their conduct and attitudes. To begin with, the fact that justification is a public activity is demonstrated by its dependence on linguistic communication, for language, by its very nature, is public and social. If a person engages in the public and social institution of language in order to discuss with other persons what policies of action, for example, ought to be pursued, he thereby enters into a discursive situation in which he is presumed to be prepared, or at least willing, to proffer his own reasoning, as well as to consider and appraise the reasoning presented by others.

There are certain "rules of the game" underlying such a discursive situation that must be assumed to be universal: The discourse must be intelligible; it must be applicable to the real world; and it must presuppose a certain self-understanding on the part of the participants.[5] In order to communicate intelligibly, each participant must adhere to customary rules of linguistic usage, and must, at least implicitly, accept certain common rules of logic (cf. Copi 1967: 36, 42–43). Without such presuppositions, no intelligible discourse and practical argumentation, including deliberation and justification, are possible. In addition, certain empirically oriented truth-conditions for assessing claims of truth and falsity, probability and improbability, and so on must be made in order for the participants to discuss the practical applicability of a proposed policy to the real world, and some rules of inductive logic must be operative, accepted and observed by the participants. Finally, in order for the discursive activity to have any point and to accomplish its practical aim of persuasion, each participant must make certain presuppositions about himself and others. He must assume that he, as well as his partners, constitutes a "center" of sentience (desire and interest), thought (conception and valuation), and agency (decision and action). Without these presuppositions, there would be no point in engaging in practical discourse with others, in offering reasons to them for their independent appraisal, in considering the weight of their reasons and arguments, or in attempting to persuade or convince another regarding a recommended course of action.

We may call each of these three sets of discursive rules, respectively, the requirements of "meaning," "truth," and "respect." It should be noted that each of these requirements, in turn, presupposes the notion of intersubjective validity. That is, the requirements of meaning, truth, and respect make possible the proposal, consideration, and appraisal of intersubjectively valid assertions or claims that can in principle be understood, assessed, and perhaps finally accepted by all the participants. In short, the notion of intersubjective validity, incorporating the requirements of meaning, truth, and (minimal) mutual respect, is necessary to practical discursive activity.

The last of the general conditions of justifiability we shall consider is the "condition of generalizability," which is our adaptation of the much discussed notion of universalizability (see, for example, Hare 1952: part 3; Hare 1963: part 1). Before elucidating this condition, there are two preliminary questions to be addressed. First, why choose *generalizability* over the more common philosophical term *universalizability?* Second, why should generalizability be treated as a general condition of justifiability, as we treat it, and not as a special condition of moral legitimacy? These two questions, and therefore their respective answers, are related.

We favor *generalizability* mainly to avoid confusion. In normal philosophical discussion *universalizability* is used in such a way as to exclude the practical reasoning of many non-Western and nonliterate peoples. Such peoples propound a particularistic or in-group morality, one that is restricted and applicable only to members of that society, and not extended, as in the Western religious and secular traditions, for example, to all persons. Insofar as a nonparticularistic morality in this sense is built into the prevalent understanding of *universalizability,* we prefer *generalizability.* It illuminates the justificatory activity of a wider range of societies than the culture-bound concept of universalizability.[6]

This preference for *generalizability* on our part is related to our view that generalizability is only a necessary condition of justifiability. For it seems clear to us that action-guides other than moral ones involve the condition of generalizability. For example, Leopold Pospisil includes among the four attributes of a legal decision what he calls "an intention of universal application" (though, from his discussion, the phrase "generalized application" appears to cover better what he means, especially in connection with the particularistic tribal societies he mentions):

[N]ot only does a legal decision solve a specific case, but it also formulates an ideal–a solution *intended* [his italics] to be utilized *in all similar situations in the future* [our italics]. The ideal component *binds all other members of the group* [our italics] who did not participate in the case under consideration. The [legal] authority himself turns to his previous decisions for consistency (Pospisil 1974: 78–81).

Pospisil's discussion clearly suggests that what we may call "legal action-guides" must minimally satisfy a condition of generalizability. If that is true, and Pospisil's analysis is most persuasive, then the condition of generalizability can hardly be a special condition of moral legitimacy.[7]

Moreover, if we may adapt an argument made by R. M. Hare, it is in the logic of the word *ought* in its typical uses that generalizability is required, rather than in the special logic of the term *moral,* which is but one of the typical uses of *ought* (Hare 1963: 37). In other words, an action-guide involving "ought" cannot possibly be justified unless the utterer is able, on demand, to generalize it (in the sense to be specified). If Hare is correct about this, and he seems to be, then not only are legal action-guides necessarily generalizable, but a very wide range of action-guiding discourse employing "ought" forms is as well. This claim, if true, further undermines any basis for considering generalizability as a special condition of moral legitimacy.

Turning now to the concept of generalizability itself, we find it can be formulated in various ways. One formulation of the concept puts it that an action-guide is generalized only if *it holds for every agent* who is under the same sort of circumstances as specified by the action-guide or its context (see Ladd 1957: 79; Monro 1967: 183–84). This we call the "sociality" interpretation. A second version, often denoted as "the generalization principle," "the principle of impartiality," and others, asserts that a well-formed action-guide must apply to any *similar* person in *similar* circumstances, and for the same agent in all relevantly *similar* situations (Singer 1958). This can be called the "impersonality" or "impartiality" interpretation. These two interpretations, which may well mutually imply one another, seem to specify what it means to generalize an action-guide. And we are suggesting that generalizability is one of the necessary conditions or requirements for justifying most, if not all, action-guides.[8]

We take up the categories of validation and vindication in the process of practical justification in Chapter 5. We indicate at this point that these categories are part of the general conditions of justifiability.

2.2. *Special Conditions of Moral Legitimacy*

We come now to a consideration of the special conditions of moral legitimacy that involve the notion that moral action-guides are in some peculiarly distinctive sense "other-regarding." This is not only the most controversial part of our reconstructive analysis but also the most crucial and, we believe, the most original. We wish to argue that other-regardingness plays an important role in our classificatory uses of the term *moral,* and, on the strength of the comparative evidence we have, is particularly relevant in identifying specifically "moral" action and deliberation in cultures other than our own.

To begin with, the expression "other-regarding" needs careful scrutiny, for its use is equivocal not only in common parlance, but also in philosophical discussion. There are at least two senses of the expression that need to be distinguished and reflected upon, and these correspond to two different ways in which we use the term *regard.* These two senses of the term are partly brought out in the following passage from an article by William Frankena, in which he designates an "other-regarding" condition as necessary, alongside other "formal" criteria—prescriptivity, universalizability, and "perhaps also supremacy"—for there to be a morality and a moral action-guide:

X has a morality or moral AG [action-guide] only if it includes judgements, rules, principles, ideals, etc. which (1) concern the relations of one individual to others, (2) involve or call for a consideration of the effects of his actions on others (not necessarily all others), not from the point of view of his own interests or aesthetic enjoyments, but from their own point of view (Frankena 1970: 155).

Frankena's two specifications correspond to two different ways in which we use the word *regard.* The second sense presupposes a personal subject or agent *who is able to consider and be aware of* the effects of his actions on someone else, whereas the first sense is nonsubjective and means only that there is *a relation* of some sort between one individual and others, whether the people involved are aware of the relation or not. It is our contention that both of these senses of *regard*—are active in our understanding of other-regard-ingness as this notion plays its role in the concept of a moral action-guide, though our interpretation diverges from Frankena's in significant respects. Let us sort out these two senses of the notion of other-regardingness as we understand them.

We follow Frankena in suggesting that moral action-guides are, so to speak, "other-impinging," in the first sense of "regard." But we mean by this term *other-impinging* something more than Frankena appears to by his phrase "concern the relations of one individual to others." Frankena's formulation is rather vague and misses an important point about our common understanding of what constitutes a *moral* problem. The point is effectively made by Eric D'Arcy when he speaks of "moral-species" terms as representing a class of human acts that "are so significant for human existence and welfare" as necessarily to be the object of moral reflection. This class of acts includes such things as murder, mayhem, rape, perjury, calumny, and the like (D'Arcy 1963: 25–39), together with positive acts, such as beneficence and generosity, that we would add. As a general rule, such acts "impinge upon" others in a quite special way: They have direct and usually dramatic (either negative or positive) effects upon the existence and/or welfare of other persons. Alongside D'Arcy's illustrative list of welfare-oriented acts, we may add a list of related emotions and attitudes that are also of universal significance in moral reasoning. On the negative side the list includes emotions and attitudes like envy, jealousy, maliciousness, and (human-oriented) anger and hatred. On the positive side it includes benevolence, sympathy, and pity. This point about moral-species terms is supported by G. J. Warnock, though we do not necessarily subscribe to all that Warnock seeks to draw out of it:

The limits [of *moral* evaluation] are set somewhere within the general area of concern with the welfare of human beings. . . . The relevance of considerations as to the welfare of human beings *cannot,* in the context of moral debate, be denied . . . it *is* so, simply because of what "moral" means (Warnock 1967: 67).

This understanding of other-regardingness as involving that class of acts, attitudes and emotions that impinge directly and dramatically upon the welfare of another human being entails some specification of the term *welfare.*[9] We prefer "welfare" to the broader notion of "interests" because it designates a subclass of "interests," namely those associated with the material needs of human beings, such as the concern for survival and for physical and psychic health and security. While it is undoubtedly true that there is "an extensive penumbral fringe of vagueness and indeterminacy" about what constitutes welfare—certainly in cross-cultural terms—nevertheless, it seems true that the "notion of 'the welfare' of human beings surely has, as one might put it, a perfectly clear and determinate core or centre" (Warnock 1967: 69). Certain actions, policies, and conditions of life are, the world round, conceived as being opposed to human welfare; these include the infliction of suffering or human debilitation or impairment viewed as ends in themselves. Other actions, policies, and conditions of life are universally understood to enhance the welfare of any person; these include the promotion of health and security. This determinate core or center of the meaning of *welfare* is no doubt the result, as Clyde Kluckhohn says, of the fact that

all cultures constitute so many somewhat distinct answers to essentially the same questions posed by human biology and by the generalities of the human situation. Every society's patterns for living must provide approved and sanctioned ways for dealing with such universal circumstances as the existence of two sexes; the helplessness of infants; the need for satisfaction of the elementary biological requirements such as food, warmth, and sex; and the presence of individuals of different ages and of different physical and other capacities. The basic similarities in human biology the world over are vastly more massive than the variations (Kluckhohn 1962: 294).

It is useful, further, to distinguish the concept of welfare, as one class of interests, from the concept of "happiness," as another. The two subclasses can be distinguished by at least two differentiating characteristics. First, happiness concepts connote the achievement of certain attitudes toward life involving a state of mind; welfare concepts are more concerned with the provision of material conditions necessary to maintain life. Second, happiness judgments are very much "agent-specific" in the sense that happiness necessarily involves the personal experience and awareness of the agent; welfare judgments have a relatively "fixed core"—that is, they are more in the nature of objective, necessary conditions for human life, and are less dependent on subjective appraisal and experience than are happiness judgments. It has been suggested in an illuminating metaphor that happiness is the "flower" of morality (von Wright 1963: 88). Correspondingly, welfare may be viewed as the "seed stock" of morality.[10]

We suggest that moral action-guides bear a special and indispensable relation to welfare concepts in two respects. First, there is a relatively fixed range of action-guides that in all societies come to be regarded as superior and legitimate (according to one or another pattern of justification), namely, the moral-species terms that rule against indiscriminate cheating, stealing, lying, or doing violence within the in-group (see Kluckhohn 1962: 276–78). (See Chapter 5 for our analysis of patterns of practical justification in religious ethics.) While a moral code is not exhausted by attention to acts of this sort, the corresponding action-guides are of basic importance, which is to say that they are "highly stringent" relative to other action-guides. It seems, then, that whatever else it is, morality is indispensably concerned with this fixed range of welfare-oriented acts and action-guides. If we encountered action-guides in a given culture that systematically minimized or disregarded the significance of the moral-species terms, we should have difficulty considering these action-guides as moral. Another feature of the same point is that action-guides will be moral only if they presuppose the centrality and stringency of the moral-species terms.

Second, there is often found in a society a range of highly stringent action-guides not intuitively connected in any direct way with the basic welfare of human beings, as we have designated the notion. Nevertheless, on reflection, such action-guides, in the minds of the adherents, do bear directly on matters of basic welfare. For example, the Navajo consider the following taboo to be highly stringent: "A man must not look at his mother-in-law and she must not look at him." One reason given for complying with this taboo is that, if it is violated, the offender will "go blind" or "will not be very strong and [his] body will be weak all over" (Ladd 1957: 230). Yet, we find upon further investigation that this reason relating to the welfare of self is logically tied up with the welfare of others and, indeed, the welfare of the whole social group. There are many illustrations of this kind.

Therefore, we conclude that while the concern with "other-impinging," welfare-oriented acts, emotions and attitudes (moral-species terms) is not the whole of morality, it is sufficiently intrinsic to be considered as a distinctive emphasis in the formulation of moral action-guides.

The importance of the second sense of *regard*—"to consider" or "to attend to"—in the process of justifying a moral action-guide is suggested by Frankena's second stipulation of what it means to have a morality or a moral action-guide. But his formulation misses the mark. If we were to abide by Frankena's specification that a moral action-guide exists only if it includes judgments, and so on that "call for a consideration of the effects of [one person's] actions on others . . . not from the point of view of his own interests . . . but from [the other's] point of view," then it seems we have to rule out as moralities many nonliterate codes of conduct.

For example, Ladd interprets or reconstructs the process of moral evaluation among the Navajo as follows:

> Every evaluation reflects the *evaluator's* interest in the actual past or anticipated effects of the action *on him personally*. . . . In effect, the grounds for evaluation are something like: "That is bad, because it will bring trouble (to me)," or "That is good, because it will help (me)" (Ladd 1957: 305).

Based on Ladd's reading, the Navajo have an apparently egoistic pattern of justification.[11] Also based on this reading, what seems lacking among the Navajo, and apparently among other groups as well, is not so much a consideration of the effects of one person's actions on others, but a consideration of these effects *from the other's point of view*. If *other-regarding* means taking the other's point of view, and if that understanding, in turn, is a requirement of what it means to have a morality, then all such "egoistic" systems are nonmoral systems.

It is just because the other-regarding requirement, as Frankena defines it, seems to be lacking from the Navajo code that Ladd drops it altogether as a defining characteristic of the concept of moral, and relies simply upon prescriptivity, superiority, and legitimacy. In our judgment, both Frankena and Ladd take unnecessarily extreme positions on this matter. Frankena defines *other-regarding,* in the second sense, overnarrowly. Ladd, for his part, overlooks evidence he himself supplies that lends support to at least one form of the other-regarding condition in the second sense:

> The basic factual belief which united egoistic premises with altruistic

conclusions is that the welfare of each individual is dependent upon that of every other individual in the group. What is good for the individual is good for everyone else, and what is good for everybody is good for the individual (Ladd 1957: 304).

Or, as he puts it elsewhere, there is a "general Navajo presumption that the welfare of others is a *necessary condition* [our italics] of one's own welfare" (Ladd 1957: 296).

There are grounds here for concluding that in the Navajo justificatory scheme, taken as a whole, the welfare of others is in fact regarded—that is, is considered or taken account of—if only assumptively and somewhat indirectly. And Ladd's use of the phrase "necessary condition" indicates that consideration of the other's welfare is not a casual matter, even if in Ladd's view it is not at the center of Navajo moral reasoning. Thus, while Frankena's formulation is too narrow to allow for the rather ulterior character of the other-regarding concern among the Navajo, Ladd's disinclination to attend to other-regardingness, in the second sense of the notion, as a special feature of moral justification (legitimacy) appears unwarranted by his own evidence. Our expectation is that among other apparently "egoistic" systems or codes of conduct, the same sort of indirect attention will often be given to the welfare of others in the justification or moral action-guides.

Our general conclusion, then, about the special conditions of moral legitimacy is that Frankena's specification of the two senses of other-regardingness needs to be revised as follows: An action-guide is moral only if it includes (together with prescriptivity, superiority, and general legitimacy, as discussed) judgments and so on that (1) concern emotions, attitudes, and acts that impinge upon the material welfare of others, and (2) involve, in the justification of its course of action, *some* consideration of the effects of the action of one person on the material welfare of others.

We need to anticipate the significance of the distinction between these two conceptions of other-regardingness for our analysis of practical justification (see Chapter 5, below). Our basic point is that an action-guide is fully moral only if it is part of a practical position that systematically includes *both* senses of other-regarding. Any such action-guide must be formulated so as to express in some way the stringency and centrality of the other-impinging emotions, attitudes, and acts. But, in addition, the reasons given to legitimate it must include reference to some consideration of the effects of the action of one person on the material welfare of others.

As we shall see, the two senses are not necessarily present in all practical positions. Other-regardingness may be present in the first sense, but not in the second. In some positions the other-impinging emotions, attitudes, and acts may be given their due, but they may not be systematically legitimated in reference to some consideration of the material welfare of others. This is the case, for example, when the other-impinging emotions are legitimated by strictly religious considerations. On the other hand, while other-regardingness in the first sense may occur without the second, the reverse does not seem possible. Since consideration of the material welfare of others includes concern for physical and psychic health and security, it is inconceivable to manifest such concern without showing due regard for the other-impinging emotions, which apply that concern to social relationships.

2.3. Moral Sanction

It is necessary to tie up a few loose ends in this account of morality and a moral action-guide. First, a word about the role of "sanction" within the reconstructive concept of a moral action-guide. Are sanctions necessarily attached to moral action-guides? If so, what function do they have, what form do they take, and how are they related to the other conceptual features of moral action-guides? A strong and typical view of the role of sanction in morality is expressed by H. L. A. Hart:

A further distinguishing feature of morality is the characteristic form of moral pressure which is exerted in its support. . . . With morals the typical form of pressure consists in appeals to the respect for the rules, as things important in themselves. . . . So moral pressure is characteristically . . . exerted . . . by reminders of the moral character of the action contemplated and of the demands of morality. . . . Emphatic reminders of what the rules demand, appeals to conscience and reliance on the operation of guilt and remorse, are the characteristic and most prominent forms of presssure used for the support of social morality (Hart 1961: 176–77).

Hart takes the position that the concept of moral sanction (pressure) is a necessary and prominent feature of a moral action-guide. According to his view, moral sanction is not merely empirically necessary to sustain a given morality, but also conceptually requisite to the notion of morality itself. It is, however, possible to accept this latter claim without ascribing the primary conceptual importance to the moral sanction that Hart does. For what is moral sanction, other than the psycho/social manifestation, the obverse or negative side, of a moral action-guide's (positive) authoritativeness? The concept of moral sanction itself cannot be understood without reference to the superiority and legitimacy of a moral action-guide. Therefore, these components are those that deserve primary conceptual emphasis—they provide the point, the rationale, for the concept of moral sanction. Thus, we agree with Hart's functional and conceptual explication of the notion of moral sanction, but hesitate to ascribe such predominance to it. For us, moral legitimacy explains and justifies moral superiority, which, in turn, granted certain facts about human nature and the human condition, gives rise to and explains the emergence of moral sanction and its role.

2.4. Moral Agents and Recipients

Another loose end is represented by the question: To whom does morality apply? This is an intentionally ambiguous question that may be construed in a variety of ways. Two significant interpretations, however, come to mind. First, who can properly be expected to comply with moral action-guides (referring to agents)? Second, who are moral action-guides designed to benefit (referring to recipients)? Although in one way or another these questions have been addressed, at least implicitly, in our account of morality and the concept of a moral action-guide, it may prove enlightening to consider them more explicitly.

The patent answer to the first question is simply "rational agents." Why and in what sense is this answer correct in our account of morality? We have argued that moral action-guides in general presuppose a certain type of legitimacy, defining a certain range of characteristic reasons, that "weighs" for or against actions, attitudes, and policies. Thus, to think and act morally is to accord such legitimation its due "weight" in deciding what to do, what attitude to adopt, what policy to pursue. Clearly, in order to recognize such legitimacy, an agent, in addition to possessing the capabilities of deciding, acting, adopting, and pursuing actions on the basis of this recognition, must be capable of so justifying. In short, to be a moral agent involves as a necessary condition being "rational," in the minimal sense that one is able to acquire knowledge about relevant circumstances, envisage alternative courses of action, grasp and weight relevant considerations for and against these alternatives according to the general conditions of justifiability and the special conditions of moral legitimacy, and to act accordingly.

We contend that these capabilities, among others, can in general be ascribed to all persons in pursuit of the object or end of morality, which is resolution of the problem of cooperation. Moreover, if this aim or point of morality represents a concern common to all (the human condition), then a rational agent cannot claim that he is the kind of agent to whom moral action-guides in general cannot be applied. This latter conditional statement appears to be analytically true, but it is not trivial. It suggests that moral action-guides can apply in the "agent sense" to virtually everyone, or at least to all rational persons. Thus, moral agency is, at least in part, definable by reference to conditions of minimal rationality. (The further contention that no rational person can claim exemption from the moral enterprise, that is, from moral action-guides in general, will not be argued here. But it merits serious reflection by students of ethics and morality.)

There are many qualifications to this brief discussion of moral agency. For example, not all persons are minimally rational (consider young children and mental defectives), so many moral action-guides cannot be agent-applicable to them. Moreover, not every moral action-guide applies in the agent sense to every moral agent; consider, for example, special role obligations here (parent/child, husband/wife, and so on). But these qualifications do not seriously mitigate the force of the general point that moral action-guides apply, in principle, and in the agent sense, to rational persons.

The second question, regarding who moral action-guides are designed to benefit, is concerned with the recipient, and seeks an understanding of morality's applicability in the recipient sense. It inquires into the conditions of relevance for moral action-guides being appropriately considered and applied by rational moral agents. More specifically, this question requests a characterization of the recipients of the consequences of the courses of action specified by moral action-guides. The answer—namely, those people whose welfare is affected by a contemplated course of action—is contained implicitly in our account of other-regardingness. But such an answer, as it stands, seems a bit shallow, for it fails to distinguish and address two important issues: (1) What is the scope of the applicability of moral action-guides in the recipient sense? (2) In virtue of what are recipients entitled to other-regarding consideration?

The first issue, concerning scope, raises the poignant matter of whether there can be (logically) particularistic or in-group moralities that are restricted and applicable only to the members of certain groups or societies and not extended to all persons. In our account of the concept of morality and of moral action-guides, such closed, in-group moralities cannot be ruled out. That is, we do not (cannot) deny that particularistic codes exist and are properly spoken of as "moral codes" (see MacBeath 1952; Fürer-Haimendorf 1967). But we do think it can be said that such codes, while perfectly comprehensible as instantiations of morality, seem to be conceptually odd. For, given our discussion of moral legitimacy, it appears that no person can be simply excluded from moral consideration: This seems almost analytically true.

This statement appealing to analyticity is not an idle remark when one seriously reflects on the point of morality as that of countervailing or resolving the problem of cooperation. It is clear that a system of action-guides cannot fully achieve this end if the scope of these action-guides is confined to restricted groups. This is so for two simple reasons. First, if moral action-guides are group-bound, then everyone is at risk vis-à-vis members of other groups. Second, if human conduct is regulated only within discrete groups, then the possibility of conflict between groups remains. In either case, action-guides with such limited range can hardly be said to satisfy or resolve the problem of cooperation. Thus, there is some reason to think that moral action-guides should give consideration to any person if the point, end, or object of morality is not to be frustrated or even self-defeating in the final analysis.[12]

The remaining issue, concerning the grounds for recipients' entitlement of other-regarding consideration, cannot be simply dispatched by talk about minimal conditions of rationality, such as were discussed in reference to moral agency. Rather, we suggest that the "beneficiaries," so to speak, of moral action-guides are more appropriately characterized as "persons" in a very unrestricted sense. For it appears to follow from our discussion of welfare that the criterion for being a recipient of moral action is simply the capacity of being subject to the conditions of human welfare. That is, to be a proper, logical subject for the ascription of welfare-type concepts is sufficient to qualify a person as a proper recipient of moral action-guides. No further conditions, such as minimal rationality or the like, need be invoked to explicate the recipients' moral claim to other-regarding consideration by moral agents.[13]

This account of the concept of moral (morality) is not offered as mere philosophical speculation. On the contrary, we intend to employ it in mapping the logic of various codes of religious ethics. In this regard, a final important point to observe about the logical features of our proposed reconstructive concept of morality and moral action-guide is that they neither specify nor imply any specific (normative) moral principles or code of conduct. This characteristic approach helps to ensure that our subsequent investigations avoid ethnocentricity and are cross-culturally applicable.

NOTES

1. Although William Frankena is credited with a classic discussion of Moore's argument (Frankena 1952; cf. Hare 1952: chap. 5), Paul Taylor's analysis of the naturalistic fallacy is among the most readable that we have encountered (Taylor 1961: 240–51). Taylor distinguishes three main versions of the fallacy. The definitional version claims that normative terms are equivalent in meaning to certain empirical terms. The deductive version asserts that normative conclusions can be derived logically from empirical premises alone. And the disagreement version holds that it is possible to resolve all normative disagreements solely by appeal to empirical facts. Taylor criticizes each version and goes on to conclude: "The underlying principle which each version of the fallacy overlooks is that empirical knowledge about what is evaluated or prescribed does not by itself provide justification of a value-judgment or prescription. There must always be, in addition, the justification of a decision to adopt a certain standard or rule" (Taylor 1961: 250).
2. By using the term *function* here, we do not intend to ally our definition with the functionalist schools in social analysis. Rather, our preliminary approach to the concept of morality is made in the spirit of Peter Strawson's remark that where we are dealing with human institutions, it is no reproach to a conceptual explication that it may be described as at least partially genetic (Strawson 1966: 294). Contrary to the views of Donald Evans, our definitions are not primarily functional, nor do they logically indicate what kinds of social scientific explanations are to be sought for the phenomena of morality and religion (Evans 1976: 6–10).

3. All such views, of course, can be traced back to the influence of Immanuel Kant's moral philosophy.
4. Some philosophers have argued that prudential considerations may override moral considerations in some cases (see, for example, Falk 1963).
5. This presuppositional approach was suggested to us by R. S. Peters (1967: chaps. 2, 3, 5–7) and by A. Phillips Griffiths (1967: 177–82). See also the fascinating and important essays by Steven Lukes, "Some Problems about Rationality," and Martin Hollis, "Reason and Ritual" (in Wilson 1970: 194–213, 221–39). As Hollis puts it, "Native logic must either turn out to be a version of our own or remain untranslatable. . . . If the natives reason at all, then they reason as we do (Wilson 1970: 232). In their *Respect for Persons*, R. S. Downie and Elizabeth Telfer offer a brief and unconvincing critique of the presuppositional method of argument (Downie and Telfer 1969: 153–55).
6. We also favor the term *generalizability* to avoid the unwarranted elision of a general condition of justifiability with what many moral philosophers treat as a special condition of moral legitimacy. In philosophical discussion "universaliza-tion" and "universalizability" are frequently used to cover not merely the notion of generalizability as we understand it but also the condition of "reversibility" (see Baier 1958: 200–04). According to this latter condition, when an action-guide is universalized by an agent, he evaluates the results of that action-guide from the point of view of the recipient of the consequences of the course of action involved. To our way of thinking, this notion of reversibility involves much more than the minimal condition of generalizability, insofar as it invokes many more specific criteria of moral legitimation pertaining to other-regardingness. In a sense, it trys to do too much; and by being so inclusive, certain important distinctions are glossed.
7. In his modern classic, *A Theory of Justice,* John Rawls discusses the insufficien-cy of the condition of generality in distinguishing "what we intuitively regard as the moral point of view" (Rawls 1971: 130–36.)
8. We have purposely excluded still a third interpretation of generalizability, namely the condition of reversibility, which is mentioned in a preceding footnote. To reiterate, according to this interpretation, an action-guide is generalized when an agent looks at its results from the point of view of the recipient or patient (see Baier 1958: 200–04). Ladd finds no evidence that reversibility is universally present (Ladd 1957: 272, 305). Therefore, as Barnsley says, "considerable difficulties arise in the application of this [interpretation] to anthropology, since so many moral codes would have to be ruled out" (Barnsley 1972: 34). Nevertheless, there seem good grounds, on the evidence, for including the weaker form of generalizability, that is, some combination of our two interpretations. As Barnsley puts it: "Moral prescriptions must be considered equally binding upon oneself, and others. In this sense, they may be said to be impersonal or social." This weaker form of generalizability "makes possible some type of genuine consensus or dissensus over moral principles" (Barnsley 1972: 45).
9. Our discussion in this chapter assumes, along with many other thinkers through-out the ages, that morality is, by definition, concerned mainly with the welfare of *human beings*. This assumption has been challenged recently by certain moral philosophers, most notably Peter Singer in *Animal Liberation* (1975). Singer goes so far as to argue that such an assumption constitutes a blatantly immoral form of discrimination called "speciesism," which is on par with racism, sexism, and the like (Singer 1975: chaps. 1, 5, 6; cf. Regan and Singer 1976). Though Singer's argument has a certain degree of force, it raises many conceptual issues that cannot be explored within the context of our investigation.
10. The discussion of the concepts of welfare and happiness makes fascinating

reading for the philosophically minded. In our research we encountered a number of brief but interesting passages. See, for example: Barry 1965: 187–90; Benn and Peters 1965: 162–70; Louch 1966: 70–79; Nielsen 1968: 9–25; Peters 1967: 91–102; Quinton 1970: 202–22; Rescher 1966: 28–30, 98–101; Runciman 1966: 260–73; Twiss 1970: 12–16; von Wright 1963: 86–113; Warnock 1967: 54–61, 66–72.

11. Ladd's egoistic reconstruction of the Navajo moral code is criticized and corrected in Chapter 6. However, there appears to be strong evidence of "egoistic systems" of conduct in many nonliterate societies; so the point of our discussion here retains a degree of cogency (see Fürer-Haimendorf 1967; MacBeath 1952).

12. It is interesting to note that even within particularistic moral codes, there is almost invariably a group of moral action-guides that recognize and regulate conduct toward strangers. For example, the Navajo explicitly interpret their own equivalent of the golden rule—"One ought to treat everyone as a kinsman"—to apply not only to the in-group but also to those outside Navajo society, that is, strangers and aliens. (See Chapter 6 for a discussion of this point.) Thus, even particularistic codes *tend* to be universally applicable in scope.

13. In deference to the moral claims and/or rights of nonhuman animals, Peter Singer suggests an even weaker criterion: the capacity for suffering and/or enjoyment or happiness (Singer 1975: chap. 1). Again, his suggestion is provocative, but it raises too many conceptual issues for exploration within the present inquiry. It should be noted, however, that our criterion is compatible with Singer's position that nonhuman animals, along with humans, share the capacity of being subject to the conditions of welfare (as we have defined them).

REFERENCES

BAIER, KURT.

    1958   *The Moral Point of View: A Rational Basis of Ethics.*
            Ithaca, N.Y.: Cornell University Press.

BARNSLEY, JOHN H.

    1972   *The Social Reality of Ethics: The Comparative Analysis of Moral Codes.* London: Routledge & Kegan Paul.

BARRY, BRIAN.

    1965   *Political Argument.* London: Routledge & Kegan Paul.

BEARDSMORE, R. W.

    1969   *Moral Reasoning.* New York: Schocken Books.

BENN, S. I., AND PETERS, R. S.

    1965   *The Principles of Political Thought.* Second edition. New York: Free Press.

CHRISTIAN, WILLIAM A.

    1964   *Meaning and Truth in Religion.* Princeton: Princeton University Press.

COPI, IRVING M.
1967   *Symbolic Logic.* Third edition. New York: Macmillan Co.

D'ARCY, ERIC.
1963   *Human Acts: An Essay in Their Moral Evaluation.* Oxford: Oxford University Press.

DOWNIE, R. S., AND TELFER, ELIZABETH.
1969   *Respect for Persons.* London: George Allen & Unwin.

DURKHEIM, EMILE.
1953   *Sociology and Philosophy.* D. F. Pocock, trans. Glencoe, Ill.: Free Press.

EVANS, DONALD D.
1976   "On Defining Morality and Religion." Unpublished paper.

FALK, W. D.
1963   "Morality, Self, and Others." In *Morality and the Language of Conduct.* Hector-Neri Castañeda and George Nakhnikian, eds. Detroit: Wayne State University Press.

FRANKENA, WILLIAM K.
1952   "The Naturalistic Fallacy." Reprinted in *Readings in Ethical Theory.* Wilfred Sellers and John Hospers, eds. New York: Appleton-Century-Crofts.
1965   "Recent Conceptions of Morality." In *Morality and the Language of Conduct.* Hector-Neri Castañeda and George Nakhnikian, eds. Detroit: Wayne State University Press.
1970   "The Concept of Morality." Reprinted in *The Definition of Morality.* G. Wallace and A. D. M. Walker, eds. London: Methuen & Co.

FÜRER-HAIMENDORF, CHRISTOPH VON.
1967   *Morals and Merit: A Study of Values and Social Controls in South Asian Societies.* London: Weidenfeld & Nicolson.

GRIFFITHS, A. PHILLIPS.
1967   "Ultimate Moral Principles: Their Justification." In *The Encyclopedia of Philosophy.* Volume 8. Paul Edwards, ed. New York: Macmillan Co. and Free Press.

HARE, R. M.
1952   *The Language of Morals.* Oxford: Oxford University Press.
1963   *Freedom and Reason.* Oxford: Oxford University Press.

HART, H. L. A.
1961   *The Concept of Law.* Oxford: Oxford University Press.

HOLLIS, MARTIN.
1970   "Reason and Ritual." Reprinted in *Rationality.* Bryan R. Wilson, ed. Oxford: Basil Blackwell.

KANT, IMMANUEL.
1959   *Foundations of the Metaphysics of Morals.* Lewis White Beck, trans. Indianapolis: Bobbs-Merrill Co., Liberal Arts Press.

KEMP, JOHN.
1964   *Reason, Action and Morality.* London: Routledge & Kegan Paul.

KIERKEGAARD, SØREN.
1941   *Fear and Trembling.* Walter Lowrie, trans. Princeton: Princeton University Press.

KLUCKHOHN, CLYDE.
1962   *Culture and Behavior.* Richard Kluckhohn, ed. New York: Free Press.

LADD, JOHN.
1957   *The Structure of a Moral Code: A Philosophical Analysis of Ethical Discourse Applied to the Ethics of the Navaho Indians.* Cambridge, Mass.: Harvard University Press.

LEISER, BURTON M.
1969   *Custom, Law, and Morality.* Garden City, N.Y.: Doubleday & Co., Anchor Books.

LOUCH, A. R.
1966   *Explanation and Human Action.* Berkeley and Los Angeles: University of California Press.

LUKES, STEVEN.
1970   "Some Problems about Rationality." Reprinted in *Rationality.* Bryan R. Wilson, ed. Oxford: Basil Blackwell.

MacBEATH, ALEXANDER.
1952   *Experiments in Living: A Study of the Nature and Foundation of Ethics or Morals in the Light of Recent Work in Social Anthropology.* London: Macmillan & Co.

MONRO, D. H.
1967   *Empiricism and Ethics.* Cambridge: Cambridge University Press.

MOORE, GEORGE EDWARD.
1903   *Principia Ethica.* Cambridge: Cambridge University Press.

NIELSEN, KAI.
1968   "On Moral Truth." In *Studies in Moral Philosophy.* American Philosophical Quarterly Monograph Series, no. 1. Oxford: Basil Blackwell.

OUTKA, GENE.
1973   "Religious and Moral Duty: Notes on *Fear and Trembling.*" In *Religion and Morality.* Gene Outka and John P. Reeder, Jr., eds. Garden City, N.Y.: Doubleday & Co., Anchor Books.

PATON, H. J.
 1963 *The Categorical Imperative: A Study in Kant's Moral Philosophy.* Fourth edition. London: Hutchinson & Co.
PETERS, R. S.
 1967 *Ethics and Education.* Glenview, Ill.: Scott, Foresman, & Co.
PHILLIPS, D. Z.
 1967 "Moral and Religious Conceptions of Duty." Reprinted in *Religion and Understanding.* D. Z. Phillips, ed. Oxford: Basil Blackwell.
POSPISIL, LEOPOLD.
 1974 *Anthropology of Law: A Comparative Theory.* Second edition. New Haven: HRAF Press.
QUINTON, A.
 1970 "The Bounds of Morality." In *Metaphilosophy* 1:202–22.
RAWLS, JOHN.
 1971 *A Theory of Justice.* Cambridge, Mass.: Harvard University Press, Belknap Press.
REGAN, TOM, AND SINGER, PETER, EDS.
 1976 *Animal Rights and Human Obligations.* Englewood Cliffs, N.J.: Prentice-Hall.
RESCHER, NICHOLAS.
 1966 *Distributive Justice: A Constructive Critique of the Utilitarian Theory of Distribution.* Indianapolis: Bobbs-Merrill Co.
RUNCIMAN, W. G.
 1966 *Relative Deprivation and Social Justice.* Berkeley and Los Angeles: University of California Press.
SINGER, MARCUS.
 1958 "Moral Rules and Principles." In *Essays in Moral Philosophy.* A. I. Melden, ed. Seattle: University of Washington Press.
SINGER, PETER.
 1975 *Animal Liberation: A New Ethics for Our Treatment of Animals.* New York: New York Review & Random House.
STRAWSON, PETER F.
 1966 "Social Morality and Individual Ideal." Reprinted in *Christian Ethics and Contemporary Philosophy.* Ian T. Ramsey, ed. London: SCM Press.
TAYLOR, PAUL W.
 1961 *Normative Discourse.* Englewood Cliffs, N.J.: Prentice-Hall.
TWISS, SUMNER B.
 1970 "Critical Notes on 'Theology and Happiness.' " In *Reflection* 67 (3): 12–16.
VON WRIGHT, GEORG HENRIK.
 1963 *The Varieties of Goodness.* London: Routledge & Kegan Paul.

WARNOCK, G. J.
    1967 *Contemporary Moral Philosophy*. London: Macmillan & Co.
    1971 *The Object of Morality*. London: Methuen & Co.
WILSON, BRYAN R., ED.
    1970 *Rationality*. Oxford: Basil Blackwell.

3 | The Concepts of Religion and Religious Action-Guide

1. INTRODUCTION

Definitions of "religion" are notoriously open to debate (see, for example, the essays and discussion in *Journal for the Scientific Study of Religion* 1962: 3–35; Christian 1941 and 1964: chaps. 3, 4; Geertz 1966; Spiro 1966; Robertson 1970; Streng 1972; Edwards 1972: chaps. 1, 2). Nevertheless, there is no need to throw up our hands in despair and proceed to study religious ethics without knowing what we are examining. The problem is to specify the proper object of the study of religion. This problem is quite complex. On the one hand, there are many phenomena we might be reluctant to include under the concept, for example, psychotherapy, Marxism, Maoism (cf. Eliade 1959: 201–13). On the other hand, some traditions ordinarily conceived as "religious" have sometimes been claimed not to be so at all, for example, Theravada Buddhism, Confucianism, Shinto (cf. Spiro 1966: 89–96). Some clarification of definition is needed before we can proceed with our inquiries into comparative religious ethics. Clarifying a definition of "religion," and adding it to our account of morality, is a necessary first step in our enterprise.

Although we are hesitant to add to the amount of literature defining *religion*, we must, for the purposes of our inquiry, attain a coherent and defensible focus on the phenomenon of religion (cf. Smart 1973: 14–15). We must present the particular considerations that justify our proposed definition, even at the risk of being wearisome. Although we give detailed justification for our proposal, however, it will not be possible to discuss in detail the many other definitions of religion that have been offered by scholars. Our proposal conforms to the canons of reconstructive definition set out in Chapter 1. Thus, we heed a general warning about definitions articulated by Michael Pye in reference to comparative religion:

A general warning may not be out of place however: namely that any definition used should not inappropriately distort the field of study from the very start—either by involving unwarranted presumptions about the "real" nature of religion, or by being so narrowly conceived as to exclude relevant data. The first danger may be avoided by emphasizing the "operational" nature of the definition required.... Too narrow a definition is usually brought about by selecting a notable characteristic of some one religion or group of religions and universalizing it as *the* specific characteristic of all religion (Pye 1972: 9).

1.1. General Object or Function of Religion

Before proposing our definition, it is useful to consider, as we did in analyzing the concept of moral (morality), certain minimal and commonly understood functional features of religion. We can acquire a preliminary understanding of religion by examining what it does in the context of human life.

It is widely assumed that religion "functions" to resolve certain distinctive problems in the lives of individuals and social groups. (Our caveat in Chapter 2, note 3 about the use of the term *function* applies with equal force to our use of the term here.) These problems are experienced as anxieties about certain "boundary situations" in human life and experience, and they are encountered at at least three points: (1) in trying to make sense out of the felt inexplicability of the natural (and social) world, its existence and purpose, and its processes and events; (2) in trying to cope with the obdurate presence of suffering and death; and (3) in trying to live with and manage the ambiguities and puzzles inherent in human conduct. For convenience, these problems may be designated as *problems of interpretability*.[1] These problems, religion's problems, pose radical challenges or "ontological anxieties" in the face of man's inclination to view the world and life as rationally comprehensible.

Religion copes with these problems in three ways: conceptually, emotionally, and practically. These three approaches may be denoted as "religion-making characteristics" (cf. Alston 1967). They consist, respectively, of adhering to a cosmology (or mythic world view), expressing certain attitudes and emotions, and acting in certain prescribed ways. The first characteristic, adhering to a cosmology, indicates that religion attempts to formulate and propound ideas on the general order of existence that provide authoritative perspectives or world views for handling those deeply disturbing concerns of life that cry out for interpretation. The second indicates that these perspectives evoke certain attitudes, dispositions, and emotions that tend to reduce the ontological anxieties mentioned. And finally, these perspectives and attitudes combine to specify certain kinds of practical activity, such as rituals and ceremonials, which in turn tend to reinforce the authority of the world view and the attitudes evoked.

In short, the three religion-making characteristics converge to produce and sustain religious persons and groups by resolving their anxieties over the problems of interpretability. Obviously there are important causal connections among these characteristics—grist for the psychology, sociology, and anthropology of religion. But while they are conceptually important and their interrelationships causally significant, these characteristics are not yet sufficiently refined to distinguish religion from other similar phenomena, such as "grand" personal and social philosophies of life like existentialism and Marxism.

1.2. A Definitional Pitfall

In attempting to define *religion*, many scholars focus their attention almost exclusively on the emotional and practical religion-making characteristics. The general trend of their analyses goes something like this: Religions and religious persons can be adequately characterized or defined by identifying the essential religious emotion and the essential religious practice. These two supposedly indispensable features of religion have been designated, respectively, as "sense of the sacred," "awe," "*mysterium tremendum et fascinans*" and as "worship," "piety," "devotion" (see, for example, Otto 1950: chaps. 4–6; Scheler 1972: 161–178; Wach 1958). Even Alexander Mac-Beath, who has an otherwise defensible definition, falls prey to this tendency when he singles out religion's "emotional element, the sense of the sacred or the uncanny and the emotional response which it evokes, what some anthropologists call the religious thrill" (Mac-Beath 1952: 298).

Using such notions as these to define *religion* is objectionable on many grounds. For one, the world's religions evoke a considerable variety of emotional expressions and behavioral practices; this diversity is not acknowledged by these notions as they are usually developed. A related objection is that using such notions to define *religion* begs, at the outset, the question of whether all religions do in fact possess certain common emotional and behavioral features. Such questions require careful empirical inquiry, not premature settlement by arbitrary stipulations. Another objection is directed to those scholars who claim that these notions are intended to cover emotional and behavioral diversity. In fact, the narrow connotations of these terms are bound to generate confusion by deemphasizing rather than highlighting the significant differences among religions. Finally, it may be charged that such definitional approaches do not adequately account for all three religion-making characteristics. Whatever happened, for example, to the cosmological feature of religion? In light of such considerations as these, we feel that the question of whether there is a distinctive religious emotion and/or a distinctive type of religious behavior should be left open by our definition.

2. Definition of Religion

We contend that any adequate definition of *religion* must take into account all three religion-making characteristics, while at the same time allowing for the empirical diversity of each. Our definition may be briefly formulated as follows. We take a *religious statement* to be *a statement expressing acceptance of a set of beliefs, attitudes, and practices based on a notion of sacred authority that functions to resolve the ontological problems of interpretability*. The conceptual diagram in Figure 2 helps to structure and clarify our elaboration and defense of this reconstructive definition.

We begin by indicating what we understand by the notion of acceptance as contained in our definition. To "accept" a set of beliefs or whatever is to affirm, implicitly at least, what we call a "basic religious claim."[2] Religious beliefs, attitudes, and practices

Figure 2. Reconstructive Concept of Religion

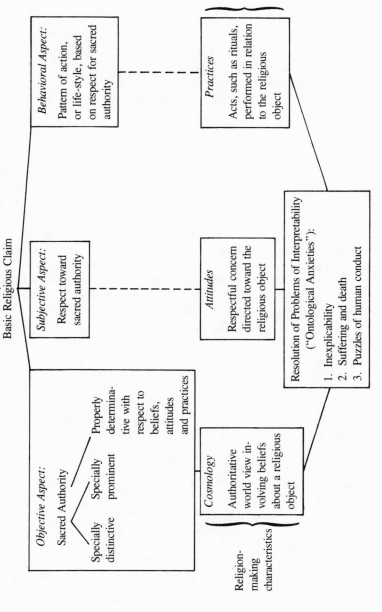

are organized in sets or systems that comprise, however loosely, a conceptual framework; such frameworks, in turn, yield basic claims that ground the fundamental convictions of various religions.[3] A particular framework, together with its basic claim, may be variously articulated and elaborated formally in scriptures, creeds, treatises and informally in sacred stories, legends, myths, art forms, and so on.

By analyzing the logical nature of this type of claim, we believe we can articulate an acceptable definition of *religion* that touches on the three religion-making characteristics. We begin this analysis by pointing out the obvious: A basic religious claim is the central belief of a religion's cosmology. It orients the authoritative perspective or world view of the religious believer. And it does this by combining three logically related aspects that correspond to the three religion-making characteristics. The objective aspect corresponds to cosmology, the subjective aspect to attitudes, and the behavioral aspect to practices. Let us examine each in turn.

A basic religious claim makes an assertion about a religious object. This asserted claim has two obvious components: It refers to a religious object and it characterizes that object in some way. The referent of the claim is the focal point of a religious belief system or cosmology (cf. Smart 1973: 67–73). From a phenomenological point of view, this object may take many forms. It may be a quality (for example, wisdom, love), a relation (for example, harmony, unity), a particular natural entity (sun, earth, sky, river, animal, and so on), a particular human individual or group (such as a king, the dead), nature as a whole (that is, Nature), a pure form or realm of pure forms (for example, Good, Truth, all Ideas), pure being (such as One, Being Itself, Ground of Being), or a transcendent active being (such as Allah, Yahweh, God). These phenomenological categories are not exhaustive, but they are sufficient to indicate the variety of possible religious objects, thereby pointing to a complex variable in the field of religious inquiry. As Ninian Smart says, "The question of what is the Focus [religious object] is a matter of empirical investigation" (Smart 1973: 68).

A basic religious claim not only refers to an object, but also characterizes it in some way. That is, a basic religious claim predicates one or more attributes, functions, or both, of an object. Its main assertive point is that its characterization is true (see Christian 1964: Chaps. 2, 12). Phenomenological inquiry provides a wide variety of such predicates, for example, "holy," "worshipful," "ultimate," "supreme." Yet it should be noted that every such characterization has three logical features in common. First, every basic religious claim asserts a special distinctiveness for its object by distinguishing it from everything else. Second, every basic religious claim ascribes a special prominence to its object, both in ontological and axiological terms. Third, every basic religious claim ascribes a high degree of authority to its object in terms of its relevance to the life of the religious subject (believer or group).

Other scholars of religion have studied certain of these features in one way or another, but none has reflected very deeply on them, and none has noted that taken together they constitute a coherent structural specification of any religious object. We are contending that a careful conceptual analysis of the logical features of a basic religious claim in its objective aspect enables us to construct a formal model of a religious object. That is, by carefully investigating the logical features of a distinctive type of claim, we can reconstruct an acceptable definition of *religion* by analyzing the other two aspects of the basic religious claim.

2.1. Concept of Sacred Authority

A basic religious claim presupposes, according to our account, that the religious object is considered to be or to have "sacred authority," a phrase that requires special attention.[4] By the adjective "sacred," we suggest two things about the way the religious object is regarded. First, it is taken to be *specially distinctive* in the sense that it is "set apart" or "marked off" from everything else in the world, thus constituting a "scope of reality" that is to *some degree beyond the volitional control of human beings.*[5] This dimension of sacredness is sometimes characterized as the "transcendence" or "otherness" of the religious object, though these particular terms have their own difficulties for broad comparative purposes.[6] Nevertheless, this condition is extremely important. It is as relevant, for example, to the sharp distinction drawn in Theravada Buddhism, as well as in various forms of pantheism, between "illusion" and "reality," as it is to the notions of "holy people" and "ghosts" held by the Navajo, or to analogous beliefs widely found among other nonliterate peoples. (See Chapters 6 and 8 for illustrations of this point).

Second, a religious object is taken as "sacred" in the sense that *special prominence* is attributed to it in the world of human experience. This means that religious objects are of unusual significance in relation to what human beings consider important. In other words, religious objects have a palpable bearing on the existence and values of human beings.

In addition to presupposing these two aspects of the notion of sacredness, a basic religious claim also presupposes that the religious object is authoritative for religious subjects. By "authoritative" we do not mean simply having "having power or force," though such capacity is present in the activities of certain "sacred authorities" in some cultures and traditions. We mean, more broadly, that the religious object is acknowledged as being in some degree *properly determinative* with respect to the beliefs, attitudes, and practices of the religious subject. (For a more extensive analysis and discussion of the notion of authority (in the legal context), see the next chapter.)

This determinative function may be conceived in at least two ways. In one case, the religious subject is normatively controlled by the religious object's performances, including commands and/or actions—for example, supernaturally initiated "mighty acts" with good or bad consequences for human life. This type of authority is especially operative in selected traditions of Judaism, Christianity, and Islam, as well as in many nonliterate religions, with their conceptions of personal supernatural forces. In another case—for example, in Theravada Buddhism, versions of pantheism, and the like—the religious subject may appeal to the religious object as normative for the shaping of attitudes, decisions, and actions.

Finally, it is our contention that religious subjects *refer* to some conception of sacred authority in order to resolve the problems of interpretability. Part of what it means to say that a religious object is "sacred" in the sense of being of "special prominence" in human affairs is that the object is taken to bear in a momentous way on the ontological anxieties of human beings, namely the problems of inexplicability, suffering and death, and the puzzles of human conduct.

We consider our definition, as elucidated so far, to be preferable to certain other relatively well-known and representative proposals, such as those of Paul Tillich, William Christian, and Melford Spiro.[7] Though there are differences between Tillich and Christian, they both build a condition of ultimacy or primacy into what constitutes a religious object. But stipulating such a condition as necessary seems decidedly counterintuitive according to common usage of the term *religion* and related cognate terms. For example, we would want to call the "holy people" and "ghosts" of the Navajo tradition "religious objects" even though they are *not* considered "ultimate" by the Navajo (as Tillich would require) and they are not considered "more important than anything else in the universe" (as Christian would seem to require). Instead, these "supernatural powers" are considered "sacred authorities," as we have specified the notion. This same application fits a broad range of religious objects whose authority is no less "sacred" for being restricted.

On the other hand, Jeremy Bentham's utilitarian "pleasure principle" can be regarded as "ultimate" for him, as "something more important than anything else in the universe," and therefore appear to qualify as a religious object based on Tillich's and Christian's definitions (Bentham 1961: 4). Further, the principle "functions to resolve the problems of interpretability." Nevertheless, it is patently odd to refer to Bentham's principle as a religious object. The reason it is odd, we suggest, is that while the principle is "authoritative" (in our second sense), and even of "special prominence," it cannot be understood as constituting a "scope of reality" that is to some degree beyond the volitional control of human beings (our first sense). On the contrary, for Bentham, the pleasure-pain calculus is itself constitutive of the conditions of human volition (Bentham 1961: 1–2). It does not refer to an independent realm assumed to exist over and above the conditions of human volition, as is assumed by primitive Christians and Theravada Buddhists (see chaps. 7 and 8, below, for a development of this point). Therefore, it does not comply with at least one of our conditions of "sacredness."

Spiro's stipulation of superhuman beings as the necessary condition of a religious object is far too restrictive. In classical Theravada Buddhism, there is no conception of a "superhuman being," and yet its basic religious claim refers to an object—namely, nirvana—that complies with our conditions of sacred authority and accordingly qualifies as a religious object. This attribution appears intuitively correct.

2.2. Religious Attitudes and Practices

We have been able to identify and characterize a key variable of religion—sacred authority—by analyzing the objective aspect of a basic religious claim. But our conceptual inquiry and explication does not end here, for other aspects of the basic religious claim are relevant to our analysis, namely, the subjective and behavioral aspects. Two implications are important in this regard. First, a basic religious claim implicitly maintains, or contextually implies, that its characterization of the religious object calls for an appropriate response from the religious subject, both in attitude and in behavior. Second, a basic religious claim implicitly maintains, or contextually implies, that its characterization authoritatively illuminates the religious subject's perception of the facts of life, as well as helping to pattern a general life-style. Both implications refer to the religious subject's attitudes and behavior, and both have close logical ties with the objective aspect. For convenience, we may designate the implications regarding the religious subject's thought, attitudes, and emotions with respect to the religious object as the basic religious claim's *subjective aspect,* and the implications concerning patterns of behavior, dispositions to action, and life-style as the *behavioral aspect.*

The subjective aspect may be simply described in terms of a very general concept—respect. Because of the religious object's sacred authority, and its concomitant features of illumination and appropriate response, the religious subject adopts a general attitude of respect for the religious object. The concept of respect employed here is very formal. It indicates that the religious subject takes the religious object seriously, that the religious object "merits" attention, and "claims" a determinative relevancy to life. As used here, "respect" does not imply any unique emotions or thrills (cf. Mac-Beath 1952: 298).

The behavioral aspect may also be described in general terms that beg no empirical questions. This aspect is also based on the religious object's character and the implications noted above. It refers simply to the dispositional correlate of the attitude of respect: the tendency of the religious subject to take serious account of the religious object in patterning a life-style, and to take account of it in a manner appropriate to its specific qualities and character.

The relations among the three aspects of a basic religious claim should be clear. From a conceptual (logical) point of view, the objective aspect grounds or justifies the subjective and behavioral aspects. The parallel between these aspects and the three religion-making characteristics should also be apparent. The objective aspect corresponds to cosmology, the subjective to attitudes, and the behavioral to practices.

3. Religious Action-Guides

The question now is whether religions, or rather basic religious claims, imply action-guides of a distinct type. That is, do conceptions of sacred authority yield any distinctive action-guides? In light of the previous discussion, an affirmative answer is indicated since basic religious claims call for appropriate attitudinal and behavioral responses on the part of their adherents. We contended that part of what it means to acknowledge a religious object as authoritative is to regard it as "in some degree properly determinative with respect to the beliefs, attitudes, and practices of the religious subject." For convenience, we may call the contextual implications regarding the attitudinal and behavioral aspects of a basic religious claim "religious action-guides." What is the logical character of these religious action-guides, and how are they related to moral action-guides? The conceptual diagram of the reconstructive concept of a religious action-guide (Figure 3) helps to structure and clarify our response to this question.

Inasmuch as we have already developed an extensive terminology with regard to the concept of a moral action-guide, we will employ that apparatus for discussing religious action-guides, noting important nuances and significant differences and introducing new notions wherever necessary. Since religious action-guides are, by definition, action-guides, we do not need to reexamine the practical or prescriptive component as discussed in Chapter 2, except to observe that the distinctive emphasis of religious action-guides is on resolving problems of interpretability rather than problems of cooperation. The authoritative component of religious action-guides, however, is another matter. Certain of its features may be handled with dispatch, but others call for careful analysis and discussion.

Those authoritative features that parallel our analysis of a moral action-guide include a religious action-guide's prima facie superiority over nonreligious action-guides. Also, the earlier discussion of autonomy and priority carries over to religious action-guides, although the distinction between "strong" and "weak" priority signals an important issue that will be explored below. The other main feature of the authoritative component of religious action-guides—

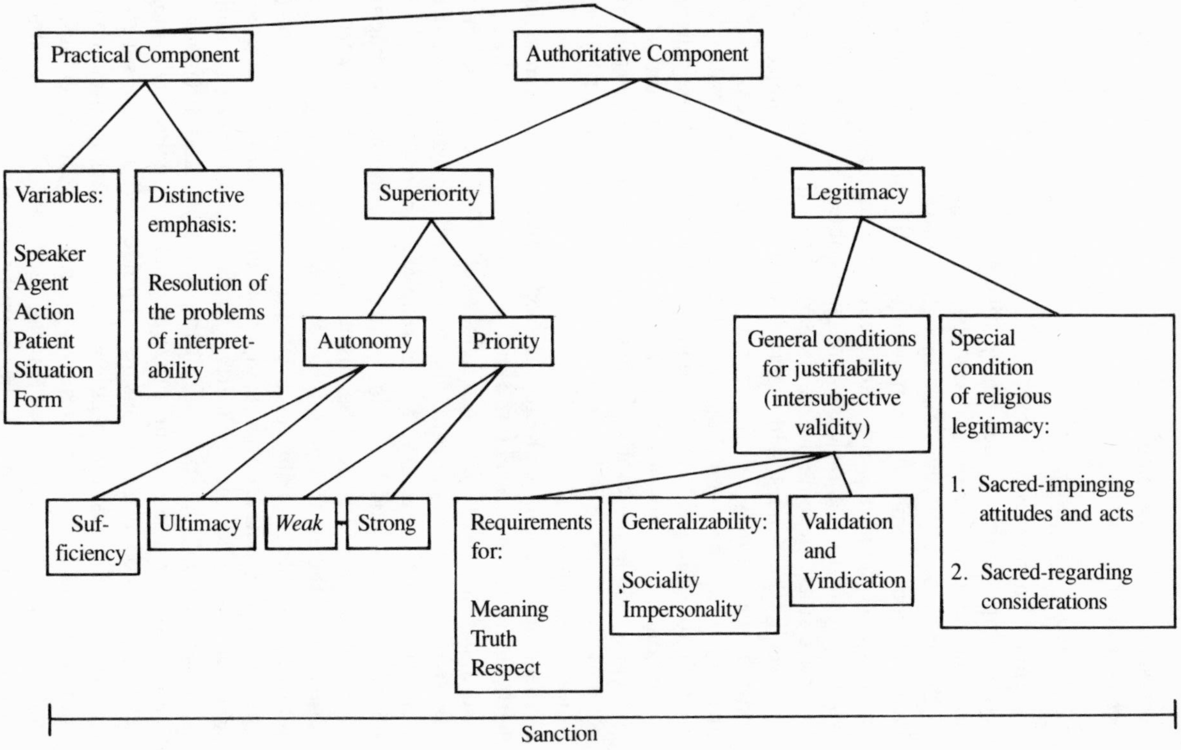

Figure 3. Reconstructive Concept of a (Purely) Religious Action-Guide

legitimacy—is the locus of important differences between moral action-guides and religious action-guides, particularly at the point where special conditions of legitimacy for each type are considered. We must therefore attend to the special conditions of religious legitimacy.

3.1. Special Conditions of Religious Legitimacy

There is a distinction in respect to religious legitimacy between a class of emotions, attitudes, and acts, on the one hand, and a class of practical reasons, on the other, that parallels the distinction drawn in respect to moral legitimacy. In other words, there are two senses of the notion of sacred-regarding that are formally similar to the two senses of other-regarding. For the sake of symmetry we may tolerate a certain amount of awkwardness and refer to the first class as sacred-impinging emotions, attitudes, and acts. The idea is that as other-impinging emotions, attitudes, and acts occupy a specially prominent and stringent place in moral reasoning, so sacred-impinging acts do in practical religious reasoning. And, as other-impinging acts characterize behavior with direct and usually dramatic effects upon the material existence and/or welfare of other persons, so sacred-impinging acts are taken as having direct or immediate effects in respect to the sacred object.

We have in mind, for example, acts (including emotions and attitudes) regarded as typically religious in Western cultures, such as prayer and worship, and, more broadly, ceremonial, ritual, and meditational practices that are aimed at a sacred object. These kinds of acts appear to be the special, though not exclusive, subject for practical religious reflection. Therefore, if we encountered a culture without an identifiable range of sacred-impinging emotions, attitudes, and acts, it could not, on our definition, qualify as possessing religious action-guides, since the *point* of religious action—namely, action carried out in direct relation with a sacred object—would be missing.

The second sense of sacred-regarding refers to a set of reasons or appeals that consciously and explicitly invoke the sacred authority in support of given practices. It is important to remember that the same sort of relationship exists between the two senses of sacred-regarding that existed between the two sense of other-regarding. It is possible to conceive of a set of sacred-impinging acts that are legitimated on grounds not involving a conscious and explicit appeal to a sacred authority. Prayer, for example, might be justified on moral rather than on religious grounds. The reverse, however, would not seem possible. If, in a given community, a notion of sacred authority is sufficiently developed so as to legitimate certain practices, it is unlikely that some of those practices would not include sacred-impinging acts.

In order to understand the logical character of the second sense of sacred-regarding, it is necessary to explore the ways in which action-guides may be derived from basic religious claims. We suggest at least four relatively distinctive types of derivation (though there may well be others): (1) charismatic revelation; (2) valuational implication; (3) role analogation; and (4) mythic warranty. It should be noted that these types of justification are by no means mutually exclusive with regard to any one religion.

Charismatic, or authoritarian, *revelation* refers to the type of justification that involves the issuing of commands, edicts, orders by the sacred authority to the obedient religious subject. The means of revelation may be many, but the logical operation of the justification is the same: having accepted the charismatic authority of the religious object, the religious subject "awaits," so to speak, "orders from on high." The religious subject "does x because the religious object says so."

Valuational implication refers to that type of justification in which the religious subject adopts an evaluative standard, identified with or implied by the religious object, makes value judgments with reference to this standard, and then derives religious action-guides from these value judgments. This type constitutes a complex category because of the variety of ways in which action-guides may be derived through evaluative reasoning. Examples of such action-guides include: "Do x because the consequences produce results in conformity with the sacred standard" and "Do x because x is itself in conformity with the sacred standard." Despite the variety, the logic of this sort of justification is determinate and distinct from the first type, insofar as the religious subject "reasons" to the religious action-guides.

Role analogation refers to that type of justification in which the religious subject derives religious action-guides by examining the implications of the subject's relationship to the religious object on the analogy of a human personal or social relationship. The religious subject discerns the appropriate religious action-guides by clarifying the implications of the role relationsip with the religious object. There are many examples, such as: "To be a slave is to attempt to please one's master. You are the slave and God is the master. Therefore, you ought to attempt to please God." The same sort of reasoning applies to all the many role images found in religious myth and literature, such as father-son, author-creature, benefactor-beneficiary, promisor-promisee.

Mythic warranty refers to that type of justification that involves appealing to general anthropological and cosmological "truths" about the nature of the universe, "truths" that are related by a sacred narrative or myth (cf. Eliade 1959: 95-113). This mythic appeal functions logically in three ways. First, it provides an intelligible background for understanding the source and meaning of life and its pathways. Second, it specifies modes and patterns of behavior that are normative for the religious subject. Third, it provides explicit backing or warrant for these normative patterns, inasmuch as the religious subject cites myths as reasons for actions and behavior.

3.2. Relation of Moral and Religious Action-Guides

Having briefly exemplified the special conditions of religious legitimacy as some form of appeal to a sacred authority, we turn now to the question of the applicability of our distinction between the special conditions of religious legitimacy and the special condition of moral legitimacy. Specifically, are religious action-guides necessarily other-regarding in the senses we have defined the term, and therefore, are they intrinsically moral, as might be argued?

It may seem at first that insofar as religious action-guides are formulated in response to the problems of interpretability, they involve a relation to and consideration of the welfare of persons and groups, and ought to be counted as fulfilling the other-regarding conditions. Such a conclusion, however, is contrary to the extensive empirical evidence we have of a divergence, and sometimes of an outright conflict, between action-guides that are justified with respect to a conception of a sacred authority (religious action-guides) and action-guides that conform to all our conditions of moral legitimacy (moral action-guides).

Such divergence is amply documented by, for example, Christoph von Fürer-Haimendorf, though the following instance is particularly striking, paralleling at the nonliterate level, the famous opposition drawn by Søren Kierkegaard between religious action-guides and moral action-guides, or, in Kierkegaard's terms, between "the religious" and "the ethical" (Fürer-Haimendorf 1967: 31, 43, 95, 140–41, 213, 216; cf. MacBeath 1952: 326; Ladd 1957: 268).[8] Fürer-Haimendorf's example describes a situation "when the demands of a god conflict with the tenets of accepted morality":

Thus there is a tradition that the men of Purka clan were once faced by their clan-gods' demand for human sacrifice, but rather than comply with this gruesome command they rushed to the nearest river, and threw the sacred whisk symbolizing the female clan-deity into the water, and hence have performed the sacrificial rites only with the symbol of the male god who accepts the sacrifice of a goat and a cow (Fürer-Haimendorf 1967: 146).

What is most interesting about this passage is, as in the case of Kierkegaard's discussion, that the conflict between the two sorts of action-guides is over *the consideration of human welfare, as we have described that notion* (in Chapter 2, section 2.2). In other words, what locates the point of tension in both cases is precisely the question of other-regardingness. It appears intelligible, then, to have an action-guide that is religiously legitimate, but that in no sense conforms to the special conditions of moral legitimacy.

Of course, we are not unaware that there are many cases in which religious action-guides are formulated not so much in disregard of the benefit or harm to others caused by the action, but in the belief that the "real" welfare of affected parties is properly redefined in supernatural terms, and that the goal of a religious action-guide supported by such a belief is, thus, "really" other-regarding, even though the action works against the "this-worldly" welfare of the affected party. Or, in the words of G. J. Warnock:

I suspect that religious views [of ethics] differ from "humanist" views not by denying the essential moral relevance of human benefit or harm, but rather by incorporating very different beliefs as to what is really good or bad for human beings. The religious believer finds in a supernatural order a whole extra dimension of preeminently important gains and losses, benefits and harm; his difference with the non-believer is not on the question whether these are of moral significance, but simply on the question whether they are real or chimerical (Warnock 1967: 79).

Providing that such a religious action-guide meets all the other criteria of a moral action-guide, might it not be correctly considered equivalent to a moral action-guide? Our response is no, since, as we have argued, the concept of welfare incorporated in our definition of morality appears to have a relatively "fixed core" that includes such objective conditions as physical survival, bodily and psychic health, security from arbitrary violence, and the like. It follows that the religious action-guide in question does not meet the conditions of other-regardingness constitutive of the concept moral, and therefore cannot be considered equivalent to a moral action-guide.

We wish to make two remarks about our conclusion, however. First, saying that such a religious action-guide is not "fully" a moral action-guide is not invidious. It implies nothing whatsoever about comparative evaluation. Second, we realize that we are opening ourselves and our conceptual explications to the charge of arbitrariness. Our rebuttal is that boundaries must be drawn somewhere if meaningful inquiry is to get started, and we think our boundaries have a strong ring of plausibility to them.

Still another "boundary line" problem in distinguishing religious action-guides from moral action-guides concerns the issue of priority. This issue refers to a tension or conflict between two action-guides, each of which, based on its own distinctive type of justification, claims superiority in terms of autonomy and priority. It is our contention that both religious action-guides and moral action-guides possess the conceptual features of superiority. How, then, are we to settle which is "really" and "finally" and "ultimately" superior? We argue, at least for the purposes of comparative religious ethics, that this is an improper question. Why should we be required to settle it in abstraction? Is it not sufficient that we have provided definitions of morality and religion that are clear enough to enable us to identify the points of tension and conflict? We contend that both moral action-guides and religious action-guides possess, at first view at least, priority in the "weak" sense; this means that either one can be overridden in specific circumstances and for "good reason" without being deprived of its title to presumptive superiority or "weightiness." Having dealt with the matter of priority in this relativistic way, we suggest that the question of whether religious action-guides or moral action-guides take precedence can only be resolved on a case-by-case basis. In short, it is an empirical matter.

If someone charges that we have left our definitions ambiguous, incomplete, and wishy-washy, we must deny the charge. Indeed, to try to settle the issue of priority in abstraction involves, we suspect, normative argumentation, and a persuasive use of terms. One example of this is Paul Tillich's discussion of the superiority of religious commitments. "In true faith," says Tillich, "the ultimate concern is a concern about the truly ultimate; while in idolatrous faith preliminary, finite realities are elevated to the rank of ultimacy" (Tillich 1957: 12). This is clearly a *normative* stipulation on Tillich's part, closely related to his own particular theological point of view. Right or wrong, such an appeal has no place in a descriptive account.

We conclude that distinctions among criteria and overlappings between religious action-guides and moral action-guides as we have indicated them are of the greatest importance in identifying many of the central issues involved in the study of comparative religious ethics.

NOTES

1. Although this phrase is our own, the problems mentioned are identified by Max Weber and many of his followers (see Weber 1946: 267–301; Parsons 1952; Geertz 1966; Berger 1967: Part 1; Bellah 1970: 3–17).
2. This expression is a modification of William Christian's "basic religious proposal." Christian's discussion of the logical structure of religious discourse and his "theory of religion" are most illuminating, and, to some degree, lie behind our argument in this chapter (see Christian 1964: 19–34, chaps. 4, 7–9; cf. Christian 1972).
3. William Christian gives the following examples of such basic religious claims: "The God and Father of our Lord Jesus Christ is the maker and ruler of all things," "Nirvana is the True State," and "We find the meaning of life by living in harmony with Nature" (Christian 1964: 109).
4. The expression warrants special attention particularly in light of its rejection or avoidance by contemporary social anthropologists. For example, Melford Spiro asserts, "It ["sacred"] is much too vague to be taken as a primitive term in a definitional chain" (Spiro 1966: 89; cf. Evans-Pritchard 1965: 65).
5. This specification obviously raises the question of how "magic" is to be defined in relation to "religion," since one of the common designations of magic is instrumental manipulation or control over sacred entities. The precise relation of magic to religion must remain an open question for us, although we are sympathetic to William Goode's proposal that they be seen as related to each other on a continuum, rather than as completely separate from each other. This would mean, tentatively, that religion and magic are similar in that "they both deal with non-human forces, sometimes called sacred," as Goode puts it (Goode 1951: 50; see 50–55). Among other distinctions, however, magic would be distinguished from

religion by its greater emphasis on human control over sacred entities. But all this remains open to further reflection and investigation. Emile Durkheim and Bronislaw Malinowski certainly failed to settle the issue, and recent discussions have not fared much better (see Durkheim 1915: 57–63; Malinowski 1954: 37–38, 69–90; cf. de Vries 1967: 189–97; van Baal 1971: 1–8; Blythin 1970).

6. For a classic example, Rudolf Otto's emphasis on the "otherness" of the divine as a defining characteristic of religion seems to have been construed rather too much in Western (theistic) religious terms (Otto 1950: Chaps. 4–6). In *Philosophers and Religious Truth*, Ninian Smart argues that "the sense of the fearful otherness of the deity [has] no place in [Theravada Buddhism]. . . . Hence, though Otto's analysis is extremely important, and illuminates a great area of religious experience and practice, it does not really cater successfully for "mysticism" (Smart 1964: 120–21). Nevertheless, Smart does admit a rather looser sense of "transcendence" as characterizing "some degree of unity" between contemplative and prophetic religion (Smart 1964: 124).

7. "Religion is the state of being grasped by an ultimate concern, a concern which qualifies all other concerns as preliminary and which itself contains the answer to the question of the meaning of our life" (Tillich 1963: 4). "A religious interest is an interest in something more important than anything else in the universe" (Christian 1964: 60). "I shall define religion as an institution consisting of culturally patterned interaction with culturally postulated superhuman beings" (Spiro 1966: 96). Tillich's definition in particular has heavily influenced scholars in the fields of religious inquiry (see, for example, Baird 1971: Chap. 2).

8. We are referring, of course, to Kierkegaard's famous discussion of the "teleological suspension of the ethical" in the face of the overriding duty to obey God, which is the point, according to Kierkegaard, of the story of Abraham and the near sacrifice of his son Isaac (Kierkegaard 1941).

REFERENCES

ALSTON, WILLIAM P.
  1967   "Religion." In *The Encyclopedia of Philosophy*. Volume 7. Paul Edwards, ed. New York: Macmillan Co. and Free Press.

BAIRD, ROBERT D.
  1971   *Category Formation and the History of Religions*. The Hague, Netherlands: Mouton & Co.

BENTHAM, JEREMY.
  1961   *The Principles of Morals and Legislation*. Revised edition. New York: Hafner Publishing Co.

BERGER, PETER L.
  1967   *The Sacred Canopy: Elements of a Sociological Theory of Religion*. Garden City, N.Y.: Doubleday & Co.

THE BIBLE.
  1962   *The Oxford Annotated Bible*. Revised Standard Version. Herbert G. May and Bruce M. Metzger, eds. New York: Oxford University Press.

BLYTHIN, ISLWYN.
   1970   "Magic and Methodology." In *Numen* 17: 45–59.
CHRISTIAN, WILLIAM A.
   1941   "A Definition of Religion." In *Review of Religion* 5: 412–29.
   1964   *Meaning and Truth in Religion.* Princeton: Princeton University Press.
   1972   *Oppositions of Religious Doctrines: A Study in the Logic of Dialogue among Religions.* New York: Herder & Herder.
DEVRIES, JAN.
   1967   *The Study of Religion: A Historical Approach.* Kees W. Bolle, trans. New York: Harcourt, Brace & World.
DURKHEIM, EMILE.
   1915   *The Elementary Forms of the Religious Life.* Joseph Ward Swain, trans. London: George Allen & Unwin.
EDWARDS, REM B.
   1972   *Reason and Religion.* New York: Harcourt, Brace & World.
ELIADE, MIRCEA.
   1959   *The Sacred and the Profane: The Nature of Religion.* Willard R. Trask, trans. New York: Harcourt, Brace & World.
EVANS-PRITCHARD, E. E.
   1965   *Theories of Primitive Religion.* Oxford: Oxford University Press.
FÜRER-HAIMENDORF, CHRISTOPH VON.
   1967   *Morals and Merit: A Study of Values and Social Controls in South Asian Societies.* London: Weidenfeld & Nicolson.
GEERTZ, CLIFFORD.
   1966   "Religion as a Cultural System." In *Anthropological Approaches to the Study of Religion.* Michael Banton, ed. London: Tavistock Publications.
GOODE, WILLIAM J.
   1951   *Religion among the Primitives.* Glencoe, Ill.: Free Press.
JOURNAL FOR THE SCIENTIFIC STUDY OF RELIGION.
   1962   "The Problem of Attempting to Define Religion." In *Journal for the Scientific Study of Religion* 2(1): 3–35.
KIERKEGAARD, SØREN.
   1941   *Fear and Trembling.* Walter Lowrie, trans. Princeton: Princeton University Press.
LADD, JOHN.
   1957   *The Structure of a Moral Code: A Philosophical Analysis of Ethical Discourse Applied to the Ethics of the Navaho Indians.* Cambridge, Mass.: Harvard University Press.
MACBEATH, ALEXANDER.
   1952   *Experiments in Living: A Study of the Nature and Foundation*

of Ethics or Morals in the Light of Recent Work in Social Anthropology. London: Macmillan & Co.

MALINOWSKI, BRONISLAW.

1954   *Magic, Science and Religion.* Second edition. Garden City, N.Y.: Doubleday & Co., Anchor Books.

OTTO, RUDOLF.

1950   *The Idea of the Holy: An Inquiry into the Non-Rational Factor in the Idea of the Divine and Its Relation to the Rational.* Second edition. John W. Harvey, trans. New York: Oxford University Press.

PARSONS, TALCOTT.

1952   *Religious Perspectives of College Teaching in Sociology and Social Psychology.* New Haven: Hazen Foundation.

PYE, MICHAEL.

1972   *Comparative Religion: An Introduction through Source Materials.* New York: Harper & Row.

ROBERTSON, ROLAND.

1970   *The Sociological Interpretation of Religion.* Oxford: Basil Blackwell.

SCHELER, MAX.

1972   *On the Eternal in Man.* Revised edition. Bernard Noble, trans. Hamden, Conn.: Shoe String Press, Archon Books.

SMART, NINIAN.

1964   *Philosophers and Religious Truth.* London: SCM Press.

1973   *The Science of Religion & the Sociology of Knowledge: Some Methodological Questions.* Princeton: Princeton University Press.

SPIRO, MELFORD E.

1966   "Religion: Problems of Definition and Explanation." In *Anthropological Approaches to the Study of Religion.* Michael Banton, ed. London: Tavistock Publications.

STRENG, FREDERICK J.

1972   "Studying Religion: Possibilities and Limitations of Different Definitions." In *Journal of the American Academy of Religion* 40(2): 219–37.

TILLICH, PAUL.

1957   *Dynamics of Faith.* New York: Harper & Row.

1963   *Christianity and the Encounter of the World Religions.* New York: Columbia University Press.

VAN, BAAL J.V

1971   *Symbols for Communication: An Introduction to the Anthropological Study of Religion.* Assen, Netherlands: Van Gorcum & Co.

WACH, JOACHIM.
    1958   *The Comparative Study of Religions.* Joseph M. Kitagawa, ed.
            New York: Columbia University Press.

WARNOCK, G. J.
    1967   *Contemporary Moral Philosophy.* London: Macmillan & Co.

WEBER, MAX.
    1946   *From Max Weber: Essays in Sociology.* H. H. Gerth and C.
            Wright Mills, trans. and eds. New York: Oxford University
            Press.

4 | The Concepts of Law and Legal Action-Guide

1. INTRODUCTION

As with the concepts of morality and religion, there has been much scholarly debate over the proper explication of the concept of law. Indeed, two centuries ago, Immanuel Kant wrote: "The lawyers are still seeking a definition of their concept of law" (cited in Bohannan 1978: Vol. 9, 73). And more recently, Paul Bohannan wrote: "It is likely that more scholarship has gone into defining and explaining the concept of 'law' than any other concept still in central use in the social sciences" (Bohannan 1965: 33). In spite of this long-standing controversy, we can provide a reconstructive definition of *law* for the purposes of our inquiry. Our reconstructive definition is intended, as a theoretical and analytical device, to delimit a category of phenomena for the purpose of pursuing comparative ethical religious inquiry.

1.1. General Object of Law

In proposing our definition of *law,* it is useful to consider certain minimal and commonly understood functional features of law and legal systems. We can acquire a provisional understanding of law by examining what it does in the context of human life—its ends and functions in social life. Very often the object or end of law is expressed in gross general terms such as "institutionalized social control" (see, for example, Benn and Peters 1965: chaps. 1, 3; Pospisil 1974: chap. 2). Though not untrue, such views risk collapsing the concept of law into an overly broad notion of social control that offers no touchstone for identifying the distinctively legal and the distinctive object or end of law. Even at this early stage, the object of law may be more precisely stated.

A more precise statement of these goals or objectives of law may be approached by examining the function of law. The simplest idea is that law functions to keep order and peace in a social group, thereby satisfying the basic social desire of maintaining general security (Pound 1922: 33). This function can be further articulated. General security of the social order is achieved by (1) regulating social institutions, (2) settling competing claims and disputes, (3) reinforcing key social norms, (4) facilitating voluntary transactions and arrangements, and (5) harmonizing the satisfaction of wants and desires within the social group. These several functions specify the distinctive object or end of law. For convenience, this object or end of law may be said to resolve the "problem of securing the social order" (cf. Eisenhower 1970: chap. 1).

1.2. Law as a Metainstitution

In responding to the problem of securing the social order, law constitutes an institution or a shared system of action-guides for regulating social behavior. The institution of law is distinct from other institutions in that it serves as a "metainstitution" or superintending institution with respect to these other social institutions. That is, the institution of law achieves its end by settling disputes, reinforcing social norms, regulating voluntary arrangements, ordering want satisfactions, and the like, that occur within the other (first-order) institutions of a social group. In short, the legal institution regulates other social institutions and modes of customary behavior.

This view of law as a distinctive metainstitution is very similar to the position held by Paul Bohannan. Bohannan conceives of law as a body of action-guides that have been *re*institutionalized within a regulative legal institution, so that the other institutions of a society can continue to function in an orderly manner.

A legal institution is one by means of which the people of a society settle disputes that arise between one another and counteract any gross and flagrant abuses of the rules . . . of at least some of the other institutions of society. . . . In carrying out the task of settling difficulties in the nonlegal institutions, legal institutions face three kinds of tasks: (1) There must be specific ways in which difficulties can be disengaged from the institutions in which they arose and which they now threaten and then be engaged within the processes of the legal institution. (2) There must be ways in which the trouble can now be handled within the framework of the legal institution, and (3) There must be ways in which the new solutions which thus emerge can be reengaged within the processes of the nonlegal institutions from which they emerged (Bohannan 1965: 35).

And this sense of law as a metainstitution, or a phenomenon of double institutionalization, may perhaps be clarified by Bohannan's comments on the notion of a legal right:

It would be better to say that legal rights have their material origins (either overtly or covertly) in the customs of nonlegal institutions but must be *overtly restated* for the specific purpose of enabling the legal institutions to perform their task. A legal right (and, with it, a law) is the restatement, for the purpose of maintaining peaceful and just operation of the institutions of society, of some but never all of the recognized claims of the persons within those institutions; the restatement must be made in such a way that these claims can be more or less assured by the total community or its representatives. Only so can the moral, religious, political, and economic implications of law be fully explored (Bohannan 1965: 36–37).

It should be noted that this preliminary interpretation of law as a distinctive type of social institution with a distinctive end in view is supported not only by social scientists but also by philosophers of law. For example, H. L. A. Hart describes law as the union of primary and secondary rules. Primary rules "contain in some form restrictions on the free use of violence, theft, and deception to which human beings are tempted but which they must, in general, repress if they are to coexist in close proximity" (Hart 1961: 89). These primary rules of obligation belong to social institutions other than law. By themselves they are defective since (primitive) systems of primary rules are open to the "vices" of uncertainty (doubt and misinterpretation), static character (unadaptability to changing circumstances), and inefficiency (difficulty in determining violations). But, according to Hart, with the introduction of secondary rules—rules of recognition (authoritative interpretation), change (official adaptation), and adjudication (authoritative determination of violations)—these defects are remedied and a "legal world" is created. As Hart puts it:

The introduction of the remedy for each defect might, in itself, be considered a step from the pre-legal into the legal world; since each remedy brings with it many elements that permeate law: certainly all three remedies together are enough to convert the regime of primary rules into what is indisputably a legal system (Hart 1961: 91).

Thus, for Hart, the distinctively legal emerges with the development of secondary rules, that is, authoritative or official rules. These rules raise up the unofficial norms and give them a legal status. What is crucial, then, about law as an institution is that its secondary rules are *rules about other rules* constitutive of, or belonging to, other social institutions. The introduction of these secondary rules helps to establish the institution of law as a metainstitution.

Seen in this light, the distinction between law and other types of action-guides, including moral action-guides, may be drawn in a preliminary fashion. The distinction may be labelled "law versus custom," assuming that "custom" covers all types of action-guides regulating normative relationships between persons in a variety of social institutions (cf. Ladd 1967). Customs, then, are action-guides prescribing the ways people must behave if social institutions are to persist over time. All institutions are composed of customs, but some customs are reinstitutionalized at a higher level, so to speak. They are restated for the purpose of achieving security of the social order and related ends. When they are so restated or reinstitutionalized, these customs are raised to the status of law and constitute yet another institution—a superintending institution.

For example, following Hart's analysis, primary rules, many of which are stringent moral action-guides, take on the additional role of law. Because of their other-regarding character, primary rules are customs that help constitute the institution of morality—they are moral action-guides. Because of their reinstitutionalization by association with authoritative secondary rules, however, these primary rules can also be viewed as, in part, comprising the institution of law—they are, under this aspect, legal action-guides.

2. Definition of Law

So far we have identified two general but minimal features of the concept of law: (1) the object or end of securing the social order and (2) the superintendency or meta-institutionalization of law. Obviously, these two conditions are not sufficiently refined to characterize in any complete way the criteria and concept of law. We turn, therefore, to our specific definition of law.

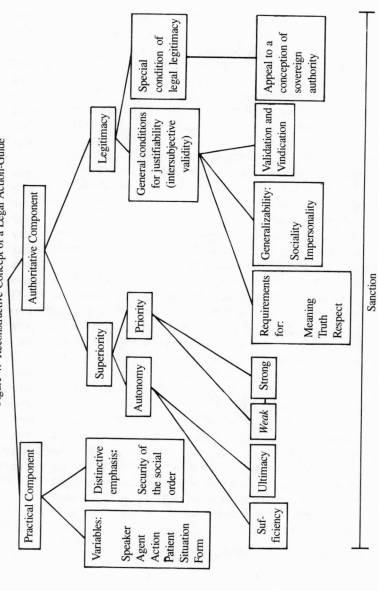

Figure 4. Reconstructive Concept of a Legal Action-Guide

We take a *legal statement* to be a *statement expressing the acceptance of an action-guide that claims superiority and that is considered legitimate in that it is justifiable and invokes a notion of sovereign authority that is at once both normative and effective (acknowledged and enforced by officials).* One implication of this reconstructive definition that we shall use in our subsequent inquiry can be formulated as follows: a legal action-guide, or a law, is a directive taken as authoritative in that it is officially both legitimate and enforceable. The conceptual diagram in Figure 4 helps to structure and clarify our elaboration and defense of the definition and its implications. Since we have already developed an extensive terminology with regard to the concept of a moral action-guide, we again employ that apparatus for discussing the concepts of law and legal action-guide.

As in the case of moral action-guides, we distinguish two primary components of a legal action-guide, the practical (prescriptive) and the authoritative. With regard to the practical component, we continue to use the expression "action-guide" because we need an inclusive phrase to cover such legal entities as decisions, commands, rules, principles, statutes, roles, rights, duties, powers, and so on. All of these are used to guide behavior within the legal sphere, as we define it. The practical component of a legal action-guide is constraining and directive in much the same way that a moral action-guide is. However, the practical emphasis is slightly different, for a legal action-guide "constrains" and "directs" in order to achieve security of the social order. In recent literature, this emphasis has acquired the popular labels of "the rule of law" and "law and order" (see, for example, Eisenhower 1970). Since legal action-guides are, by definition, action-guides, it is not necessary to examine the practical component any further. It need only be said that different theories of law, though tending to restrict legal action-guides to one or another category of action-guide (for example, command) and to one or another modality of security (such as maximization of free self-assertion), support our analysis (cf. Golding 1975: chap. 2; Pound 1922: chap. 2).

2.1. Authority of Legal Action-Guides

The authoritative component of the concept of a legal action-guide, unlike the practical component, calls for more careful and detailed discussion, if only because many scholars argue that authority is the key concept in the analysis of law. We agree with this judgment, though we offer a distinctive, if not original, analysis of the authoritative aspect. Certain features of this aspect may be treated with dispatch, but others require careful elucidation.

Following our analyses of moral action-guides and religious action-guides, the authoritative component may be broken down into the two broad, logical features of superiority and legitimacy. Although moral action-guides and religious action-guides generally take precedence, respectively, over nonmoral and nonreligious action-guides, this fact does not mean that legal action-guides have no degree of superiority over other types of action-guides. Nor does this fact imply that legal action-guides lack the characteristics of priority and autonomy. These misleading inferences must be countered immediately.

The superiority of a legal action-guide refers to its characteristic features of autonomy and priority. The autonomy of legal action-guides marks the fact recognized by legal positivists that legal action-guides are sufficiently and properly justified according to distinctive legal norms (the apparent circularity will dissipate when we examine the features of legitimacy). The autonomy of a legal action-guide rests, as Hans Kelsen and others point out, on the logical requirement that in tracing the validity of a legal action-guide we ultimately come to a basic legal norm (whatever that may be) from which the validity of all other action-guides of a given legal system is derived (Kelsen 1966: 1–7; cf. Golding 1975: 39–43). The seeming paradox that the existence of laws (legal action-guides) presupposes the existence of law (basic legal norm) is dissolved by the logical requirement that no legal conclusions can be derived from premises which do not themselves contain a legal element. Of course, with the basic legal norm one reaches the limits of the logic of legal positivism. And one might attempt to derive the validity of the basic legal norm from a set of moral principles, for example. But then one has left the legal sphere and the legal system in question and is now pressing "metalegal" questions. The result is that the autonomy of legal action-guides is left intact. Thus, the autonomy of a legal action-guide can be specified by the conjunctive features of its sufficiency—that is, once a legal action-guide is accepted for legal reasons, no further nonlegal justification is needed (unless metalegal questions are raised)—and its ultimacy—that is, a legal action-guide cannot in principle be justified on nonlegal grounds (otherwise it would not be law).

The other aspect of a legal action-guide's superiority, its priority, indicates that legal action-guides tend to take precedence over other action-guides belonging to nonlegal institutions. The priority of legal action-guides, however, must be qualified by the modal "weak," as discussed in regard to moral action-guides and religious action-guides. Therefore, our contention is that legal action-guides possess, at least at first view, priority in the weak sense. This means that no legal action-guide can always be ignored or subordinated without losing its status as a legal action-guide.[1] But nonlegal action-guides can and do take precedence over legal action-guides under specified conditions in many cases of conflict. One need only think of cases of civil disobedience, conscientious objection, religious conscience clauses, and the like, to see that legal action-guides have weak priority in the sense indicated.

The case is so clear with regard to moral versus legal conflicts that Burton Leiser is able to claim the following:

> I conclude, then, that there is no necessary order of priority between law and custom, one taking precedence in certain contexts, and the other in others. But whenever a given practice is required either by custom or by law, but forbidden by moral considerations, the moral rule takes precedence (Leiser 1969: 91).

However, in Leiser's view, this priority of the moral over the legal is less clear in the case of the religious versus the legal:

> Thus, for example, I may have a positive duty to marry several wives in order to "be fruitful and multiply and fill up the earth," as the Bible commands. But the law prohibits my doing so. It seems to me that most people would agree that here the legal prohibition must take precedence . . . (Leiser 1969: 92).

Although religion should not be equated with morals, since there are certain important differences, a useful analogy may be drawn from the experiences of the Jews in the Soviet Union. If a Jewish housewife is forbidden to kindle her Sabbath candles by a fire ordinance, she and her family will miss this traditional observance. They may long for it, and they will regret having to forego the ceremony; but they will feel that the law must take precedence, and they will find some other ways in which to express their religious fervor.

The religious injunction, then, does *not* take priority over the legal prohibition (Leiser 1969: 95).

We suggest, then, that in order to do justice to the apparent tensions between these different sorts of authoritative action-guides, that priority in the weak sense represents an appropriate understanding of the legal action-guide.

2.2. Conditions of Legal Legitimacy

The second main feature of the authoritative component of legal action-guides—legitimacy—is a crucial part of our reconstructive definition. It is the locus of important differences between legal action-guides, on the one hand, and other types of action-guides, on the other, particularly at the point where special conditions of legitimacy are identified. In order to keep our analysis of this feature succinct, we draw attention to an important point made in conjunction with moral action-guides: namely, action-guides other than moral ones involve the condition of generalizability (see section 2.1 of Chapter 2). Now, we wish to extend this claim to say that a legal action-guide in principle meets the general conditions for justifiability (intersubjective validity) set out for the concept of a moral action-guide. This contention is supported by virtually all recent legal scholarship, though it finds its most eloquent statement in Lon Fuller's discussions of the conditions for success in the law-making enterprise—that is, his "implicit laws of lawmaking" (Fuller 1964: chap. 2; cf. Golding 1975: 46–50). Fuller's conditions of generality, promulgation, clarity, noncontradiction, constancy, publicity, and so on, are obviously equivalent to our notion of the "rules of the game" underlying all practical discursive activity, and they incorporate the requirements of meaning, truth, and respect articulated in connection with moral action-guides.

More important for our purposes than these general conditions of justifiability is the special condition of legal legitimacy. The proper identification and characterization of this condition of the "distinctively legal" has been extensively debated. Many scholars are inclined to adopt the view that the criterion for the distinctively legal—the special condition of legal legitimacy—is logically bound up with the notions of sanction, enforcement, and the like. For example, according to Max Weber, the special criterion of a legal action-guide is "a 'coercive apparatus,' i.e., that there are one or more persons whose special task it is to hold themselves ready to apply specially provided means of coercion (legal coercion) for the purpose of norm enforcement" (Weber 1954: 13). As Pospisil and many others have pointed out, however, while sanction and coercion and enforcement may be important criteria of law and legal action-guides, they are not the sole criteria (Pospisil 1974: chap. 3). Nor do they articulate any special notion of legal "legitimacy." As Philip Selznick, H. L. A. Hart, and even Weber himself (in other passages) indicate, the distinctive criterion for law is logically tied to the notion of authority, rather than coercion (Selznick 1969: 3–34; Hart 1961: 91–96; Weber 1947: 329–33).

In our view, legal legitimacy involves a justificatory appeal to a conception of a sovereign authority. That is to say, legal action-guides are based on, or appeal to, a sovereign authority. In order to clarify the logical character of this justificatory appeal, it is necessary to do two things. First, the notion of sovereign authority (legal sovereign) must be elucidated. Second, it is necessary to explore the ways in which action-guides may be derived from a conception of a sovereign authority (legal sovereign).

The intuitive idea behind our proposal stems from our provisional analysis of the object of law and its institutionalized form. Law is a system of action-guides designed to settle disputes, reinforce norms, regulate transactions, and order want satisfactions, among other objectives. Such a system needs criteria of validity to determine which action-guides belong to it. And it needs a supreme norm (or leader) to provide, directly or indirectly, the criteria of validity for all other action-guides in the system, a norm not itself open to challenge within the system. This norm and these criteria of validity are needed (logically) if legal issues, such as disputes and rule violations, are to be settled with certainty and finality. Thus, the concept of a sovereign authority or legal sovereign meets the judicial need for an ultimate point of reference.

Our proposal is not only intuitively plausible because logically necessary, but it also has the support of many scholars. Consider, for example, the following representative statements by Ernest Barker, W. J. Rees, Hans Kelsen, and Stanley Benn, among many others:

There *must* exist in the State, as a legal association, a power of final legal adjustment of all legal issues which arise in its ambit (Barker 1951: 59).

Laws can only be effectively administered if there exists some final legal authority beyond which there is no further legal appeal. In the absence of such a final legal authority no legal issue could ever be certainly decided (Rees 1950: 501).

The legal order . . . is therefore not a system of norms coordinated to each other, standing, so to speak, side by side on the same level, but a hierarchy of different levels of norms. The unity of these norms is constituted by the fact that the creation of one norm—the lower one—is determined by another—the higher—the creation of which is determined by a still higher norm, and that this *regressus* is terminated by a highest, the basic norm which, being the supreme norm of validity of the whole legal order, constitutes its unity (Kelsen 1945: 124).

This notion of the "supreme norm" is essential to any study of the rules governing decisions within a normative order. It is of primary importance for the practising lawyer, and for the jurist (Benn 1967: 71).

This intuitive idea behind our proposal may be helpful, but it does not in itself furnish an adequate analysis of sovereign authority in the legal context. The conceptual diagram in Figure 5 may help to structure our analysis.

A legal sovereign is a supreme norm or agent which has authority, as a matter of right, over all other institutions, action-guides, or persons within the legal system. If this formulation seems a bit obscure, or perhaps somewhat circular, consider the following more lengthy characterization. In relation to other derived legal action-guides, there is a basic action-guide (norm) or action-guiding agency that is regarded as sovereign. Sovereignty means supremacy, but supremacy of what? To say that the norm or agent is sovereign is to say that this norm or agent has the final authority; there is no further appeal to any more ultimate norm or agent; all other legal action-guides are subordinate to the final authority of this norm or agent. Moreover, although it makes sense to speak of authority without power, it must be recognized at the same time that authority that ceases to be effective tends after a time to lose its authoritative status. So, since the principal object of law is to maintain order and security, there seems little point in ascribing de jure authority to the basic norm or agency unless that norm or agency has a fair chance of attaining its object. If a legal system is to be valid law, it must in general be effective. This implies that, in the case of the legal sovereign (norm or agent), de jure authority

Figure 5. Sovereign Authority (Legal Sovereign)

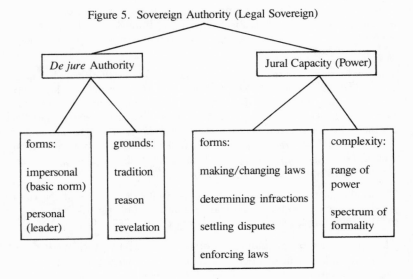

must be conjoined with effective jural capacity, that is, power (cf. Raphael 1970: chap. 3).

Consequently, considered as a key aspect of the special condition of legal legitimacy, the concept of sovereign authority (or legal sovereignty) has two primary components: de jure authority and jural capacity. In the present context "de jure authority" is intended to specify a basic norm or agent that is accorded the right to serve in the role of "auctor," that is, that which brings about or is responsible for the existence of an object (in this case, a legal action-guide) (Peters 1967: 85–86). The de jure authority may take one of two forms: an impersonal basic norm or legal action-guide (for example, a constitution), or a personal leader or leadership group (for example, a king, a senate). Both types of de jure authority may have their legitimacy grounded in a variety of ways. For example, following Weber, these legitimating grounds may involve appeal to tradition, practical reason, or revelation (Weber 1947: 324–29). Weber's typology of legitimating grounds could be expanded and improved (see Peters 1967), but here we only wish to make the point that the sovereign authority (or legal sovereign) has de jure authority legitimated in some meta-legal recognizable way.

The other main component of the concept of sovereign authority in the legal context is "jural capacity or power." Here we are maintaining that the (effective) de jure authority of a legal sovereign logically requires the capacity or ability to do or to support distinctive types of jural activities. In the case of an impersonal sovereign authority, the legal sovereign (norm) must be acknowledged and appealed to in order to have jural capacity and to be effective. In the case of a personal sovereign authority, the legal sovereign (leader or leadership group) must have the ability to make others conform to the legal action-guides constituting their jural activities. There may seem to be a qualitative difference between these two types of legal sovereign, but this difference is overshadowed by the fact that both require the acknowledgment and agency of others in order to be genuinely effective. The effective agency of others is nicely captured by Weber's contention that "the concept of law . . . depends upon an enforcement staff," that is, an official or group of officials who act to insure that the legal sovereign is acknowledged and effective (Weber 1954: 6).

There are at least four kinds of jural capacity associated with a sovereign authority in a legal context: (1) making or changing subordinate legal action-guides, (2) determining infractions of legal action-guides, (3) settling disputes by reference to legal action-guides, and (4) enforcing the maintenance of legal action-guides (cf. Golding 1975: chap. 1). These capacities are relatively clear and noncontroversial, and they need no explication. Jural capacity of whatever kind varies in its degree of complexity according to two variables: range of effective power and spectrum of formality. Effective power ranges from limited influence over behavior to coercive enforcement. Formality ranges from imprecise formulation to codified statutes and judicial procedures. Once again, the typology could be refined and expanded (cf. Pospisil 1974: 58–61), but the main point is that the sovereign authority's legitimated de jure authority is also de facto authority in the sense that the legal sovereign has the capacity to effect jural activity.

Legal legitimacy, then, involves a justificatory appeal to a conception of a sovereign authority of the sort just articulated. In order to understand more fully the logical character of this justificatory appeal, it is necessary to explore briefly the ways in which legal action-guides may be derived from a sovereign authority (or legal sovereign). We suggest that the distinctive types of derivation of legal action-guides parallel those cited for religious action-guides. Generally speaking, the types of derivation correspond logically to the forms of the legal sovereign: personal and impersonal. For example, with respect to personal forms of the legal sovereign, legal action-guides are typically justified as the commands, orders, or requirements of a competent human authority (leader or leadership group). Such legal action-guides are justified according to their source or origin, though they must also satisfy the general conditions of justifiability applicable to all action-guides. A favored example of such an authoritative source cited in jurisprudential literature is the fictional character King Rex (see, for example, Hart 1961: chap. 4; Fuller 1964: chap. 2). Of course, there are many real life examples in legal and anthropological literature (see Hoebel 1954; Bohannan 1957; Pospisil 1974).

With respect to impersonal forms of the legal sovereign, legal action-guides are typically justified either by reference to tradition—that is, authorization by custom, antiquity, and the like—or by appeal to formal norms from which legal action-guides can be derived in various ways—deduction, interpretation, and even selection (if the norm is really a set of basic norms). The appeal to tradition is fairly straightforward and needs no elaboration.

Other modes of derivation are simply types of valuational implication, as introduced in connection with the legitimation of religious action-guides (see Chapter 3, section 3.1). Since the next chapter is devoted to analyzing these patterns of reasoning and derivation, we will not detail them here. What is said there about the appellate patterns of validation and vindication in practical moral reasoning applies *mutatis mutandus* to the justification of legal action-guides.

2.3. Legal Sanction

Before we discuss the logical relations among moral action-guides, legal action-guides, and religious action-guides, we should say something about the role of sanction in the reconstructive concept of a legal action-guide. Our discussion of the jural capacity or power of sovereign authority implies that sanctions are necessarily attached to legal action-guides, or at least to legal systems or "sets" of legal action-guides. Thus, the attribution of sanction is a logical feature of the concept of a legal action-guide.[2]

This logical point is so truistic that in analyses of law it is often stated aphoristically; for example, "Law has teeth for the case of breach or trouble" (Llewellyn and Hoebel 1961: 287). The truth of this conceptual remark cannot be seriously disputed; sanction and the possibility of coercion are conceptually requisite in the notions of law and legal action-guide. Legal sanctions—whether physical, psychological, or social—are logically related to the quality of authoritativeness of legal action-guides. That is, the concept of legal sanction cannot be accounted for adequately without reference to the superiority and legitimacy of a legal action-guide. As suggested by our analysis of sovereign authority, legal legitimacy explains and justifies legal superiority, which in turn, granted certain facts about human nature and society, explains the emergence of sanction and its role in law. Consider H. L. A. Hart's view of the matter, which is very close to our own:

No doubt the advantages of mutual forbearance are so palpable that the number and strength of those who would cooperate voluntarily in a coercive system will normally be greater than any likely combination of malefactors. Yet, except in very small closely-knit societies, submission to the system of restraints would be folly if there were no organization for the coercion of those who would then try to obtain the advantages of the system without submitting to its obligations. "Sanctions" are therefore required not as the normal motive for obedience, but as a *guarantee* that those who would voluntarily obey shall not be sacrificed to those who would not. To obey, without this, would be to risk going to the wall. Given this standing danger, what reason demands is *voluntary* cooperation in a *coercive* system . . . the traditional question whether every legal system *must* provide for sanctions can be presented in a fresh and clearer light, when we command the view of things presented by this simple version (Hart 1961: 193, 194–5).

Inasmuch as the notion of legal sanction is intimately related to the jural capacity of enforcement, we can infer that a legal action-guide is a directive taken as authoritative in that it is officially both legitimate (having de jure authority) and enforceable (having jural capacity or power). This inference provides a handy reformulation of the concept of a legal action-guide, and we have occasion to use it in our case studies in Part II (especially Chapter 7).

3. Legal, Moral, and Religious Action-Guides

Having briefly examined the special condition of legal legitimacy, along with other criteria characterizing the concept of a legal action-guide, we must now consider the question of the applicability of our analysis to moral action-guides and religious action-guides. This consideration poses two distinct problems. First, are legal action-guides necessarily other-regarding, in the senses in which we have specified the term, and therefore are legal action-guides intrinsically moral in character? Second, can legal action-guides be counted as religious, and, conversely, when can religious action-guides be properly characterized as legal?

3.1. Legal Action-Guides and Moral Action-Guides

At first, it may seem that insofar as legal action-guides are formulated in response to the problem of securing the social order, they involve a relation to and a consideration of the welfare of persons and groups, and, as a result, ought to be counted as fulfilling the other-regarding conditions of morality. Such a conclusion, however, is contradicted by extensive empirical evidence of divergences and outright conflicts between action-guides justified with regard to a sovereign authority (legal action-guides) and action-guides that conform to all the conditions of morality (moral action-guides). This disparity is amply documented in social philosophy and social anthropology. Burton Leiser cites a typical counterexample from the 1960s:

Thus, the following conversation, typical of so many that are heard on college campuses today [year 1969], may be instructive:

JONES: You ought to refuse to be inducted into the Army.
SMITH: But my draft board called me.
JONES: Nevertheless, you should refuse.
SMITH: Surely I ought not to refuse. The law stipulates that every person who is called by his draft board must report for induction.
JONES: I know that you have a *legal* obligation to submit to induction. But that's all it is—just a *legal* obligation. You have a *moral* obligation *not* to submit to induction; and therefore, you ought to refuse to be inducted.

The priority of the moral norm to the legal norm is clearly assumed by Jones. If the conversation were to continue, Smith would not be likely to dispute that. The argument would revolve, not around the question of the priority of moral to legal norms, but about whether Smith does or does not have a moral duty to refuse to submit to induction (Leiser 1969: 89–90).

Leopold Pospisil, fond of pricking intellectual balloons, cites many counterexamples from his fieldwork among the Kapauku Papuans of West New Guinea; he concludes his discussion with this empirically based, philosophical observation:

> Second, since the area is defined by a "moral obligation" criterion, it hardly can be called jural. There is a significant difference between the two terms. Law, logically, heuristically, and empirically, always entails legal, not moral obligations (Pospisil 1974: 49).

This is a remarkable claim to be made by a field-based researcher, and is all the more persuasive because of its source. On the whole, then, it appears intelligible to have action-guides that are legally legitimated, but that in no way satisfy the special conditions of moral legitimacy.

There are many cases in which legal action-guides are formulated and justified in such a way that they meet the criteria for a moral action-guide. We introduced a class of such action-guides under the guise of H. L. A. Hart's "primary rules of obligation" (see above, section 1.2). Hart initially describes these rules in the following way:

> There are certain conditions which, granted a few of the most obvious truisms about human nature and the world we live in, must clearly be satisfied. The first of these conditions is that the rules must contain in some form restrictions on the free use of violence, theft, and deception to which human beings are tempted but which they must, in general, repress, if they are to coexist in close proximity to each other. Such rules are in fact always found in the primitive societies of which we have knowledge, together with a variety of others imposing on individuals various positive duties to perform services or make contributions to the common life (Hart 1961: 89).

His discussion of these rules is continued under the rubric of the "minimum content of natural law":

> The argument is a simple one. Reflection on some very obvious generalizations—indeed truisms—concerning human nature and the world in which men live, show that as long as these hold good, there are certain rules of conduct which any social organization must contain if it is to be viable. Such rules do in fact constitute a common element in the law and conventional morality of all societies which have progressed to the point where these are distinguished as different forms of social control. With them are found, both in law and morals . . . universally recognized principles of conduct which have a basis in elementary truths concerning human beings, their natural environment, and aims (Hart 1961: 188–89).

It should be clear that Hart's primary rules are equivalent to the "relatively fixed range of action-guides that in all societies come to be regarded as superior and legitimate," which we introduced in our discussion of moral action-guides (see Chapter 2, section 2.2). This equivalence implies that, according to Hart's conception of a legal system, some legal action-guides are indisputably moral in character. This equivalence is sometimes expressed as "the social morality embedded in the law" (cf. Muir 1975: 25–30). This conclusion does not discomfit us as long as it is recognized that many other legal action-guides are not moral in nature, and as long as it is recognized that Hart's primary rules have a dual character, satisfying as they do the criteria for both moral action-guides and legal action-guides.

3.2. Legal Action-Guides and Religious Action-Guides

The questions of whether legal action-guides can be intrinsically religious and whether religious action-guides can ever be properly characterized as legal have received scant attention from scholars working in fields relevant to comparative religious ethics. The major exception is the brief but pointed discussion by Leopold Pospisil. Pospisil is concerned with the second of these two questions, namely, whether religious action-guides, such as religious taboos, can be legal in character. Pospisil states his position in no uncertain terms:

Obligatio [which states the rights of one party to a dispute and the duties of the other] is a relation between two parties who are both represented by living individuals. Hence all obligations toward the dead and toward the supernatural are excluded from legal consideration unless the interests of the dead or of the supernatural are represented by living people. . . . I maintain that a religious taboo "with no officials to enforce it" is not law, no matter how firmly such a taboo is established and believed in as a procedure for social control, but is a strictly religious phenomenon (Pospisil 1974: 84).

In conclusion let me restate that the attribute of obligatio . . . is also a measure that dissociates religious customs from religious law. We are confronted with the latter only when the interests of the supernatural are represented by a living individual such as a priest or shaman. Religious law will never be left to the decision and punishment of the supernatural only, as may be true in a violation of a purely religious custom. A religious taboo is law only if all four of the legal attributes are present (an authority's decision, intention of universal application, *obligatio,* and sanction); otherwise it should be classified as a religious custom (Pospisil 1974: 87).

Pospisil's position has a direct bearing on our second question as we stated it, for he invokes an aspect of the notion of legal sovereignty to make his case—jural capacity. Hence, "a religious taboo 'with no officials to enforce it' is not law ... but is a strictly religious phenomenon." His case is provocative but weak since he fails to provide a definition of religious action-guide, taboo, custom, or phenomenon. Despite this shortcoming, however, Pospisil leads us in the right direction.

Employing our more developed concepts of a legal action-guide and a religious action-guide, we come to the following conclusions. First, a legal action-guide is hardly intrinsically religious since the appeal to a sovereign authority need make no reference to any notion of sacred authority. Second, a religious action-guide may also be a legal action-guide if it invokes the notion of a legal sovereign that is logically related to its appeal to a conception of sacred authority. For example, many religious action-guides in the Judaic and Christian traditions make not only a religious appeal to a sacred authority (for example, God) but also a legal appeal to a related sovereign authority (such as rabbinic and ecclesiastical courts, kings and princes)—this is similar to Pospisil's point. Third, a religious action-guide may also be a legal action-guide if it equates the notions of sacred authority and sovereign authority in its legitimating appeal. For example, God as a legal sovereign is a dominant motif throughout the history of the Judaic tradition and much of the Christian tradition.

The frequency and ease with which religious action-guides in many traditions may also be characterized as legal action-guides suggests that the problem in our case studies is not so much distinguishing religious action-guides from legal action-guides, but rather distinguishing the moral and religious elements in action-guides that also happen to be legal in character. The latter task is the principal concern of comparative study in religious ethics, in any case.

NOTES

1. Compare this claim with Leopold Pospisil's treatment of "dead rules": "Thus the field of law consists of principles abstracted from the decisions of authorities. These may be identical in content with corresponding abstract rules (*leges*) in which case we may regard the rules as being actually enforced. Those rules that are not enforced—the dead rules—are, by their lack of exercise of social control, omitted from the legal field; they have no corresponding principles abstracted from decisions" (Pospisil 1974: 37).
2. Compare this claim to Pospisil's assertion that "sanction is certainly an essential criterion of legal decisions" (Pospisil 1974: 89).

REFERENCES

BARKER, ERNEST.
   1951   *Principles of Social and Political Theory*. Oxford: Oxford University Press.
BENN, STANLEY I.
   1967   "The Uses of 'Sovereignty.'" Reprinted in *Political Philosophy*. Anthony Quniton, ed. London: Oxford University Press.
BENN, S. I., AND PETERS, R. S.
   1965   *The Principles of Political Thought*. Second edition. New York: Free Press.
BOHANNAN, PAUL J.
   1957   *Justice and Judgment Among the Tiv*. London: Oxford University Press.
   1965   "The Differing Realms of the Law." In *American Anthropologist* 67(6): 33–42.
   1968   "Law: Law and Legal Institutions." In *International Encyclopedia of Social Science*. Vol. 9. David L. Sills, ed. New York: Macmillan.
EISENHOWER, MILTON S.
   1970   *The Rule of Law: An Alternative to Violence*. A Report to the National Commission on the Causes and Prevention of Violence. Nashville: Aurora Publishers Inc.
FULLER, LON F.
   1964   *The Morality of Law*. New Haven: Yale University Press.
GOLDING, MARTIN P.
   1975   *Philosophy of Law*. Englewood Cliffs, N.J.: Prentice-Hall.
HART, H. L. A.
   1961   *The Concept of Law*. Oxford: Oxford University Press.
HOEBEL, E. ADAMSON.
   1954   *The Law of Primitive Man: A Study in Comparative Legal Dynamics*. Cambridge, Mass.: Harvard University Press.

KELSEN, HANS.
    1945   *General Theory of Law and State*. A. Wedberg, trans. Cambridge, Mass.: Harvard University Press.
    1966   "On the Pure Theory of Law." In *Israel Law Review* i: 1–7.

LADD, JOHN.
    1967   "Custom." In *The Encyclopedia of Philosophy*. Volume 2. Paul Edwards, ed. New York: Macmillan Co. and Free Press.

LEISER, BURTON M.
    1969   *Custom, Law, and Morality: Conflict and Continuity in Social Behavior*. Garden City, N.Y.: Doubleday & Co., Anchor Books.

LLEWELLYN, KARL N., AND HOEBEL, E. ADAMSON.
    1961   *The Cheyenne Way*. Second edition. Norman: University of Oklahoma Press.

MUIR, J. S. C.
    1975   "In the Matter of Karen Quinlan." Superior Court of New Jersey, Chancery Division, Morris County. Unpublished Opinion.

PETERS, R. S.
    1967   "Authority." Reprinted in *Political Philosophy*. Anthony Quinton, ed. London: Oxford University Press.

POSPISIL, LEOPOLD.
    1974   *Anthropology of Law: A Comparative Theory*. Second edition. New Haven: HRAF Press.

POUND, ROSCOE.
    1922   *An Introduction to the Philosophy of Law*. New Haven: Yale University Press.

RAPHAEL, D. D.
    1970   *Problems of Political Philosophy*. New York: Praeger Publishers.

REES, W. J.
    1950   "The Theory of Sovereignty Restated." In *Mind* 59: 501–17.

SELZNICK, PHILIP.
    1969   *Law, Society, and Industrial Justice*. New York: Russell Sage Foundation.

WEBER, MAX.
    1947   *The Theory of Social and Economic Organization*. A. M. Henderson and Talcott Parsons, trans. New York: Oxford University Press.
    1954   *On Law in Economy and Society*. Edward Shils and Max Rheinstein, trans. Cambridge, Mass.: Harvard University Press.

5 | Structure of Practical Justification in Religious Ethics

1. INTRODUCTION

In the preceding chapters we defined *morality, religion,* and *law* in such a way as to bring out a feature of central importance in the comparative study of religious ethics: *practical justification.* We suggested that religious and moral codes of conduct can be compared with reference to the different ways in which each code justifies its action-guides. But although we suggested this point of comparison, we did not analyze in detail the general characteristics of practical justification, nor some of the types or patterns of justification that can be found cross-culturally. That is our task in this chapter.

Our respective definitions of "morality" ("moral action-guide") and "religion" ("religious action-guide")—not to mention "law" ("legal action-guide")—demonstrate the centrality of practical justification for these phenomena as we conceive them. We understand the concept of practical justification as an activity that involves *the giving of authorizing reasons for the performance of an action.*[1] For example, we defined a "moral statement" as one "expressing the acceptance of an action-guide that claims superiority, and that is considered *legitimate,* in that it is *justifiable* and *other-regarding*" (note italics). Correspondingly, we defined a "religious statement" as one "expressing acceptance of a set of beliefs, attitudes, and practices based on a notion of sacred authority that functions to resolve the ontological problems of interpretability." We are most interested in religious statements as they function to *support or warrant* actions and practices, or what we call "religious action-guides."

At the outset we wish to emphasize something that we tried to make clear in our discussions of definitions, namely, the autonomy of moral and religious justifications (see Chapter 2, section 2, and Chapter 3, section 3). Reasons can be given for acting in particular ways—like those given by Jeremy Bentham in support of utilitarianism—that meet the conditions of moral legitimacy or justification, but that are not in any sense religious reasons, according to our definition (see Chapter 3, section 2.1). In contrast, actions can be supported by authoritarian reasons, such as are found in early Christian literature, or by "mystical" reasons, such as are found in classical Theravada Buddhism, that are grounded in conceptions of sacred authority, in our sense of the notion (see Chapter 3, section 2.1). These reasons meet our conditions for religious legitimacy, but need not, for example, be other-regarding, as we specify this condition for moral legitimacy. They would not, in other words, meet our special conditions of moral legitimacy. Of course there can be complex interweavings of religious and moral justifications in specific empirical cases. Nevertheless, for analytical purposes it is important to keep our distinction clearly in mind.

Some discussions of the relation between moral and religious justifications have blurred this important distinction. For example, in his influential article "Some Remarks on the Independence of Morality from Religion," Kai Nielsen fails to get the distinction right (Nielsen 1966). Nielsen begins by making a general and familiar point about the logic of prescriptive statements, with which we agree. He contends that it is (logically) impermissible to draw conclusions about what actions one ought to perform from a set of descriptive facts, whether these facts be supernatural or not. From the belief that there exists a supernatural being who is in the habit of giving orders, nothing at all follows about whether or not the orders of that being ought to be obeyed. A believer who obeys such orders must first adopt a proposition like, "It is right to obey the orders of such a supernatural being as this one." In short, he must first adopt a *prescriptive* premise.

Fair enough. But when Nielsen goes on to contend that any such prescriptive premise is necessarily a moral one, that "a moral understanding must be logically prior to any religious assent," he is, in our view, mistaken (Nielsen 1966: 151). For it is possible to conceive of a set of action-guides that is religiously, but *not* morally, justified. Consider the following example:

General prescriptive premise: It is right to consider the author of the world as a sacred authority in the sense that his commands ought to be obeyed above all other imperatives.

Descriptive premise: God is of such character that he is the author of the world, he gives commands, and the commands he gives are nonmoral (that is, they exclude all reference to other-regardingness).

Action-guiding conclusion: God is a sacred authority whose commands, which are purely religious action-guides, ought to be obeyed above all others.

There is no prior commitment here to a moral premise, though there is a commitment to a prescriptive premise. This means that general prescriptive premises can be moral *or* religious (or they can be some combination). But they are not necessarily (by the logic of the case) one or the other.

Nielsen might respond that this is finally a matter of definition. And so it is, though we believe that we have been more careful than Nielsen in specifying our terms and in giving plausible reasons for the reconstructive definitions we adopt. But aside from the intrinsic virtues (if there are any) of our definitions, and, consequently, of our way of distinguishing between religious and moral legitimacy or justification, we contend that the ability to make the distinction is true to the logical dynamics of religious and moral phenomena in various cultural settings. Practitioners themselves often articulate a tension between religious action-guides and moral action-guides, and without some distinction such as ours, it would be impossible to do justice to the tension (see Chapter 2, section 2.2, and Chapter 3, section 3.1 and 3.2).

It is necessary to make an initial distinction between the *content* and the *structure* of a code of conduct, whether the code be moral, religious, or legal, or whether it be some combination of these. The content of a code is the substantive beliefs and action-guides that comprise it. The structure is the way in which the code is logically arranged so as to provide authorizing reasons that aim to induce acceptance of the action-guides of the code and, indeed, the code as a whole. In short, the structure comprises the pattern of justification inherent in a code of conduct.

We propose that although the specific content of practical codes varies, the structure of justification among all codes involves several formal features that exist in a fixed relationship with each other. There are three general features of justification: situational application, validation, and vindication. As the conceptual diagram in Figure 6 indicates, these features are related to each other in an appellate fashion; that is, they constitute three ascending levels of appeal in the process of providing justification.[2]

2. SITUATIONAL APPLICATION

The action-guides contained in a code of conduct must be applied to concrete situations. Application involves specifying (1) the character of the act and (2) the condition of the actor or agent. With

Figure 6. The Structure of Practical Justification

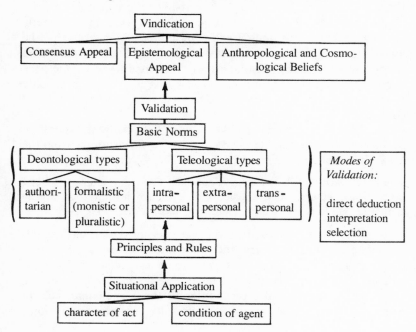

respect to the character of the act, a specific action-guide indicates what is to be done, to whom, in what way, under what circumstances. With respect to the condition of the agent, codes of conduct, especially moral and religious codes, specify certain attitudes, dispositions, motivations, virtues, and traits of character an agent ought to manifest in performing prescribed actions.

For example, in the case of Theravada Buddhism, Winston King cites the following five conditions as indications for determining the application of the moral prohibition against killing:

(1) It must be a living being [that is destroyed]; (2) it must be known [by the killer] that it is a living being; (3) there must be a desire or an intention (*cetanā*) to kill that living being; (4) an endeavor must be made to kill that living being; and (5) that living being must be killed through the efforts made [by the would-be killer]. A person who commits an act of killing, fulfilling all the above conditions, may be said to be guilty of killing (King 1964: 120).

Note that conditions 1, 4, and 5 describe in general terms the character of the prohibited act of killing. These conditions identify the victim (a living being), what must be done to it (it must, in one way or another, be destroyed), and the killer (the agent directly causing death). Conditions 2 and 3 describe the conditions of the agent. He must be cognizant of what he is doing, and he must intend to kill the living being. Insofar as all these conditions are met, the perpetrator is guilty of an immoral act; that is, he has specifically violated a central action-guide in the Theravada Buddhist moral code.

The distinction between the character of the act and the condition of the agent can be heightened, as in the following example from the New Testament of Christianity:

You have heard that it was said, "You shall not commit adultery." But I say to you that every one who looks at a woman lustfully has already committed adultery with her in his heart (Matthew 5:27–8).

Here reference is made both to the character of the proscribed act, namely, performing adultery, and to the intention and disposition of the agent, namely, that he not even desire to engage in adultery, whether or not he actually performs it. The distinction between the character of the act and the condition of the agent is particularly emphatic. There are, in early Christianity, certain motivations, certain dispositions, certain attitudes that are considered wrong in themselves, regardless of whether they are carried out in practice or exhibited in overt behavior. Religious and moral literature is full of similar examples.

With respect to the two features of situational application, there is a debate among moral philosophers that is relevant not only to moral philosophy but also to the analysis of moral and religious codes of conduct. The issue is whether it is possible to speak of the intentions, attitudes, and motives of the agent in complete independence from the disposition *to act* in certain ways, whether it is possible to speak of virtues in complete independence from action-guides (see Gert 1966: chap. 8; Warnock 1971: chap. 6; Outka 1972: chap. 5; Frankena 1973: chap. 4). In examining moral and religious codes, is it possible to divorce the respective descriptions of virtue, or the recommended character traits appropriate to the agent, from the kinds of action prescribed by a code of conduct? In the above example from the New Testament, the dispositions of the agent are singled out for special attention, but they are not completely divorced from an action that is considered wrong. On the contrary, an adulterous desire is identified by the kind of action it could lead to.[3] The question is whether this is the typical pattern.

Fortunately, the student of descriptive and comparative ethics need not settle this debate but only take note of it. It points to a genuine tension in religious and moral literature, and our hypothesis is that it is dealt with differently by different traditions. It is conceivable, for example, that a religious tradition, perhaps a mystical one, might develop a concept of religious virtue that is concerned primarily with the inner dispositions of the agent—"the imaginations of the heart"—without much, if any, explicit reference to external action. In specific traditions, it is probably more a matter of emphasis than exclusive attention to either agent or act. But the distinction is important in that it enables us to chart the comparative differences of emphasis among different religious and moral codes.

3. VALIDATION

As we have just suggested, action-guides must be applied situation by situation. They must also be capable of being justified on request.

Practical justification involves two general steps: validating and vindicating.

To illustrate how the procedure works, let us imagine an incident in which a teenage boy, who is a member of a hypothetical religious community, gives evidence that he is about to strike his father. A bystander intervenes and reminds the boy that he ought not to hit his father in these circumstances. What has the bystander done? In the first place, the bystander has applied situationally what he understands to be the "fitting" action-guide: He has identified the father and son as the relevant parties and he has pointed out the restrictions concerning the action. In the second place, the bystander, were he a "good" member of the hypothetical religious community—that is, one who knew well the details of the prescribed code of conduct and also understood it or grasped "how it worked"— would be prepared to give reasons why the boy ought not to strike his father.

These reasons would be arranged in an appellate pattern, moving from the more specific to the more general. As in a well-developed legal system, where a specific application of the law is appealed from a lower court of restricted jurisdiction to an ascending series of higher courts with expanding jurisdiction, so the bystander would be prepared to appeal to a series of "higher" and "more general" levels of reasons to support his original prescription to the boy, "Do not strike your father."

On the first level, the bystander might simply appeal to a rule like, "One ought not strike one's parents." In support of that rule, he might point out that the act of striking a parent is prohibited because it constitutes incontrovertible proof of the repudiation of parental authority. Repudiation of parental authority, in turn, is always condemned because it is a violation of a general imperative, "Never dishonor your parents," an imperative that is regarded as highly stringent by our hypothetical community.

"Never dishonor your parents" is to be unconditionally obeyed because it is taken as a direct commandment uttered by the god of the community. And direct commandments of God are to be obeyed because the community has accepted as its underlying prescriptive premise, "Whoever has the power to create man has a right to have what he commands obeyed and what he forbids avoided by his creatures." With this appeal to the "rights of the Creator," we have reached the logical end of the validating procedure. We have uncovered the community's basic norm and the sequence of subsidiary norms that establish the validity of the original action-guide, "Do not strike your father."

Since it is assumed that all codes of conduct can be reduced to a basic norm, or set of norms, part of the analysis of religious and moral codes involves identifying these. As Herbert Feigl puts it, "No matter how long or short the chain of validating inferences, the final court of appeal will consist in one or the other type of justifying principles" (Feigl 1952: 675).

3.1. Types of Basic Validating Norms

As Feigl's comment suggests, it is possible to conceive of several types of basic norm, and part of the task of the student of comparative religious ethics is to identify which type of basic norm characterizes a given religious and/or moral code. In proposing the particular types we do, we emphasize two things. First, only after specific case analysis can it be determined whether the relevant type of basic norm is religious or moral in character. In other words, the types may apply to both religious and moral codes. Second, our list of proposed types is not assumed to be exhaustive. It will undoubtedly need to be extended and refined, although at the present stage of our investigations, it is sufficient to cover what seem to be the prominent types of basic norm.

Following philosophical convention, we divide the types of basic norm into two major classes, *deontological* and *teleological*. Deontological norms specify certain general characteristics or conditions according to which the rightness (or wrongness) of actions is determined, without regard to the consequences produced by performing such actions. By contrast, teleological norms specify general characteristics and conditions according to which the rightness (or wrongness) of actions is determined on the basis of the consequences produced by performing these actions.[4]

Deontological basic norms may, in turn, be subdivided into *authoritarian* and *formalistic* norms. Authoritarian norms denote that actions are right and ought to be obeyed if they are commanded or required by a competent authority—that is, actions are justified by the source or origin from which they come, rather than by their intrinsic characteristics. Moreover, authoritarian norms may be personalized, as in the case of a human or supernatural figure who is acknowledged as entitled to direct action. Our previous hypothetical illustration of practical reasoning yields a clear example of an authoritarian basic norm. In that case, as we saw, the emphasis was on the source of the command, not on the character of the command itself.

Other examples of at least an implied form of a personalized authoritarian basic norm can be found in the New Testament, and particularly in the Synoptic Gospels, though such examples frequently compete with other types of basic norm (see Chapter 7).

Authoritarian norms may also be impersonalized, as in the case of traditionalistic prescriptions—insofar as actions are authorized by custom and by antiquity, they are to be obeyed. The Anglican theologian Richard Hooker gives voice to a traditionalistic form of authoritarianism when he writes:

And to be commanded we do consent, when that society whereof we are part hath at any time before consented, without revoking the same after by the like universal agreement. Wherefore as any man's dead past is good as long as he himself continueth; so the act of a public society of men done five hundred years [ago] standeth as theirs who presently are of the same societies (Hooker 1868: 195).

Formalistic basic norms, in contrast to authoritarian ones, emphasize the intrinsic characteristics and conditions—the "form"—of actions as determinative of their rightness, rather than the origin or source from which an action-guide emanates. So far as moral justification goes, Immanuel Kant's basic norm, or "supreme principle of morality," as he calls it, is formalistic in our sense of the term.[5] The conditions of "pure practical reason," such as consistency, universality, respect for persons, and the like, are those conditions according to which the rightness of acts is validated.

Similarly, one of the basic norms implied in the Letters of St. Paul is formalistic. When, in the early chapters of Romans, Paul argues that men ought to have given thanks to God for the blessings of creation, and later when he contends that men ought to be grateful for God's mercy and saving grace, which was freely given despite man's lack of appreciation and respect, Paul is trading on the following basic norm, along with appropriate inferences:

1. Beneficiaries ought to show thanks for blessings received, by attending to the requests and interests of the benefactor.
2. God is a benefactor and man a beneficiary.
3. Therefore, man ought to attend to the requests and interests of God.

In this argument, the basic norm (1) constitutes a set of criteria stipulating what sort of acts are considered right. It specifies that when one agent (a benefactor) acts in a certain way (beneficially) toward a recipient (a beneficiary), the recipient is thereby obligated to requite the benefactor in certain ways (by attending to the benefactor's requests and interests). Accordingly, actions complying with this "form" are subject to its prescriptive implications.

While Kant's "supreme principle" and the preceding illustration from St. Paul are examples of basic norms that are moral, by our definition, it is also possible to construct a purely religious example of a formalistic basic norm. A religion might stipulate that actions are valid according to whether they are motivated by certain sacred dispositions, such as "piety" or "blessed unconcern," as in the Buddhist tradition, dispositions that are understood as excluding all regard for the "material" welfare of others (see Chapter 8).

Whether they are moral or religious, formalistic basic norms can be *monistic* or *pluralistic* in character. In spite of his various formulations, Kant pictured his basic norm in monistic terms, which means that he thought of it as providing one unified criterion for validating moral action: "The three aforementioned ways of presenting the principle of morality are fundamentally only so many formulas of the very same law, and each of them unites the others in itself" (Kant 1959: 54). A philosopher like W. D. Ross, however, posits several basic norms, which he calls "prima facie duties," from which selections must be made in particular cases, that is, from among the duties of fidelity, reparation, gratitude, justice, beneficence, self-improvement, and nonmaleficence (Ross 1930: 20–22). In the same way, a religion might indicate one unique and ideal attribute, like love, for validating action, or it might posit several basic attributes that do not all come to the same thing, and among which choices must be made in specific cases.

Teleological basic norms, or those that specify the sort of consequences that render actions right or wrong, may be subdivided three ways, depending on who is affected by the specified consequences, and how that person is affected. An *intrapersonal* basic norm is essentially an egoistic norm. Accordingly, a state of affairs is designated as desirable from the agent's point of view, exclusive of all reference to the desires or welfare of others. To the degree that the actions achieve the agent's interests, as defined, they are valid. Thomas Hobbes seemed to propound this sort of basic norm, though, as in the case of most egoists, he advanced a *modified* form of (ethical) egoism. In the pursuit of each agent's own maximum pleasure, Hobbes believed, it is usually expedient to take the interests of others into account. This is a factual condition that does modify, in practice, Hobbes's otherwise consistent egoism (see Taylor 1975: 46–53; cf. Olson 1965).

According to John Ladd, the Navajo appear to validate their action-guides in terms of an intrapersonal or egoistic basic norm of the same modified sort. Each agent's worldly gratification is taken as the final reason for abiding by the action-guides of the Navajo code. Yet, as with Hobbes, the Navajo assume that "the welfare of others is a necessary condition of one's own welfare" (Ladd 1957: 296).

The particular character of the desired state of affairs can vary of course. The agent's "good" might be hedonistic and materialistic, as in the case of Hobbes and Ladd's reconstruction of the Navajo code. Or the agent's "good" might be defined in transcendental or spiritual terms, and all actions would then be validated to the degree to which they contributed to the realization of the agent's spiritual satisfaction. This distinction between this-worldly and other-worldly benefits can apply to the extrapersonal and transpersonal basic norms as well.

It is difficult to know with certainty whether the apparently egoistic or intrapersonal references in religious traditions like Theravada Buddhism and Christianity can be construed as implying an intrapersonal basic validating norm. The more complex the tradition, the more complex the set of basic norms operative in the practical reasoning of that tradition, and the more difficult it is to sort out the different strands of appeal in each tradition. Along with the clear evidence in Christianity of deontological basic norms of both the authoritarian and formalistic types, it is possible that there is also a teleological intrapersonal norm, in which the end or good of the self is defined in other-worldly terms. The references in the teachings of Jesus to supernatural rewards and punishments for individual deeds and misdeeds lend some plausibility to this idea. It is also possible, though, that the allusions to rewards and punishments in the New Testament are more in the nature of "motivating" or "exciting" reasons, rather than of validating reasons, or reasons that establish the rightness of an action (see Chapter 7). The appeal to personal interest may do nothing more than prompt the believer to do his duty, a duty determined on other grounds, such as by the command of God. This interpretation seems satisfactory, though it does not eliminate all ambiguity or uncertainty. The relation of motives to the norms and beliefs that justify the action-guides of a moral code is an involved question to which we shall return in section 4.

In the case of Theravada Buddhism, the matter is somewhat clearer, though it is not completely free of ambiguity. There the references to the self's materialistic gratification do appear to come closer than in early Christianity to constituting one sort of basic validating norm, among others, in Buddhist practical life—namely, a teleological intrapersonal norm. This norm applies to only one segment of life, which is governed by "karmic reality." Nevertheless, in the appropriate range of behavior, morally good or right action is very near to being determined according to the yield of hedonistic satisfaction (beauty, health, prosperity) for the self. As Winston King says:

If an action is called "good" because it will produce a materialistically pleasant state of being in the future, and only for that reason, then what does it signify to call it "good," except that it is *good for* producing such results? Hence we must say that charitableness is good, not in and for itself, and hatred bad, not in and for itself, but because each type of attitude in the end produces a pleasant or unpleasant psychological state of being in the loving or hating man (King 1964: 73).

King goes on to qualify this conclusion, and the matter bears extensive investigation (King 1964: 73–79). Yet, as we say, karmic action in Theravada Buddhism appears to "come very close" to being validated by a teleological intrapersonal basic norm (see Chapter 8, section 3.1.).

An *extrapersonal* basic norm includes a concern for the welfare of others in addition to the self-concern of the agent. With respect to moral justification, the version of utilitarianism articulated by Jeremy Bentham presents a clear example. The basic validating principle, "the greatest happiness for the greatest number," designates that while hedonistic satisfaction is the end to be maximized by all correct actions, it must be produced aggregatively. Unlike the intrapersonal norm, regard for the welfare of others is built into the basic norm itself.

Alexander MacBeath gives an illustration of what may be an extrapersonal basic norm among the Bantu:

> It is their conception of the good of the group, as that good is embodied in their institutions, that sets them their duties and prescribes their obligations. It requires of them that they subordinate their personal advantage and private inclinations to the larger good, the good of the group as a whole, a good which they also recognize as their own (MacBeath 1952: 189).

If MacBeath is right, the Bantu notion of "the interest of the clan" is itself the validating principle of Bantu action-guides. In this case the conception of "good" is obviously collective.

A *transpersonal* basic norm designates a state of fulfillment above and beyond the typical consciousness of the acting person. While an other-worldly intrapersonal norm also identifies a state of satisfaction that is "transcendental," so to speak, and thus beyond everyday experiences, it nonetheless assumes the notion of a self-conscious agent who himself succeeds in experiencing the desired form of bliss. By contrast, actions that are validated by means of a transpersonal norm have, as their final end, the "extinction of the self," at least as the concept of self is ordinarily understood. Mystical religious traditions, such as forms of Buddhism, Hinduism, and Taoism, clearly espouse this kind of basic norm.

Transpersonal norms are, by definition, nonmoral, although they may be religious in character. The concept of morality, as we understand it, presupposes conscious selves in relation to each other, who consider, up to a point, the "effects of the action of one person on the material welfare of others" (see Chapter 2, section 2.2). Obviously, transpersonal states do not involve such presuppositions. The concepts of self and of others are themselves problematical in regard to such transpersonal states, as is the notion of regarding the material welfare of others. Transpersonal norms, however, may be religious according to our definition. They may imply, as they do in Buddhism, Hinduism, and Taoism, "a set of beliefs, attitudes, and practices based on a notion of sacred authority that functions to resolve the ontological problems of interpretability" (see Chapter 3, section 2).

3.2. Modes of Validation

In addition to resting on basic validating norms, practical systems involve various kinds of procedures for applying the basic norms to lower-order rules and to specific cases. Following the methodological discussion of John Ladd, these procedures can be labelled "modes of validation," and separated into three main types: *the mode of direct deduction, the mode of interpretation,* and *the mode of selection* (Ladd 1957: 152–62).[6] This is not, of course, an exhaustive typology.

In describing the three types of validation, we stress that a particular mode of validation may apply to several kinds of basic norm. For example, the mode of direct deduction, in which particular practical judgments are simply deduced in standard syllogistic fashion from the assumed basic norm, applies to Bentham's way of proceeding, as well as to our hypothetical example of an authoritarian code (in Chapter 5, section 3). In the case of our hypothetical example, it is possible to reconstruct the chain of argument in the form of a series of syllogisms that illustrate the mode of direct deduction:

1. Whoever has the power to create human beings has the overriding right to have what he commands obeyed, and what he forbids avoided by everyone (all human beings).
2. God created human beings.
3. Everyone ought to obey what God commands, and avoid what He forbids.
4. God forbids dishonoring parents.
5. One ought not to dishonor parents.
6. Repudiating parental authority dishonors parents.
7. One ought not to repudiate parental authority.
8. Acts of striking parents repudiate parental authority.
9. One ought not to strike one's parents.
10. This man before you is one of your parents.
11. You ought not to strike him.

The same sort of reconstruction could be performed on an argument made by a Benthamite utilitarian, or by representatives of other directly deductive practical systems, no matter how long or short the chains of syllogistic reasoning might be in particular cases.

According to Ladd's reconstruction, the Navajo moral code presents an example of the mode of direct deduction (Ladd 1957: 279–80):

1. All actions producing misfortune for you are wrong.
2. "Bothering your sister" will produce misfortune for you (incest sickness).
3. Therefore, "bothering your sister" is wrong.

or

1. Don't do anything that will produce misfortune.
2. Stealing (and getting caught) will produce misfortune.
3. Therefore, don't steal.

If the mode of direct deduction is logically strict and tight in form, the mode of interpretation is a somewhat vaguer way of validating practical judgments. While it, like the mode of direct deduction, assumes one basic norm, and finally substantiates practical judgments with respect to it, the content of the basic norm is open-ended, and subject to discretionary interpretation in the application of the norm to concrete situations. The mode of interpretation, then, implies two reference points: the basic norm itself and the principle of interpretation, or better, of discretionary application.

For example, Christians often speak of "love" (*agape*) as the highest norm or principle of the ethics of Christianity. As such, that norm is understood always to rule out certain kinds of actions, like the willful inflicting of unnecessary suffering, and always to encourage other actions, like helping those in need. But those outer negative and positive limits still leave much to the discretion and imagination of individual Christians faced with having to make specific decisions. Thus, it may be claimed that while Christian love does not "provide all the answers," it does indicate general limits of action, and it also specifies those personal characteristics of agency, such as compassion, humility, empathy, and open-mindedness, that give a Christian the capacity to apply the rather vague basic norm to the real world. These characteristics are procedural in that they do no more than designate how the individual is to go about validating a particular decision he is faced with (cf. Gustafson 1968).

For obvious reasons the mode of interpretation puts special emphasis on the "virtue" or the personal dispositions of the agent.

This is true whether the mode of interpretation applies to a purely religious code, to a purely moral code, or to some combination of both.

The third mode of validation is the mode of selection. Whereas both previous modes of validation were monistic in assuming one final criterion of validation, the mode of selection is pluralistic in assuming a set of basic norms, among which some choices must be made in specific cases. Earlier we mentioned W. D. Ross and his conception of a set of prima facie moral duties, which may in practice conflict, and which therefore invite some procedure for adjusting the conflict (Ross 1930). In Ross's case, however, there is no overarching principle by which to adjudicate among conflicting duties; instead, the final selection is to some degree arbitrary or random. Insofar as that is true, we speak of a "random mode of selection" according to Ross.

Ross's basic norms are deontological (of the formalist kind), but it is possible to conceive of a set of ends or values in teleological terms, that are also subject to the mode of selection. Which of the desirable ends to pursue in given cases would have to be determined by some procedure of selection.

4. VINDICATION

In discussing the next, and last, aspect of practical justification, let us recall once more our example of the rebellious boy and the bystander. We carried the process of justification up to the basic validating norm—"Whoever has the power to create human beings has the right to have what he commands obeyed . . . ,"—and we saw that this basic norm was the end of the line as far as validation is concerned.

Nevertheless, it is apparent that even though no further validating reason can be requested (on pain of an infinite regress), it is still intelligible to ask why one should accept this sort of authoritarian norm (or any other norm) as basic, and be disposed to act on it. The answer the bystander would give to this question is: We should do it for *vindicatory* reasons, that is, reasons that are "suggestive considerations" (rather than logically compelling ones), intended to persuade the boy to accept and act on the recommended action-guide and the related practical code. For example, the bystander might first suggest empirical evidence for the existence of God and for his great creative power. Then, he might go on to ask the boy whether he does not find the prospect of such a God to be awesome, to be something that inspires in him a disposition to obedience. He might add to these vindicatory maneuvers what he believes is the common acceptance of a close connection between the concept of author and the concept of authority (cf. Peters 1967: 85–86).

When we are concerned with vindication, we are operating on what might be called the "metapractical" level. In respect to moral discourse, we turn, on this level, to metaethical matters, namely to a discussion of those salient considerations that might persuade one to adopt one kind of basic ethical norm and one particular mode of validation, rather than another. Formally speaking, the same sort of concerns are addressed in regard to the metapractical aspects of religious or legal discourse, or any other form of practical discourse for that matter.

4.1. Types of Vindicatory Appeal

Consensus appeal: Whenever an author claims that the Ten Commandments, for example, ought to form the foundation of a moral code because they "have the weight of mankind behind them," he is resorting to a consensus appeal. While this was an important appeal in certain historical periods, it seems, for better or for worse, to have fallen on hard times under the impact of "cultural relativism," among other things. Certain anthropologists, like Clyde Kluckhohn, have revived the appeal in recent years (Kluckhohn 1964: 296–97).

Epistemological appeal: In attempting to vindicate a basic norm, someone might appeal to one or another epistemological theory. For example, he could, along with certain intuitionists, hold that the basic norms for practical judgments are self-evident, and thus readily available to any right-thinking or right-feeling human being. Some intuitionists believe that we "know" the basic norms, as well as how to apply them, in the same way that we know the first principles of mathematical or logical systems and the procedures for working the systems. For others, such as those of the moral sense school, we perceive the basic norms, as well as the procedures for applying them, in the same way we perceive other sensations (for two good discussions of these positions, see Garner and Rosen 1967: Chap. 12; Hudson 1967).

Religious thinkers, on occasion, make an appeal to self-evidence, as when Jesus refers his hearers to "the signs of the times," and suggests that those who do not perceive what is going on before their eyes are willfully blind. Similarly, St. Paul seems to be offering a related sort of appeal when he writes: "[The Gentiles'] conduct shows that what the law commands is written on their hearts. Their consciences also show that this is true, since their thoughts some-times accuse them and sometimes defend them" (Romans 2:15).

A second example of the epistemological appeal is what we may call the appeal to "implicit acceptance" (see Ladd 1957: 179–81). It is a modification of the self-evidence appeal. On the one hand, it does not assume that the recommended set of norms is intuitively obvious or perceivable by some special sense. Extensive systematic reflection is required in order to become persuaded of the rightness of the norms. On the other hand, the hearer is invited, through the process of reflection, to see whether he can "make sense of" his way of acting and his way of thinking about acting without assuming the recommended set of norms. In other words, he is challenged by this maneuver to admit that he has implicitly accepted the set of norms in his thinking and acting, and, furthermore, that the norms are necessary in order to make his practical experience intelligible. This was Immanuel Kant's way of vindicating his supreme principle of morality, and it has been reactivated by modern philosophers like Richard Peters (Kant 1959; Peters 1966). Religious thinkers like Gautama Buddha also appear to have employed versions of the implicit acceptance appeal.

A third example of the epistemological appeal is the emotivist argument that moral convictions, along with other value commit-ments, are irreducibly subjective and noncognitive, and thus inac-cessible to adjudication and resolution (see, for example, Stevenson 1944). Prescriptivism is in part a modification of the basic emotivist claims (see, for example, Hare 1952).

General anthropological and cosmological beliefs: When Jeremy Bentham and John Stuart Mill attempt to vindicate a basic norm like "Always seek the greatest happiness of the greatest number," they make claims of the following sort. Man is so constituted, they argue, that he naturally and inevitably seeks happiness in the form of pleasure, and the recommended norm is only a generalization of that fact. Consequently, for them the basic practical norm is rooted in the nature of man. Thomas Hobbes's maneuver would be exactly the same. It would be easy to list any number of psychological and sociological theories about the nature of man that might be used to persuade people regarding one or another basic norm.

Similarly, religious theories about man and about the universe have again and again been employed to vindicate one or another religiously oriented basic practical norm. For example, the Buddhist cosmological conception of karma, as the law of cause and effect that governs all natural and human events, supplies backing for at least some of the action-guides put forward by Buddhism. Or, as Ladd points out, the Navajo beliefs about the laws of physical and human nature significantly affect and support their particular form of modified egoism, on his reconstruction of their code (see Chapters 6 and 8 for further discussion of these examples).

4.2. Aspects of Persuading: Convincing and Motivating

Vindication, then, is an effort to persuade others of the acceptability of the recommended validating norms and procedures. Before concluding our discussion of the structure of practical justification, we must take note of a certain ambiguity about the concept "persuade," which haunts much philosophical literature, and which directly affects the interpretation of religious and moral codes of conduct.

Webster's New World Dictionary indicates that "persuade" has two meanings: "1. to cause (someone) to do something, especially by reasoning, urging, or inducement; 2. to induce (someone) to believe something; convince." In other words, "to persuade" involves supplying reasons that both *convince* someone of the rightness of a belief and also succeed in inducing or *motivating* someone to act in certain ways. It involves what Francis Hutcheson referred to as "justifying reasons" and "exciting reasons" (Selby-Bigge 1964: I, 404–18; cf. Frankena 1958). Since, therefore, vindicating is the business of persuading, both convincing and motivating are obviously implied in the task.

We contend that there is a conceptual link between those reasons for adopting a basic norm that "induce to believe" or convince, on the one hand, and those reasons that motivate one to try to put the basic norm and all that follows from it into practice. This means that although the kind of connection that exists may vary from case to case, the justifying reasons and the exciting reasons must be compatible with each other. If not, it would be hard to speak of a coherent or consistent vindicatory position. When serious divergence exists, it is probable that two different sets of justifying and motivating reasons are present.

For example, a member of our hypothetical religious community might try *to convince* someone to believe in the basic norm of the community by appealing to certain cosmological and anthropological "facts" that, it is believed, provide evidence for the existence and power of the community's god. But he might also try *to motivate* his listener to appropriate and live by the basic norm by appealing to the listener's self-interest. He might suggest that since God has enormous power, he can in fact back up His commands and prohibitions with severe sanctions. The listener, like everyone else, thus runs the risk of strong penalties for disobedience, just as he stands to gain from obedient behavior.

The question is whether, in this case, the motivational appeal, or exciting reason, is consistent with the convincing considerations, or justifying reasons. At first, it does not appear that they are. It does not seem that the basic norm—"The creator has the overriding right to have his commands obeyed"—or the cosmological beliefs that support it, are necessarily compatible with an appeal to the self-interest of the creatures. Conceivably, the self-interest of the creature might dictate one set of action-guides and the commandments of the creator quite another. For instance, the creator might command someone to forfeit all worldly and supernatural benefits for the sake of the creator's own glory.

If such a discrepancy occurred, then there would be a conflict between the justifying reasons and the motivating reasons, and the individual would have to make a choice. He would have to follow one of two courses of action. On the one hand, he might side with his motives and set about developing a new basic norm with a correlative set of convincing considerations at the level of vindication. The new basic norm would be egoistic or intrapersonal in character, and it would, as such, fall into line with the motivational appeals to self-interest. Of course the individual holding such a belief would subsequently be required to pick and choose among the divine commandments, adopting those that serve his interests, but eschewing those that do not (like the command to forfeit all personal benefit to the greater glory of God). We have already seen that egoistic or intrapersonal basic norms are fully conceivable, as are vindicatory appeals to "the egocentric nature of man" (Frankena 1973: Chapter 2).

On the other hand, the individual might retain his original authoritarian basic norm and then seek to bring the motivational appeals into line with it. Such an attempt might take a strong form. It might call for nothing less than "a broken spirit and a contrite heart," according to which the individual would be inclined to "do what he was told" simply on the authority of the creator. Or, the attempt might take a less rigorous approach to motivation. It might appeal to self-interest within limits. That is, it might accept the authority of the creator as overriding, but at the same time appeal to self-interest as a supplementary motive, so long as self-interest did not conflict with the wishes of the creator. "The creator possesses the supreme authority to determine what is right, though, on the whole, your interests will be advanced by obeying what he declares to be right," turns out to be an intelligible, if probably unstable, compromise between the convincing and the motivating reasons. It is likely, as we suggested in our reference to early Christianity, that this is just the sort of compromise that exists in the New Testament materials between justifying and motivating (see above, section 3.1.; also see Chapter 7).

As we said at the outset, the links between the two sorts of reasons can vary from case to case, and the analysis of particular religious and moral codes must be specially sensitive to these possible variations. At the same time, the links are there and must be carefully traced. It does not make sense to divorce completely the notion of justification from the notion of motivation.

5. THE RELATIONS BETWEEN MORAL AND RELIGIOUS ACTION-GUIDES

There are two points in the structure of practical justification at which the problem of relating moral and religious practical principles and assumptions is pertinent: the level of validation and the level of vindication. It is necessary to distinguish them.

5.1. The Level of Validation

A basic practical validating norm may, as we suggested in section 1, be defined either in regard to moral legitimacy or religious legitimacy. In respect to moral legitimacy, the basic validating norm will include an explicit reference to other-regardingness in the second sense (see Chapter 2, section 2). In respect to religious legitimacy, the basic validating norm will include an explicit reference to sacred-regardingness in the second sense (see Chapter 3, section 3.1). Thus, attitudes and acts in a given practical code may be validated by a moral norm or by a religious norm, among others.

It is important to remember, as we have pointed out, that while other-impinging attitudes and acts, and sacred-impinging attitudes and acts play a distinctive role, respectively, in moral and religious justification, they are logically detachable from explicit appeals to moral considerations or explicit appeals to religious considerations. Accordingly, a set of prohibitions against murder, stealing, or cheating might, in a given code, be validated by a religious norm, while a set of prescribed prayer or worship rituals might be validated by a moral norm. Of course, these are only some of the conceivable combinations of morality and religion in respect to validation. We offer the following typology of other possible combinations.

5.2. A Typology of Possible Relations Between Morality and Religion in Respect to Validation

Unmixed Types.

1. *Moral System.* In such a system there is no reference to or reliance on sacred-regardingness, either in connection with the kind of attitudes and acts that are prescribed, or the kind of legitimating appeal that is made. On the other hand, there is reference to moral attitudes and acts that are validated by an explicitly moral norm. This system is exemplified by "secularist" moral philosophers like Jeremy Bentham, Kai Nielsen, P. H. Nowell-Smith, and many others.

2. *Religious System.* This system is the complete reverse of the moral system. Here there is no reference to other-regardingness in either sense. Rather, religious attitudes and acts are prescribed and legitimated by an appeal to a sacred authority. A purely mystical

form of religion that had extruded all consideration of human material welfare would be an example of this system.

Mixed Types.

1. *Moral-Religious System.* On the basis of our suggestions in Chapter 2, section 2, we can conceive of a system of validation according to which sacred-impinging acts are justifed by a moral norm. This type implies, of course, that the other-regarding acts prescribed in the system are also validated by the same moral norm. Immanuel Kant clearly exemplifies this type.

2. *Religious-Moral System.* This type is the reverse of the Moral-religious system. Other-impinging acts, together with whatever sacred-impinging acts there are in the system, are validated by a religious norm. An example is the Old Testament tradition, to the extent that both tables of the Ten Commandments (the first, religious, the second, moral) are validated by reference to a sacred authority.

It must be remembered that these types of moral and religious validation can themselves be combined in various ways in a given practical tradition. Frequently, practitioners in the real world are content to live with several of the logical possibilities. In one way or another such pluralism is characteristic of the Navajos, the primitive Christians, and the Theravada Buddhists. In fact, part of the richness of developed practical traditions undoubtedly inheres in the elaboration and combination of various systems of validation. This kind of combination is possible so long as the various systems within a tradition do not, in practice, conflict with each other. Such conflict is always possible, since a claim to superiority (and priority) lies at the heart of moral and religious legitimacy respectively. In the Christian tradition, for example, such conflict has sometimes broken out between the claims of independent moral reason ("natural law"), on the one hand, and the claims of religious revelation, on the other (see Chapter 7, section 3.2).

5.3. The Level of Vindication

We could proceed to develop a still more elaborate typology with respect to the background considerations that might vindicate each of the various types of possible validational positions listed above. For a complete comparison of practical systems that would indeed be important. For our more limited purposes, however, it is sufficient to concentrate on the level of validation, because the validational norm in any system of justification constitutes the basis for the logical autonomy of the system. That is, we decide, from a logical point of view, whether a system of practical justification is finally a moral or religious one depending on the content and character of its validational norm (see Chapter 2, section 2). It is obvious that the level of vindication adds another dimension to the complexity of analyzing and comparing morality and religion.

NOTES

1. One definition of "justification" in *Webster's New World Dictionary* is "to show an adequate reason for something done." That captures our meaning quite well.
2. Our position is, roughly, that this formal structure of justification is a "descriptive universal" among ethical systems, though we need further empirical confirmation for this view. We believe it is, however, a reliable hypothesis that moral and religious discourse in various cultures proceeds according to an appellate pattern, from relatively specific prescriptions and rules to broader norms and principles of validation and, finally, to ultimate reasons by which the entire system is vindicated or justified (see Ladd 1957: part 2; Taylor 1961).
3. Compare this contention to the following description of the relation between moral principles and virtues: "Nor does it seem terribly contentious to suggest that displaying a given moral virtue, say fairness, is to regulate one's conduct in accordance with the principle of fairness and to employ that principle in deliberation and justification. To put it the other way round, a principle of action is far from being affectively and behaviorally neutral or "inert"; rather it becomes (or is) active as a principle insofar as a person is disposed to employ it in his thought (deliberation and justification) and action (conduct). It is hard to see how moral principles can get off the ground except through the development of dispositions to think and act in accordance with them (moral virtues). And one cannot easily conceive of moral virtues except as dispositions to think and act in certain distinctive sorts of ways characterized by moral principles. The point is that moral virtues are systematically related to various moral principles of action which specify them, for virtues identify those capacities and desires which a person who acts on certain principles must have. Moral virtues and principles, in short, are intimately related" (Twiss 1974: 260).
4. In *Five Types of Ethical Theory*, C. D. Broad defines "deontological theories" as follows: "Such and such a kind of action would always be right (or wrong) in such and such circumstances, no matter what its consequences might be." Broad defines "teleological theories" in this way: "[They] hold that the rightness or wrongness of an action is always determined by its tendency to produce certain consequences which are intrinsically good or bad" (Broad 1959: 206–07).
5. Kant's formulations of this basic norm include the following: "Act only according to that maxim by which you can at the same time will that it should become a universal law"; "Act so that you treat humanity, whether in your own person or in

that of another, always as an end and never as a means only"; "Act according to the idea that the will of every rational being makes universal law, to which it is subject in such a way that it might be regarded also as self-legislative and only for this reason subject to the law" (Kant 1959: 39–54).
6. These types are borrowed, more or less in their original form, from Ladd's discussion. Ladd does add a fourth type, "extreme particularism," which is peculiar in that it does not presuppose any basic norm at all, but determines the moral thing to do anew in each set of circumstances (cf. Prichard 1949: 1–17). For the sake of simplicity, we simply bypass this fourth type here. Also, we alter one of Ladd's modes of validation from "the mode of application" to "the mode of direct deduction," since all the modes *apply* the basic norms to situations in one way or another.

REFERENCES

THE BIBLE.
    1962   *The Oxford Annotated Bible*. Revised Standard Version. Herbert G. May and Bruce M. Metzger, eds. New York: Oxford University Press.

BROAD, C. D.
    1959   *Five Types of Ethical Theory*. Paterson, N.J.: Littlefield, Adams & Co.

FEIGL, HERBERT.
    1952   "Validation and Vindication: An Analysis of the Nature and the Limits of Ethical Arguments." In *Readings in Ethical Theory*. Wilfrid Sellers and John Hospers, eds. New York: Appleton-Century-Crofts.

FRANKENA, WILLIAM K.
    1958   "Obligation and Motivation in Recent Moral Philosophy." In *Essays in Moral Philosophy*. A. I. Melden, ed. Seattle: University of Washington Press.
    1973   *Ethics*. Second edition. Englewood Cliffs, N.J.: Prentice-Hall.

GARNER, RICHARD T., AND ROSEN, BERNARD.
    1967   *Moral Philosophy: A Systematic Introduction to Normative Ethics and Meta-ethics*. New York: Macmillan Co.

GERT, BERNARD.
    1966   *The Moral Rules: A New Rational Foundation for Morality*. New York: Harper & Row.

GUSTAFSON, JAMES M.
    1968   "Moral Discernment in the Christian Life." In *Norm and Context in Christian Ethics*. Gene H. Outka and Paul Ramsey, eds. New York: Charles Scribner's Sons.

HARE, R. M.
  1952   *The Language of Morals.* Oxford: Oxford University Press.
HOOKER, RICHARD.
  1868   *Laws of Ecclesiastical Polity.* Book I. R. W. Church, ed. Oxford: Oxford University Press.
HUDSON, W. D.
  1967   *Ethical Intuitionism.* London: Macmillan & Co.
KANT, IMMANUAL.
  1959   *Foundations of the Metaphysics of Morals.* Lewis White Beck, trans. Indianapolis: Bobbs-Merrill Co., Library of Liberal Arts.
KING, WINSTON L.
  1964   *In the Hope of Nibbana: An Essay on Theravada Buddhist Ethics.* LaSalle, Ill.: Open Court Publishing Co.
KLUCKHOHN, CLYDE.
  1964   "Ethical Relativity: *Sic et Non.*" In *Culture and Behavior.* Richard Kluckhohn, ed. Glencoe: Free Press.
LADD, JOHN.
  1957   *The Structure of a Moral Code: A Philosophical Analysis of Ethical Discourse Applied to the Ethics of the Navaho Indians.* Cambridge, Mass.: Harvard University Press.
  1973   *Ethical Relativism.* John Ladd, ed. Belmont, Calif.: Wadsworth Publishing Co.
MACBEATH, ALEXANDER.
  1952   *Experiments in Living: A Study of the Nature and Foundation of Ethics or Morals in the Light of Recent Work in Social Anthropology.* London: Macmillan & Co.
NIELSEN, KAI.
  1966   "Some Remarks on the Independence of Morality from Religion." Reprinted in *Christian Ethics and Contemporary Philosophy.* Ian T. Ramsey, ed. London: SCM Press.
OLSON, ROBERT G.
  1965   *The Morality of Self-Interest.* New York: Harcourt Brace Jovanovich.
OUTKA, GENE.
  1972   *Agage: An Ethical Analysis.* New Haven: Yale University Press.
PETERS, R. S.
  1966   *Ethics and Education.* London: George Allen & Unwin.
  1967   "Authority." Reprinted in *Political Philosophy.* Anthony Quinton, ed. London: Oxford University Press.
PRICHARD, H. A.
  1949   *Moral Obligation: Essays and Lectures.* Oxford: Oxford University Press.

ROSS, W. D.
  1930   *The Right and the Good.* Oxford: Oxford University Press.
SELBY-BIGGE, L. A.
  1964   *British Moralists: Being Selections from Writers Principally of the Eighteenth Century.* Volumes I and II. L. A. Selby-Bigge, ed. New York: The Bobbs-Merrill Co.
STEVENSON, CHARLES L.
  1944   *Ethics and Language.* New Haven: Yale University Press.
TAYLOR, PAUL W.
  1961   *Normative Discourse.* Englewood Cliffs, N.J.: Prentice-Hall.
  1975   *Principles of Ethics: An Introduction.* Encino, Calif.: Dickenson Publishing Co.
TWISS, SUMNER B., JR.
  1974   *The Dialectic of Moral Communication: A Conceptual Inquiry.* Unpublished Ph.D. dissertation. Ann Arbor, Mich.: University Microfilms.
WARNOCK, G. J.
  1971   *The Object of Morality.* London: Methuen & Co.
WEBSTER'S NEW WORLD DICTIONARY OF THE AMERICAN LANGUAGE
  1952   Cleveland and New York: The World Publishing Co.

II | APPLICATION

6 | Religion and Morality of the Navajo

1. KEY CONCEPTS IN NAVAJO IDEOLOGY

Before examining the content and structure of the Navajo moral code, it is necessary to understand four key concepts in the Navajo cultural system. To adapt an analogy developed by Gary Witherspoon, culture is like a rule book that creates the world or environment in which the game of morality takes place (1975: 3–5; cf. Geertz 1966). In order to follow this game and to understand the way it is played, it is necessary to understand at least some aspects of the relevant cultural rule book—in this case, certain underlying premises of the Navajo philosophy of life. In particular, four such premises or key concepts need to be introduced: harmony, kinship, welfare, and rationality.

1.1. Harmony

The Navajo view the universe as an orderly unitary system in which all events occur in accordance with lawful processes. Their conception of the universe is essentially one of a machine that runs according to certain rules.[1] Originally established by the Navajo divinities, the Holy People, these rules are designed to maintain equilibrium or ultimate harmony in the universe (Vogt 1951: 35–36). In other words, to the Navajo, the universe is a coherent whole in which all components are interrelated and constitute an equilibrium of forces. These notions of order, system, equilibrium, and

harmony imply a teleological evaluative conception of what constitutes the proper state of affairs—the way things ought to be. This
teleological conception is expressed in the Navajo notion of *hózhǫ́*,
namely, that state of affairs where each thing is in its proper place
and functioning in harmony with everything else (Kluckhohn 1949:
369–70). This notion is the central idea in the Navajo cultural
ideology or philosophy of life. It has moral, aesthetic, and religious
meaning insofar as it refers to an equilibrated state of affairs that is
simultaneously good, beautiful, and blessed. When this state of
affairs, this harmonious order, is disrupted, sickness and social
friction arise that must be rectified by restructuring the harmonious
order of the world. Navajo religious curing ceremonies are designed
to re-create and restructure the world for patients suffering from
sickness. Navajo moral principles and rules are designed either to
avoid or to rectify the trouble arising from social friction.

Thus, the main aim of Navajo religion is to maintain and restore
harmony within the frame of health. And the main goal of the
Navajo moral code is to promote harmonious social relations and
ensure social equilibrium. Whether both of these aims are logically
subsumed under the overarching goal of *hózhǫ́* is a question that
will be taken up later (section 2.2), as will the question of the extent
to which Navajo religion and morality are logically related (section
3.3).

1.2. Kinship

It is said that the key to understanding social relations among the
Navajo is understanding their kinship system (Shepardson and
Hammond 1970). Indeed, recent anthropological study suggests
that access to the Navajo moral order is provided by their culturally
related kin universe (Witherspoon 1975). The same point is made in
reference to Navajo religion: namely, the striking characteristic of
the Navajo pantheon of sacred beings is its kinship organization
(Reichard 1974: 61–62). Consequently, the symbols and rules of the
Navajo kin universe may well have a significant bearing on how to
understand their moral principles and rules and their religious
taboos and ceremonials. The Navajo kinship system provides two
preeminent models for human relations.

The first model is kinship solidarity in the strict sense, which is
symbolized by the mother-child bond, the primary bond in the

Navajo kinship system. This model provides the following normative framework for human relations. Just as the mother is the one who gives life to her children through birth, and sustains their life with loving care, assistance, protection, and nourishment, so kinsmen are those who sustain each other's life by mutual help, protection, and sharing of material goods. The second model is that of affinal relations, symbolized by the bond between husband and wife. This model provides another type of normative framework for human relations, one of exchange and reciprocity in which the notions of equity and contractual obligation are emphasized. Both of these kinship models are applied to the Navajo in general, the *dinê*, all people. On the one hand, the *dinê* are bound together by affinal relations that cut across maternal descent lines. On the other hand, there is ethnographic evidence that suggests the Navajo attempt to relate to everyone in terms of the first model of kinship solidarity (Witherspoon 1975: 88; Kluckhohn and Leighton 1974: 298–99). Both of these models have implications for the Navajo moral code that will be explored below.

1.3. Welfare

One of these implications, however, warrants immediate attention. Inasmuch as the *dinê* and indeed all people are viewed as having kinship solidarity in the strict sense, the first kinship model implies a unique concept of welfare. It is a basic Navajo belief that the welfare of each individual is dependent on the welfare of every other individual. That is, what is good for the individual is good for everyone else, and, conversely, what is good for everyone is good for each individual (Ladd 1957: 303–04; Witherspoon 1975: 96–97). This belief results in the view that no one is in competition with his fellows. Quite the reverse in fact—the success of others is thought to contribute to one's own welfare; and doing good for oneself is inseparably related to doing good for others. Indeed, the welfare of others is a *necessary condition* of one's own welfare. This concept of welfare implies that the Western philosophical distinction between egoism and altruism is not, and cannot be, recognized as either valid or intelligible by the Navajo.

The symbolic representation of this welfare conception in Navajo culture is the sheep herd (Witherspoon 1975: 96–98; Kluckhohn and Leighton 1974: 105–07; Downs 1964: 93–102). The sheep herd is the most important cooperative enterprise among the Navajo, and it is in the care of this herd that the potentially divergent interests of individuals are converged into a notion of a cooperative undertaking for the welfare of each and all. Clearly, this distinctive concept of welfare is logically responsible for shaping Navajo patterns of moral validation, for at the very outset the validational patterns and norms of ethical egoism are ruled out as logical possibilities.

1.4. Rationality

The fourth element of the Navajo cultural system that requires a brief introduction is the element of practical reason, which is deeply rooted in Navajo culture. The Navajo stress the importance of rationality in all practical discourse (Ladd 1957: 203–06, 219–25). This emphasis is symbolized by the prevalence of public discussions used to decide what policies of action ought to be pursued, as well as by the highly prized virtues of sobriety, self-control, knowledge, and rhetorical ability (Kluckhohn 1956: 385–86). The types of reasoning and arguments employed by the Navajo indicate that they appeal to certain norms of rationality that are distinctively non-Western. These norms affect Navajo moral reasoning at the validational and vindicatory levels and take the logical form of principles of causality and reasoning. They may be formulated as follows (see Ladd 1957: 220–25).

1. Principle of temporally remote causal efficacy: A cause may be temporally quite remote from its effect.
2. Principle of spatial proximity: A cause must be physically proximate to its effect.
3. Principle of part for whole: Action affecting a part of an entity usually affects the entity as a whole.
4. Principle of general effects: Causes are infectious in the sense that the effects of an agent's action involve not only his own welfare but also the welfare of others around him.
5. Principle of many reasons: More than one cause may be responsible for an effect, and more than one reason may justify a course of action.
6. Principle of like producing like: Certain types of action performed by an agent will cause similar actions to be directed toward him.[2]

Although some of these principles do not conform to our Western ethnocentric notion of rationality, they help to define the Navajo conception of what counts as rational. To understand the content and structure of Navajo moral reasoning, these principles must be taken into account and not rejected by any ethnocentric bias toward a different set of rational norms.

2. CONTENT OF THE NAVAJO MORAL CODE

Most anthropological discussions of the content and structure of the Navajo code are quite disorganized. For example, moral and religious elements are not distinguished, mainly because defining criteria for moral and religious action-guides are not articulated. Moreover, although there is some ethnographic agreement on what action-guides are adopted by the Navajo, there is little attempt to relate these action-guides to each other in any intelligible way (see Matthews 1899; Haile 1943; Kluckhohn 1949; Vogt 1951; Hobson 1954). And, with one exception, the issue of practical justification is simply not addressed in any systematic fashion (see Ladd 1957). In order to bring coherence to these data and issues, we begin our analysis by characterizing the aim of the Navajo code. Then we analyze the code's content and structure by employing the methodology proposed in Part I.

2.1. *Moral Elements of the Navajo Code*

The essential aim of the Navajo moral code is to promote harmonious social relations and to provide the action-guides necessary for achieving social equilibrium. This aim is ordinarily conceived by the Navajo in a negative way: to avoid social friction and troublemaking actions and thereby to maintain harmony in the social world. This negative formulation seems to indicate prima facie that the Navajo code is a limited morality, "an ethic of constraint," in the sense that it is concerned only with drawing a sharp line between permitted and unpermitted acts and with defining a limited area of prohibited conduct (Ladd 1957: 300–02). This prima facie view, however, is contradicted on three counts. First, the basic validating norm of the code is given positive formulations by the Navajo. So that, second, the code incorporates "an ethic of direction" with positive injunctions and recommended virtues. And, third, the code itself is conceived as defining proper behavior that is prerequisite to attaining an even higher religious goal (Reichard 1974: 49). This third point suggests that the Navajo code has two distinctive aims: one characteristically moral, the other distinctively religious. It further suggests that an analysis of the content of the code ought to distinguish between its moral elements and its religious elements and ought to examine the logical relations between the two.

In introducing the distinctively moral content of the Navajo code, we will be specifying in a preliminary way two features of code's structure of practical justification: situational application and validation. In fact, we begin by describing the logical terminus of the validational pattern—the basic moral norm.

2.1.1.   Basic Moral Norm of K'é.   The basic moral norm of the Navajo code is *k'é* or what may be called "moral harmony." This norm is internally complex, and it may be formulated in a variety of ways. First, in its most general formulation *k'é* expresses the ideal relationship among all persons in the social universe of the Navajo. Second, translated literally *K'é* means love, kindness, peacefulness, friendliness, cooperation, and all the positive aspects involved in kinship solidarity (Witherspoon 1975: 37). Third, in its kinship connotations *k'é* can refer to both kinship models and their implications: the maternal bond and loving care, assistance, protection, and sustenance, on the one hand; and the affinal bond involving equity in exchange, reciprocity, and mutual obligations, on the other. The norm of *k'é* is indeed complex, and the mode of validation logically appropriate to it may well be the mode of interpretation, since the content of *k'é* is open-ended and apparently subject to discretionary interpretation.

It is possible to advance this preliminary characterization of the norm of *k'é* by observing three things. First, because of its logical relations to the notions of social solidarity, communal welfare, and harmony *k'é* can be formulated more precisely with the aid of these categories. Second, though it is a general concept, *k'é* is specified by the notions of (1) giving and sharing, characteristic of kinship solidarity and (2) equity and reciprocity, characteristic of affinal relations. Third, the open-textured character of *k'é* permits the derivation, by the interpretive mode of validation, of more specific moral principles, rules, virtues, and character traits.

Following from the first point, then, it is reasonable to formulate the norm of *k'é* in at least three ways. Each of these formulations has its counterpart in Navajo ethnography. First, *k'é* prescribes the maximization of social solidarity and the minimization of social friction; translated into Navajo terms this becomes: "Help others" and "Avoid trouble" (Ladd 1957: 237–38, 253–54; Reichard 1974: xxxvii–xli, 123–33). Second, *k'é* prescribes advancing the welfare of self and of others; in Navajo terms this is: "Care for yourself" and "Care for others" (Ladd 1957: 252–54; Kluckhohn and Leighton 1974: 298–99; Witherspoon 1975: 96–97). Third, *k'é* prescribes the maintenance of a stable equilibrium among persons and groups; in Navajo terms: "Don't disturb social harmony" and "If the harmony is disturbed, restore it" (Kluckhohn 1949: 366; Vogt 1951: 36). These formulations are virtually equivalent, or at least mutually reinforcing. If they are further interpreted in light of the other two points about kinship-affinal solidarity and the interpretive mode of validation, a distinctive set of moral principles and rules, on the one hand, and a distinctive set of moral virtues and character traits, on the other, may be derived. These principles, rules, virtues, and traits can also be found in the discourse of Navajo informants.

2.1.2. Moral Principles and Rules. Three high-level, general moral principles and three corresponding sets of lower-level, specific moral rules may be derived from the basic norm of *k'é*. The three principles may be formulated as follows: (1) "Care for yourself"; (2) "Avoid and rectify any trouble with others"; and (3) "Help others by treating them as your kin" (Kluckhohn 1956: 384–86; Ladd 1957: 237–38, 249–50, 252–54; Witherspoon 1975: 94–96).

The first principle is concerned with advancing the welfare of self, but it is also other-regarding in three senses. First, according to Navajo ideology, the welfare of self is logically tied to the welfare of others: caring for self is logically prerequisite for advancing the welfare of others. Second, the class of acts that the Navajo associate with this principle is other-impinging. Third, as indicated by the Navajo concept of welfare, the justification for this principle takes into account the welfare of others.

The lower-level moral rules implied by this principle include prohibitions against excess in any activity, against drinking and drunkenness, against gambling (gambling away family resources), and against being lazy (in not keeping up one's health and in not using family resources to the best advantage) (Kluckhohn 1956: 385, 387–88; Ladd 1957: 252–53; cf. Hobson 1954). All of these rules clearly come under the aegis of "caring for yourself," and, as indicated in the parenthetical qualifications, all are intended to be other-regarding. The Navajo ascribe special importance to this first principle and its subsumed rules, for their satisfaction is a necessary precondition to fulfilling the other two principles and their subsumed rules. For example, being drunk results in loss of superego control, which in turn increases the likelihood of social friction, getting in trouble with others (Kluckhohn 1956: 385; cf. Ladd 1957: 253).

The second general moral principle is concerned specifically with problems of social friction: "Avoid and rectify any trouble with others." This principle is other-regarding in two senses. First, it subsumes other-impinging moral-species terms, namely, that class of acts so significant for human social existence and welfare as necessarily to be the object of moral reflection. Second, it is other-regarding to the extent that its justification and the derived rules take into account the welfare of others. In this case, the Navajo employ utilitarian arguments. As Ladd says, "The arguments used . . . are utilitarian in the sense that they . . . argue that an action is wrong because it promotes trouble for everyone" (Ladd 1957: 238). And with regard to this principle and these rules Kluckhohn agrees: "Most of these are the prohibitions necessary to orderly life in any group. . . . Morals are relative to situation and to consequences rather than absolute. Everything is judged in terms of its consequences" (Kluckhohn 1956: 387–88). The lower-level moral rules implied by this principle constitute a relatively fixed range of quite stringent prohibitions against killing, fighting, stealing, adultery, ridiculing others, lying, and other forms of deception (Kluckhohn 1956: 387; Ladd 1957: 239–45; cf. Haile 1943). These rules also include injunctions specifying forms of rectification, compensation, assurances, and so on for breach of these prohibitions (see Ladd 1957: 249–52).

The third moral principle is the Navajo equivalent to the golden rule: "One ought to treat everyone as a kinsman" (Kluckhohn 1949: 374; Witherspoon 1975: 96). Obviously, this principle is other-regarding in the other-impinging sense (in this case, beneficent acts) and in the justificatory sense. The Navajo ideal embodied in this principle is that one ought always to help other people and be generous to them. The interesting feature is the way in which this principle is conceived, for the Navajo explicitly interpret this principle to apply not only to the *dinê* within the in-group but also to those outside Navajo society, that is, to strangers and aliens (Reichard 1974: xxxix). Thus, this principle not only subsumes role relations to children, parents, and affinal relatives but also enjoins beneficent action to the aged, to aliens, and in fact to anyone who requests or needs help. Moreover, explicit inquiry into the range of this principle has elicited the altruistic notions of self-sacrifice and aiding another, even a stranger, at the risk of one's own welfare (Ladd 1957: 255, 295–96). This altruistic notion is very definitely present in the Navajo code and is expressed in the forms of "sharing one's food at risk of starving oneself" and "never abandoning anyone in dire need" (Ladd 1957: 295). Witherspoon sums up this principle quite nicely:

> The sharing of food is a symbol of solidarity . . . the sharing of food is a primary social obligation. This extends even to outsiders and to non-Navajo. . . . The refusal to share food is a denial of kinship, and one of the worst things to be said about a person is, "She refused to share her food" or "He acts as though he had no kinsmen"—meaning about the same thing (Witherspoon 1975: 88).

2.1.3. Moral Virtues and Character Traits. In addition to these moral principles and rules, it is important to observe that the Navajo derive moral virtues and traits of character from the basic norm of *k'é*. In fact, most of the ethnographic data about Navajo morality are expressed in terms of virtues and character traits, as contrasted with rules and principles (Kluckhohn 1956). Two reasons account for this phenomenon. First, the moral principles and rules distinguished above may well represent analytical constructs that are not strongly indigenous to native Navajo thinking and action. For example, according to Navajo thinking, the prohibitions logically derived from the second moral principle are not that distinct from each other; rather, they tend to fall into a general class of "trouble-making actions" (Ladd 1957: 238). Second, the Navajo rarely appeal to abstract morality in the form of principles and rules; instead, they appeal more often to patterns of behavior and conduct invested in mythic figures who exhibit certain traits of character, for example, the benevolence of Changing Woman, the hospitality of Monster Slayer, and so on (Kluckhohn and Leighton 1974: 297; Reichard 1974: 63–79; cf. Spencer 1957; Wyman 1970).

Moral virtues and traits of character are, however, derived from the basic moral norm of *k'é*. And, as indicated in Part I, it is difficult on philosophical grounds to conceive of moral virtues except as dispositions to think and act in ways that can be characterized by moral principles and rules of action. So in the present context it appears plausible to differentiate three broad virtues and sets of specific character traits that logically correspond to the three moral principles distinguished above: (1) the virtue of prudence, (2) the virtue of social control, and (3) the virtue of benevolence. The first virtue subsumes the traits of rational competence, independence of mind, industry, and self-reliance; the second, sobriety, control over impulses, truthfulness, trustworthiness, and dependability; and the third, generosity, kindness, peacefulness, and friendliness (Kluckhohn 1956: 385–88; Kluckhohn and Leighton 1974: 297–303). Since other-regardingness in the other-impinging sense and in the justificatory sense has been established for the moral principles and rules, it would be unnecessarily redundant to work through a similar demonstration for these virtues and traits of character. Their other-regarding nature is sufficiently evident to warrant the appellation of "moral."

The only additional point worth mentioning in regard to k'é and the moral virtues is that this account implies certain minimal conditions of moral competence. Thus, the basic norm of k'é and its application imply the rational ability to follow certain kinds of reasoning and the ability to keep the consequences of courses of action in mind in making decisions (Ladd 1957: 279–71). These abilities constitute necessary conditions for operating within any validational mode in applying the norm of k'é to more specific principles, rules, and situations. They establish minimally necessary conditions for what may be called "moral selfhood" in the Navajo code (cf. Kluckhohn and Leighton 1947).

2.2. Religious Elements of the Navajo Code

The teleological norm of hózhǫ is a central concept in Navajo thought and action. As indicated earlier, this notion has moral, aesthetic, and religious meaning inasmuch as it denotes a harmonious state of affairs that is simultaneously good, beautiful, and blessed. It needs to be observed, however, that the religious meaning of hózhǫ is the dominant one (Kluckhohn 1949: 369–70; Wyman 1950: 346).[3] Hózhǫ represents primarily a state of integration or harmonious relation with the sacred powers and authorities in the Navajo universe. Consequently, the main aim of Navajo religious practices is to carry man along the road of life from birth to dissolution in such a way that he is kept in harmonious relation with the sacred authorities in the universe (Reichard 1974: 35–37). Since this state of blessed harmony is not permanently attainable for various contingent reasons, the specific goal of Navajo religious ceremonials is the restoration of such harmony whenever it is disturbed. Further, since the breakdown in harmony typically results in sickness, the majority of Navajo religious action-guides are concerned with what has been called the "type anxiety of health" (Kluckhohn 1942). Religious taboos are designed to avoid illness; religious ceremonials are designed to cure illness. These taboos and ceremonials are derived from the (religious) norm of *hôzhą́*.

2.2.1. *Sacred Authorities in Navajo Religion.* In order to understand the religious implications of the norm of *hôzhą́*, it is necessary to sketch the characteristics of Navajo religion—particularly the role played by the sacred authorities. To begin, it should be observed that the Navajo religion constitutes a thoroughgoing mythic world view that specifically addresses the problems of interpretability encountered by all religions: explicability of the world, problems of suffering and death, and problems of human conduct. Thus, for example, Navajo cosmogony tries to account for everything in the universe by relating it to man and his activities (Reichard 1974: 3–25). Problems of suffering and death are handled specifically by Navajo ritual practices, taboos and ceremonials, that aim to prevent or to cure sickness (Wyman 1950: 349–59; Ladd 1957: 228–37). Problems of human conduct are addressed by those Navajo myths that describe the metamorphosis of the *dinê* in emerging into this world and emphasize the ideals of stability, knowledge, and cooperation enjoined by the gods and the ancestors of the Navajo (Reichard 1974: 13–19).

The basic religious claim of the Navajo mythic world view is that there is a pantheon of supernaturals, deities, or Holy People. Further, these Holy People created the Navajo, the *dinê,* or the Earth Surface People and taught them how to exert control over themselves and their natural and social environment in order to maintain harmony and achieve *hôzhą́* (Reichard 1974: 13–49). The beings that comprise the Navajo pantheon have sacred authority in all the senses articulated in Part I. They are set apart or marked off from the ordinary world by the concept of supernatural power and immunity (that is, holiness), and they constitute a scope of reality that is to some degree beyond the control of humans: The Holy

People are ontologically and axiologically different from the Earth Surface People. The qualification "to some degree" beyond human control is necessary because some human control of the Holy People by ritual invocation and propitiation is both possible and effective. The Navajo pantheon also has sacred authority in the sense that special prominence is attributed to the Holy People in the world of human experience, thought, and action. All of these beings have a palpable bearing on the existence and values of the *dinê*. Finally, the Navajo pantheon is authoritative in the sense of being acknowledged as properly determinative for the beliefs, attitudes, and practices of the *dinê*. In some cases—for example, in certain ritual situations— the Holy People exert normative control over the *dinê*. In other cases the Holy People and their mythic actions are appealed to by the *dinê* as normative; for example, in reasoning from mythological precedent.

Following Gladys Reichard, the Navajo pantheon consists of the following types of sacred beings or sacred authorities (Reichard 1974: 50–79):

1. persuadable deities, such as the Sun or Changing Woman, whose motives are benevolent and who are invoked in rituals to help out the *dinê*;
2. undependable deities, such as First Man or First Woman, whose motives are mischievous and who can be persuaded ritually to help the *dinê* only with difficulty;
3. messenger deities, including all animals, who bridge the supernatural distance between the *dinê* and Holy People and play a major role in ritual instruction and in successful achievement of ritual ceremonies;
4. mythical protagonists, such as the Hero Twins, who serve as intermediaries between the *dinê* and Holy People and teach the *dinê* to perform important rituals;
5. unpersuadable deities, such as Monsters, who are essentially evil and who must be remembered in ceremonies by exorcistic rites;
6. natural forces conceived as deities, some of which are dangerous, such as lightning and whirlwinds, and others of which are favorably disposed to the *dinê* such as rain and certain crops;
7. deities falling between good and evil, such as Old Age and Poverty, which have mythological reasons for existing and whose presence helps to counter certain problems of interpretability.

Two points should be noted about the structure of the Navajo pantheon. The first is that the pantheon has a kinship organization, though it is not as consistent as a Navajo family or clan (Reichard 1974: 61–62). This feature reinforces the view that the Navajo kinship system is an important key to understanding their social relations and morality. The second point is that Reichard hypothesizes that the Navajo pantheon may be a sun cult, insofar as the Sun is a central correlating deity who exists to help the *dinê* to achieve harmony (Reichard 1974: 75–79). Whether or not this hypothesis is finally substantiated, it does serve to emphasize the significance of the norm of *hôzhǫ* in the Navajo religion.

Two other types of sacred authorities are not considered part of the Navajo pantheon and yet are specially distinctive, prominent, and authoritative in the requisite senses. These are ghosts and witches (Ladd 1957: 218; cf. Kluckhohn 1944). Ghosts are the malignant parts or spirits of dead people; they are invariably dangerous and to be avoided. Witches are human beings who possess supernatural powers and use them for evil purposes; they are either to be avoided or else ritually killed. These two classes of sacred beings or authorities need to be mentioned if only to make sense out of certain Navajo religous taboos and rituals. It has also been suggested that ghosts play a role in Navajo moral reasoning, but this point will be taken up later (Ladd 1957: 218).

2.2.2. Norm of Hôzhǫ and Religious Action-Guides. The reason for specifying the nature of the Navajo pantheon and other sacred powers is that for the Navajo virtually every element in the universe has the potential of being or becoming a sacred authority. Some of these beings are dependable or at least persuadable; some may be persuaded or coerced only with difficulty; and some are wholly dangerous and to be avoided. In order to achieve and maintain the state of *hôzhǫ,* the Navajo must maintain harmonious relations between themselves and these beings with sacred authority or at least avoid them lest the harmony be upset. Consequently, within the Navajo religion the norm of *hôzhǫ* or religious harmony may be formulated in at least two ways: (1) Maintain harmonious relations with the Holy People (and other sacred authorities); and (2) If these harmonious relations should be disturbed, restore them immediately. Inasmuch as the Holy People take on a kinship structure, and man is related to the Holy People, it might be hypothesized that kinship and affinal formulations could be developed for the norm of *hózhǫ́,* that is, formulations employing the notions of giving/sharing and exchange/reciprocity. The ethnographic data available, however, are not sufficient to project and defend such speculative formulations.

The two valid formulations for the norm of *hózhǫ́* or religious harmony imply two broad categories of religious action-guides: (1) taboos that prescribe ways of avoiding friction and thus maintaining harmonious relations with the Holy People and other sacred authorities; and (2) ceremonials (Chantways) that prescribe ways of restoring harmonious relations with sacred authorities (Kluckhohn and Leighton 1974: 200–23). Typically, taboos cite some kind of sickness as the likely effect of their violation. This citation is expressed by the Navajo term *bahadzid,* which means "for it there is fear and reverence"; *bahadzid* carries the connotations of danger and the numinous (Ladd 1957: 226–27; Kluckhohn and Leighton 1974: 200–01).

Taboos may be divided into two general classes: Those whose violation would antagonize some specific sacred being or authority, and those whose violation would bring sickness to any being in the universe, including the sacred beings, who broke the taboo. The first class of taboos includes prohibitions against killing certain animals, against imitating and thereby antagonizing dangerous natural forces, against antagonizing ghosts and witches, and so on. The second class of taboos includes prohibitions against incest, against contact between son-in-law and mother-in-law, against contact with menstrual blood, and so on. It should be emphasized that these taboos derive logically from Navajo religious theory and in most cases have mythological warrant (Ladd 1957: 230–31; Spencer 1957).

The restoration formulation of the norm of *hózhǫ́* implies distinctive types of ceremonials that share the common feature of being designed for curing disease and sickness (Kluckhohn and Leighton 1974: 202–21). Chantways constitute the largest group of these ceremonials, and their structure typifies the rest (Wyman 1950: 349–50). All Chantways share three structural elements. First, they all include Blessingway rites that invoke positive blessings and general well-being from the persuadable Holy People. Second, they all include invocatory offerings designed to attract those Holy People specifically relevant to the sickness in question. Third, they all include exorcistic rituals designed to drive out the evil causing the sickness. According to Wyman, Chantways may be divided into three main groups: (1) Holyway chants used for sickness traced to etiological factors associated with the Navajo pantheon; (2) Ghostway or Evilway chants used for sickness caused by ghosts or witches; and (3) Lifeway chants used for injuries resulting from accidents (Wyman 1950: 350). Together with the taboos, these Chantways constitute the bulk of specifically religious action-guides in the Navajo code.

These Navajo taboos and Chantways should be viewed as specifically religious action-guides because their legitimation involves justificatory appeal to the Navajo conception of sacred authority. This appeal takes the form of valuational implication as articulated in Part I (see Chapter 3, section 3.1.). The taboos are clearly derived from the Navajo conception of sacred authority by the use of valuational implication. For example, the taboo against killing certain animals takes the logical form of "Do not kill these animals because the consequences of doing so will result in disharmony with the sacred standard." This disharmony in turn takes the form of courting *bahadzid,* that is, dangerously antagonizing these animals qua sacred authorities. This courting of *bahadzid* directly contravenes the norm of *hózhá,* religious harmony. For another example, the incest taboo takes the logical form of "Do not have incestuous relations because having such relations does not conform with the sacred standard." This nonconformity directly contradicts the standards of behavior established by the Holy People and reported in the myths of the Navajo. In both examples the Navajo reason to their religious action-guides from a notion of sacred authority.

Valuational implication is also employed to derive the Chantways from the Navajo conception of sacred authority. With regard to the Chantways, the arguments take the following forms: (1) "Perform the Chantways because the consequences of doing so result in establishing harmony with the sacred standard" (conceived as specific sacred beings and/or the state of *hózhá);* and (2) "Perform the Chantways because doing so conforms with the sacred standard" (conceived as ritual patterns established by the Holy People in mythic events). In the case of both taboos and Chantways, then, it seems clear that these are religious action-guides justified by specific appeal to the Navajo conception(s) of sacred authority.

3. STRUCTURE OF PRACTICAL JUSTIFICATION OF THE NAVAJO CODE

In examining the structure of practical justification in the Navajo code, an important feature of Navajo culture needs to be kept in mind—namely, although the Navajo themselves prize rationality in practical discourse, they appeal to some norms of rationality that are different from those in the literate Western cultural tradition (see above, section 1.4). In particular it should be emphasized that the Navajo operate according to the principle of many reasons: More than one reason may justify a course of action, and these reasons may not be, or have to be, entirely consistent. Further, it is by no means clear that the Navajo distinguish between moral and religious phenomena. Their view of the universe is, after all, that of an orderly unitary system (see above, section 1.1). It is also not clear that the Navajo reason in the form of tight syllogistic argument in their practical discourse. (Who does?) And they are certainly not aware of all or even some of the philosophical distinctions that will be used to reconstruct their patterns of reasoning. Life is not all that logical and tidy. With these caveats in mind, we turn to the issues of practical justification raised by the moral and religious elements of the Navajo code.

3.1. Structure of the Moral Aspects of the Navajo Code

In regard to the moral aspects of the Navajo code, at least three questions must be raised and answered. They are as follows. First, what is the logical character of the basic moral norm of *k'é?* That is, what type of validating norm is it? Second, how is the justificatory procedure of applying *k'é* to lower-level principles, rules, and specific cases to be characterized logically? That is, what mode or modes of validation are used? Third, at the metapractical level, what type or types of vindicating appeals are used? That is, what is the logical character of such ultimate appeal(s)?

3.1.1. Logical Character of the Basic Moral Norm of K'é. Earlier it was argued that the basic moral norm of *k'é* can be formulated in three alternative ways, corresponding to its logical relations with the notions of social solidarity, communal welfare, and harmony (see above, section 2.1). These formulations and their Navajo linguistic equivalents are:

Religion and Morality of the Navajo

Religion and Morality of the Navajo 141

1. Maximize social solidarity and minimize social friction: "Help others" and "Avoid trouble."
2. Advance or maximize the welfare of self and the welfare of others: "Care for yourself" and "Care for others."
3. Maintain a stable equilibrium or state of harmony among persons and groups: "Don't disturb social harmony" and "If social harmony is disturbed, restore it."

According to these formulations, the norm of *k'é* is teleological in character in that it specifies conditions according to which rightness and wrongness are determined on the basis of the consequences of actions. These consequences pertain to the advancement or retardation of social solidarity, communal welfare, and social harmony. The norm of *k'é* is evidently extrapersonal since it logically includes a concern for the welfare of others and the community along with the self-concern of the agent. In fact, the welfare of self and of others are united logically in the distinctive Navajo concept of communal welfare (see above, section 1.3). In short, the norm of *k'é* is utilitarian, for a course of action is right if it promotes everyone's welfare and wrong if it promotes trouble for everyone.

This logical characterization of the basic moral norm of the Navajo code is at odds with, and flatly contradicts, the conclusions drawn by Ladd (Ladd 1957: 277–81). A number of reasons account for this divergence. First, Ladd does not identify *k'é* as a norm, much less a basic norm, of Navajo moral reasoning. Recent ethnographic data contradict Ladd on this point (Witherspoon 1975). Second, although Ladd recognizes that the Navajo employ utilitarian arguments, he reinterprets these arguments in egoistic terms (Ladd 1957: 238–48). Hence he misuses his own ethnographic data. Third, although he correctly articulates the Navajo concept of welfare, Ladd fails to appreciate its significance for properly characterizing Navajo moral reasoning (Ladd 1957: 303–04). This failure constitutes a basic oversight on his part. Fourth, Ladd fails to take seriously ethnographic data that do not fit into his reconstruction of the Navajo moral code (Ladd 1957: 286–92, 295–97). Instead of questioning the cogency of his reconstruction, Ladd merely expresses the opinion that eventually this counterevidence will be interpreted by his egoistic reconstruction. This point suggests that Ladd's reconstruction is not open to falsification—a serious flaw from the scientific point of view. Fifth, Ladd has an ideological ax to grind against all social definitions of morality, that is, against the criterion of other-regardingness (Ladd 1957: 235, 313). And this apparently biases his view of Navajo morality. Sixth, Ladd does not distinguish between moral and religious action-guides. Since some religious action-guides (namely taboos) may appear to be egoistic, and since Ladd views taboos as the most significant moral action-guides in the Navajo code, he is ineluctably misled into his egoistic reconstruction of Navajo morality (Ladd 1957: 235, 261). Here Ladd is simply not sufficiently sensitive to the differentiating criteria for the concepts of morality and religion and to the conceptual refinements made in the philosophy of religion and in comparative religious ethics.

3.1.2. Validating Procedures in the Navajo Moral Code. The issue of what mode(s) of validation are employed in the Navajo moral code has already been raised in connection with describing the content of Navajo morality (see above, section 2.1). The answer suggested earlier is that the interpretive mode of validation seems logically appropriate and in use. This view is supported by two observations. First, the norm of *k'é* appears to be sufficiently open-textured as to require discretionary interpretation in its application to lower-level principles, rules, and specific cases. Second, it appears that in its emphasis on virtues and character traits the norm of *k'é* specifies the minimal conditions necessary for operating within an interpretive mode of validation (see above, section 2.1). Hence it may seem that the issue is clear-cut and settled.

However, it is possible to argue a case for the validational mode of direct deduction. For example, there is ethnographic evidence to suggest that the Navajo would justify the moral principle of "avoid and rectify trouble with others" and the rules it subsumes (see above, section 2.1) in the following manner (Ladd 1957: 238–41, 279–80):

1. Minimize social friction (*k'é*).
2. *K'é*, then, specifies "avoiding trouble".
3. Trouble is avoided only if prohibitions against killing, stealing, lying, and so on are in force and followed.
4. Therefore, do not kill, steal, lie, and so on.

This type of argumentation can be reconstructed in the cases of the other moral principles and rules, as well as in the case of moral virtues and character traits. Ladd makes excellent use of this mode of direct deduction even though his identification of the Navajo basic moral norm is incorrect (1957: 24–84). Moreover, Kluckhohn argues a strong case for viewing the Navajo as rationalists par excellence in matters of morality (Kluckhohn 1956: 388–89). On balance, therefore, it appears that the Navajo use or would use the validating mode of direct deduction in many cases. One cannot but suspect, however, that this representation of Navajo moral reasoning may involve an ethnocentric Western bias for the way in which such reasoning ought to take place. Of course, there is the distinct possibility that the Navajo may employ more than one mode of validation, particularly since they adhere to the principle of many reasons (see above, section 1.4). The best that one can conclude at this point, therefore, is that the Navajo may well employ two modes of validation: interpretation and direct deduction. The issue of whether one of these validating procedures predominates must remain an open question.

3.1.3. *Vindicating Appeals in the Navajo Moral Code.*   The vindicating appeals made by the Navajo in support of the basic moral norm of *k'é* make an enormously complex issue. In reviewing the ethnological literature that may be relevant to this issue, it appears that the studies of Navajo religion and mythology have the greatest bearing (cf. Reichard 1974; Spencer 1957; Kluckhohn 1949). None of this literature, however, appears to address the issue of vindication in any conclusive fashion. Therefore, the following reconstructions are tendered only as plausible (or "possible") hypotheses.

There appear to be two types of vindication for the basic moral norm of *k'é*. One type is religious in character; the other type is more rational and secular. But even this relatively simple and straightforward characterization must be qualified. For, as will be seen, the "secular" rational vindication of *k'é* ultimately refers back to a more basic type of religious vindication.

The religious vindication of *k'é* involves a complex mythic appeal to the sacred authority of the Navajo pantheon. Only the general character of this mythic appeal can be sketched here. Speaking formally, this vindicating appeal falls within the mode of articulating general anthropological and cosmological beliefs about the nature of the universe. More specifically, this mythic appeal to the

Navajo pantheon functions logically in three ways. First, it provides an intelligible background for understanding why the ultimate moral norm for the Navajo should have kinship connotations. Second, it specifies modes and patterns of behavior that are normative for interpreting the content of *k'é*. Third, it provides explicit backing or warrant for regarding *k'é* as the basic moral norm by citing certain myths as reasons.

In the case of intelligible background, the mythic appeal refers to or invokes the mythology of Enemyway and highlights accounts of family councils held among kin-related Holy People (Witherspoon 1975: 57–60; cf. Haile 1938). This appeal attempts to dramatize concepts and forms of kinship relations that provide background for understanding the deep-rooted norm of *k'é* in the cultural kinship universe of the Navajo. It suggests that the norm of *k'é* derives from the kinship relations and organization of the Navajo pantheon itself. As a secondary theme, this appeal also mythically legitimates rationalism and public discussion among the *diné*.

In the case of normative patterns of behavior, the mythic vindicating appeal refers to the mythology surrounding the figure of Changing Woman who symbolizes the mother-child bond and the virtue of benevolence (Reichard 1974: 50–62; cf. Kluckhohn 1949: 364–66). This and related mythology shows how the Holy People maintain kinship and affinal behavior patterns as well as a balance of harmonious relations, that help give form and content to the norm of *k'é*. Reichard is quite explicit on this point and goes so far as to say, "Proper behavior was defined by the gods along with life-giving and life-preserving principles" (Reichard 1974: 49).

In the case of explicit backing, the mythic appeal refers to the Emergence myth, which describes how the Holy People advised, coerced, and otherwise guided the *diné* to adopt the ideals of social stability, cooperation, promise-keeping, and the general avoidance of "trouble" as moral norms of conduct for life in this world (Reichard 1974: 13–25; cf. O'Bryan 1956). This myth provides explicit justification for the basic moral norm of *k'é* and its derived content in terms of high-level principles and virtues. And it is important to observe that this is the basic myth of the Navajo. Indeed, Wyman says that the Navajo emergence story is "their nearest analogue to the Christian Bible" (Wyman 1950: 358).

Insofar as the Navajo mythic tradition embodies the essential core of rationalism, it encourages and indeed justifies the use of practical reason in the moral life. This theme is clearly exhibited by the virtue of public and rational discussion represented in accounts of family councils among the Holy People over matters of practical and moral concern. The Navajo mythic tradition, then, sanctions the use of practical reason in making and justifying moral decisions. As has been shown already, Navajo practical reason leads to the view that the concept of welfare concerns both self and others (see above, sections 1.3 and 1.4., especially the principle of general effects). It is not at all implausible to suggest that the principle of general effects points to the logical appropriateness of employing not only utilitarian reasoning but also the utilitarian norm of *k'é* in the sphere of social and moral relations. Furthermore, the Navajo view of the universe as an orderly unitary system governed by general laws spotlights the concept of harmony and suggests that a norm like *k'é* is an appropriate basic norm for action in the social world (see above, section 1.1). The cumulative effect of these observations is that the Navajo have a second type of vindicating appeal for the norm of *k'é*—the appeal to autonomous practical reason (cf. Ladd 1957: 203–06). To the extent that this use of practical reason is legitimated by the mythic tradition itself, however, the vindicating religious mythic appeal appears to represent the more fundamental mode of vindication.

3.2. Structure of the Religious Aspects of the Navajo Code

In regard to the religious aspects of the Navajo code, a number of questions must be raised and answered. First, what is the logical character and status of the norm of *hózhǫ́*? That is, is it exclusively religious or does it incorporate the notion of moral harmony, *k'é*? Second, are the religious action-guides of the Navajo (their taboos and ceremonials) purely religious in character or do they have moral import as well? What is their logical character? Third, can anything further be said to elucidate the ways in which the Navajo derive these religious action-guides from the norm of *hózhǫ́* and other conceptions of sacred authority? For example, following Ladd (see above, section 3.1), are these modes of derivation and justification egoistic in character?

3.2.1. Logical Character of the Norm of Hózhǫ́. It has already been pointed out that the Navajo norm of *hózhǫ́* has religious, moral, and aesthetic meaning, though the religious meaning clearly predominates (see above, section 2.2). In short, it has been argued that *hózhǫ́* represents a state of integration or harmonious relation with the sacred authorities in the Navajo universe. The fact that this norm is principally religious is implied by Witherspoon's discussion of the concept.

The Navajo often say "shił hózhǫ́" which means "With me there is beauty, happiness, and harmony"—in other words, "Things in my world are in proper place and harmonious order." When this order is disrupted, *sickness* [our italics] arises and must be treated . . . (Witherspoon 1975: 8).

Witherspoon's view that sickness arises from the disruption of the harmony of *hózhǫ́* clearly implies that he considers *hózhǫ́* to be a distinctively religious goal: The Navajo religion is essentially concerned with harmony within the frame of health and sickness.

This religious interpretation of *hózhǫ́* is confirmed by Kluckhohn when he says: " 'Hózhǫ́' is probably the central idea in Navajo religious thinking" (Kluckhohn 1949: 369). And yet Kluckhohn himself later says that *hózhǫ́* has moral meaning also (Kluckhohn 1949: 369). Moreover, in his discussion of Navajo religion, Wyman includes in the concept of *hózhǫ́* not only the restoration and maintenance of health but also the well-being and security of self and others (Wyman 1950: 346). These latter statements raise the question of whether the norm of *hózhǫ́* logically incorporates or implies the moral norm of *k'é*. This question in turn poses the issue of whether the basic norm of the Navajo code is of a mixed sort, rather than being distinctively moral.

The answers seem to be supplied by Reichard. It is her view that "invocation and propitiation of the gods and the forces of nature (for the ritual restoration and maintenance of *hózhǫ́*) are useless unless one is in rapport with his fellowmen" in the sense of behaving properly toward them (Reichard 1974: 49). This view suggests that being moral is a necessary condition for successfully achieving and maintaining the state of *hózhǫ́* through religious ritual. If this is the case, then it appears that the moral norm of *k'é* must be logically distinct from the religious norm of *hózhǫ́*. And this claim implies that the basic norm of the Navajo code is the moral norm of *k'é*, a distinctively moral norm. It must also be admitted, though, that the notion of *hózhǫ́* has some sort of primacy over the norm of *k'é*.

Hózhǫ́ represents a more ultimate teleological goal in Navajo thought and action than the more restricted goal of *k'é*, conceived as moral harmony. The implications of this admission are explored below. For the present, it is sufficient to note that the norm of *hózhǫ́* refers to an exclusively religious state of harmony and that it does not logically subsume the distinctively moral norm of *k'é*.[4]

3.2.2. Logical Character of Religious Action-Guides.

The issue of whether Navajo religious action-guides, in the form of taboos and Chantways, are purely religious or rather have moral import as well is raised specifically by Ladd's analysis of Navajo taboos (Ladd 1957: 228–37). Ladd's position is that these taboos are explicitly moral in character and have a distinctively moral justification. He argues that the principal justification for taboos is that they specify certain actions as *bahadzid* which, if performed, would result in sickness for the agent. Further, since it is Ladd's view that the basic moral norm is egoistic—"Never do anything leading to your own misfortune"—he calls these taboos "moral prescriptions."

There are at least three major difficulties with this position. First, as indicated earlier, Ladd misidentifies the basic moral norm of the Navajo—it is not the intrapersonal, egoistic, teleological principle he suggests, but rather the utilitarian norm of *k'é* (see above, section 3.1). Second, as indicated earlier, the notion of *bahadzid* is a distinctively religious concept of numinous danger potentially disruptive of the state of *hózhǫ́* (see above, section 2.2). So the appeal to actions being *bahadzid* is not prima facie a moral appeal at all. A third and final point is this: It has been shown that taboos are religious action-guides logically derived from the prima facie religious norm of *hózhǫ́* and other Navajo conceptions of sacred authority, not from the moral norm of *k'é* or any other moral norm for that matter (see above, section 2.2). Thus, there is every reason to suppose that these action-guides, along with the ceremonial curing rituals, are purely religious in character.

3.2.3. Derivation of Religious Action-Guides.

The issue of what mode(s) of derivation or justification are employed by the Navajo in regard to religious action-guides has already been addressed and been given a definitive answer: valuational implication (see above, section 2.2). A few additional comments are in order, however. Ethnological analyses of Navajo religion and mythology indicate that there are two types of justification for *hózhǫ́* and the derived taboos and Chantways: (1) mythical appeal to cosmological beliefs about the Holy People and sacred authorities in general; and (2) appeal of practical reason to supernatural sanctions and consequences. Since it has been demonstrated that both types of appeal take the logical form of valuational implication, this point will not receive any further elaboration (see above, section 2.2). Here we are concerned with the metapractical level of religious justification that is equivalent to the level of vindication in the structure of Navajo moral reasoning.

In the first type of justification, mythic beliefs about the Navajo pantheon qua sacred authority are invoked to provide content for the norm of *hózhǫ́* and to cite precedent for the derivation of taboos and ceremonials from the norm of *hózhǫ́*. More specifically, Navajo Chantway mythology describes how the Holy People behave in relation to each other in order to maintain harmony or *hózhǫ́*, for example, how First Woman avoided incestuous relations with the Sun. The same mythology articulates the curing ceremonials necessary for restoring harmony, for example, ceremonials to cure Coyote after he violated the incest taboo (Ladd 1957: 230–31; Spencer 1957). Thus, in the first type of justification the Navajo cite mythological precedent in support of the position that taboos and ceremonies are logically connected with the achievement and maintenance of *hózhǫ́* (cf. Reichard 1974: 3–7). In the second type of justification, the Navajo employ the principles of practical reason in conjunction with supernatural sanctions and consequences cited in myths (see above, section 1.4). Thus, in accordance with their various causal principles, most especially that of general effects, the Navajo cite the adverse consequences of blindness and craziness in support of the son-in-law/mother-in-law and the incest taboos (Ladd 1957: 230–31; Spencer 1957). And they appeal to the same principles in articulating and supporting those ceremonies necessary to restore harmony (*hózhǫ́*) after violations have taken place (Wyman 1950: 345; Kluckhohn 1949). This sort of rational appeal to supernatural sanctions and consequences conforms to the logical pattern of utilitarian reasoning, as in the case of moral justification. We say utilitarian rather than egoistic, for as Wyman and many others point out in regard to Navajo religion, "individualism is more apparent than real" (Wyman 1950: 347; Kluckhohn and Leighton 1974: 235–40; Reichard 1974). Thus, for example, taboos should not be violated not merely because such breaches would be *bahadzid* for the violator but also, and more importantly, because violations would have undesirable consequences for other people associated with the agent (Ladd 1957: 228–31).

3.3. Overlap of Moral and Religious Aspects of the Navajo Code

The central issue that remains to be examined is the extent, if any, of the overlap between the moral and religious aspects of the Navajo code. Do any of the moral principles, rules, virtues, or character traits have a distinctively religious justification, in addition to their moral one? To answer this question in any definitive way requires an extensive knowledge of Navajo language, social life, ceremonies, and myths. Some relevant considerations can be adduced, however, if only to provide a tentative hypothesis in lieu of a final answer. Three points require explicit discussion: Do the Navajo think of the Holy People in their pantheon as moral authorities? Do the Navajo invoke any distinctively religious or mythic warrants in justifying any of their moral principles or virtues? In justifying any specific principles or virtues, do the Navajo ever appeal to esoteric or concealed beliefs that may be distinctively religious in character?

3.3.1. Do the Holy People Function as Moral Authorities? There appears to be some consensus among social anthropologists on how to answer this first question. The Navajo do not think of the Holy People as moral authorities or moral legislators (Ladd 1957: 267–68). Kluckhohn is apparently quite explicit on this point: "Nor does the Navajo invoke the supernaturals for moral guidance" (Kluckhohn 1962: 176). This view is not as straightforward as it might first appear, however, for elsewhere Kluckhohn elaborates on this denial in the following way:

Certain other acts are commanded or prohibited on the basis that one or more of the Holy People did or did not behave in similar fashion, but never in the modes which would seem "natural" to Christians: "Do this to please the Holy People because they love you," or "Don't do this because the Holy People punish wrongdoing" (Kluckhohn and Leighton 1974: 297; cf. Kluckhohn 1949: 372).

Kluckhohn is saying that the Navajo do not appeal to the Holy People for moral guidance as Christians may appeal to God for guidance. This is an important qualification of his original statement.

The implications of this qualification are twofold. The Navajo do not view the Holy People as moral authorities who issue commands as a theistic god may issue commands: On this point all anthropologists seem to agree. But the Navajo may well view the Holy People as role models that help to define proper moral behavior. Thus, Reichard is able to assert, "Proper behavior was defined by the gods along with life-giving and life-preserving principles" (Reichard 1974: 49). This assertion leads directly into the second point.

3.3.2. *Are There Mythic Religious Warrants for Navajo Morality?*   Apparently, the Navajo do invoke mythic religious warrants in support of their moral principles and virtues. This claim is clearly implied by Reichard's assertion, and it is supported by other scholars as well: for example, Matthews refers to the virtues and paradigmatic actions of the supernaturals in Navajo myths (Matthews 1899); Kluckhohn refers to patterns of conduct invested with symbolic significance and having their warrant in tradition (Kluckhohn 1949: 366); and Spencer devotes an entire book to the value themes and standards in Chantway myths appealed to by the Navajo (Spencer 1957). It is Reichard's considered view that "the Navajo layman resorts for his answer to myth . . . he cites myth for his reasons"; and again, in regard to moral ideals "the Navajo reason from mythological precedent" (Reichard 1974: xlvii, 13–16). The sole dissenting view is expressed by Ladd in his assertion that "the Holy People are not relevant to moral discourse" (Ladd 1957: 217). Ladd, however, is inconsistent on this matter, for he bases this claim on the suggestion that beliefs about the Holy People are esoteric. And yet he himself later admits that "information about all of these beings is available to the Navajo layman" (Ladd 1957: 219). Ladd's position does not stand up under careful scrutiny.

The implication of this cumulative evidence is, therefore, that the Navajo have both moral and religious reasons that justify their moral principles and virtues in some cases. Inasmuch as these moral notions have autonomous forms of moral and religious justification, they may be logically characterized as religious and moral action-guides (see Chapter 5, section 5).

An even stronger claim *may* be made about the logical nature of Navajo morality. In order to make and support this claim, two observations must be made. First, in light of the earlier discussion about the vindicating appeals for the basic moral norm of *k'é*—

where even the secular use of practical reason was seen to have mythic warrant—it must be observed that religious elements play a dominant role in the Navajo moral code (see above, section 3.1). Second, specific moral principles and virtues may also be justified by mythic religious appeals. The overwhelming impression of these logical observations issues in a claim: The Navajo code may well be justly characterized as a religious-moral code. That is to say, conceived as a whole, the code appears to be finally grounded on religious premises.

We would be more comfortable with this conclusion if it could be clearly shown that the Navajo norm of *hôzhǫ́* logically subsumes the moral norm of *k'é*. As things now stand, *k'é* has been shown to have the backing of both religious and at least quasiautonomous rational appeals: This makes the situation ambiguous. If, however, it could be demonstrated that the concept of *hôzhǫ́* logically includes *k'é*, the dominant religious character of the Navajo code would be clinched. While this thesis is quite attractive to us, it is not conclusively supported by available ethnographic data. In the final analysis, it appears that the Navajo possess what we may call a *dual system of both moral and religious action-guides*. To reiterate: Only if *hôzhǫ́* could be conclusively shown to subsume *k'é*, could the system be logically characterized as a religious-moral system (see Chapter 5, section 5.2).

3.3.3. Is Navajo Morality Justified by Concealed Beliefs? In arguing for his egoistic reconstruction of the Navajo code, Ladd raises the important question of whether any specific moral principles or rules are justified by esoteric or concealed religious beliefs (Ladd 1957: 207, 297). This question is significant, for an affirmative answer would provide further evidence for viewing the Navajo code as essentially religious. Ladd takes the position that esoteric knowledge and beliefs do not constitute an essential component of the Navajo code (Ladd 1957: 207). In his effort to reconstruct the code along egoistic lines, however, Ladd speculates frequently about the existence of concealed beliefs—especially about ghosts—that might support, for example, the prohibition against killing and the supposed altruistic injunctions to help the aged and the needy (Ladd 1957: 240, 255, 291, 295–96). Ladd's point is that the egoistic fear of ghosts might count as a concealed religious reason for the prohibitions and injunctions in question. The point is well taken since, if true, it would support the position that the Navajo justify some specific moral rules on religious grounds. Unfortunately, as Ladd recognizes, there is insufficient ethnographic data to support this view.

Ladd's inquiry tends to raise the more general issue of whether Navajo moral principles and rules are justified by reference to esoteric beliefs about sacred authorities. This issue is potentially significant because if many of the reasons for Navajo moral principles and rules were esoteric, then their code would be authoritarian in character. But, as has been indicated, the Navajo religion is not esoteric; Reichard's extensive research supports this denial (Reichard 1974). And, therefore, the Navajo moral code is not authoritarian (cf. Ladd 1957: 265–68). This lack of authoritarianism is precisely why Kluckhohn says that the Holy People may shape and guide Navajo morality, "but never in the modes which would seem 'natural' to Christians" (Kluckhohn 1949: 372).

3.3.4. Conclusion.   One final point needs to be made about the logical character of the Navajo moral code. We have suggested that the cumulative evidence indicates that the code is finally grounded on religious premises concerning sacred authority and the goal of *hózhǫ́* (see above, section 3.3). Yet at the same time, we indicated that the vindicating appeals for the moral norm of *k'é*—mythic religious and rational secular—make the situation quite ambiguous. We shall conclude by reiterating a point made at the outset of this discussion of the structure of practical justification, for this point explains why the situation is, and probably ought to be left, ambiguous. The point is this: The Navajo operate according to the principle of many reasons. Therefore, according to Navajo thinking, more than one reason and more than one type of reason may justify an action-guide. Further, Navajo norms of rationality may not demand that these reasons and types of reasons be made totally consistent with each other. This observation, together with the fact that the Navajo do not clearly distinguish between moral and religious phenomena, explains the ambiguity (see above, section 3). Moreover, it suggests that to press any harder to get rid of the ambiguity may do an injustice to the nature of Navajo moral and religious reasoning. At some point we must stop and say, this is simply the way things are.

NOTES

1. By using the terms *orderly, lawful,* and *machine,* we do not mean to suggest that the Navajo have a static conception of the universe. Quite the contrary, the Navajo universe is a very dynamic one. Consider, for example, Gary Witherspoon's recent characterization: "[T]he perspective or dimension of movement dominates and pervades the Navajo view and classification of the world. The Navajo world is a world of motion—a world of action in which all beings and entities are either acting or being acted upon; a world of change in which both individual entities and systems are constantly going through phased cycles and processes of deformation and restoration; a world of things in motion . . ." (Witherspoon 1977: 140).
2. Another basic Navajo principle is that physical and mental phenomena are inseparable. Although this metaphysical notion underlies the principles of causality, it does not significantly affect our representation of the Navajo moral code. For an excellent discussion of Navajo metaphysics, see Witherspoon 1977: 8–62.
3. Witherspoon observes that the Navajo do not possess a category of religion. His point is a linguistic one: "The term 'nahaghá' [ritual] bears no semiotic or syntagmatic relationship to the word 'religion' " (Witherspoon 1977: 14). His observation, while true, does not rule out the use of our concept of religion for the purpose of analysis.
4. Witherspoon's most recent work on the Navajo seems to suggest that *k'é* can be subsumed logically under the norm of *hózhǫ́*: "The Navajo emphasis on harmony and order as expressed by the term *hózhǫ́* is an emphasis on relatedness. It is impossible to have order and harmony among unrelated entities. *K'é* terms refer to forms of social harmony and order that are based in affective action. Rather than seeking to emphasize their independence, self-reliance, and separateness, and rather than seeking to escape bonds with others that involve continuous obligations of assistance and generosity, Navajos seek to relate themselves to others in their world, and seek to join in the vast system of interdependence that characterizes the social harmony and order of their world . . . Although careful, deliberate, and proper action can reduce the danger, and various ceremonies can create a substantial degree of immunity to the ill will of various Holy People, only generosity, kindness, and cooperativeness expressed in affective action can reduce one's vulnerability to the ill will of other earth surface people. Through the affective actions found in forms of *k'é* solidarity a Navajo can transform potential ill will into good will" (Witherspoon 1977: 88–99). Although Witherspoon's comments clearly suggest that *hózhǫ́* logically subsumes *k'é,* his remarks are inconclusive. In refusing to employ such analytical concepts as religion and morality, Witherspoon presents us with an ambiguous position: *K'é,* may be subsumed by *hózhǫ́,* but equally *k'é* may only be a precondition for achieving *hózhǫ́.* We find it unfortunate that Witherspoon's otherwise incisive ethnology fails to clarify this important issue.

REFERENCES

DOWNS, JAMES F.
1964   *Animal Husbandry in Navajo Society and Culture.* Berkeley and Los Angeles: University of California Press.

GEERTZ, CLIFFORD.
1966   "Religion as a Cultural System." In *Anthropological Approaches to the Study of Religion.* Michael Banton, ed. London: Tavistock Publications.

HAILE, FATHER BERNARD.
1938   *Origin Legend of the Navaho Enemy Way.* New Haven: Yale University Press.
1943   "Soul Concepts of the Navaho." In *Annali Lateranensi* 7: 59–94.

HOBSON, R.
1954   *Navaho Acquisitive Values.* Papers of the Peabody Museum of Harvard University. Volume 42, No. 3.

KLUCKHOHN, CLYDE.
1942   "Myths and Rituals: A General Theory." In *Harvard Theological Review* 35: 45–79.
1944   *Navaho Witchcraft.* Papers of the Peabody Museum of Harvard University. Volume 22, No. 2.
1949   "The Philosophy of the Navaho Indians." In *Ideological Differences and World Order.* F. S. C. Northrop, ed. New Haven: Yale University Press.
1956   "Navaho Morals." In *Encyclopedia of Morals.* Vergilius Ferm, ed. New York: Philosophical Library.
1962   "Navaho Morals." In *Culture and Behavior.* Richard Kluckhohn, ed. New York: Free Press.

KLUCKHOHN, CLYDE, AND LEIGHTON, DOROTHEA.
1947   *Children of the People: The Navaho Individual and His Development.* Cambridge, Mass.: Harvard University Press.
1974   *The Navaho.* Revised edition. Cambridge, Mass.: Harvard University Press.

LADD, JOHN.
1957   *The Structure of a Moral Code: A Philosophical Analysis of Ethical Discourse Applied to the Ethics of the Navaho Indians.* Cambridge, Mass.: Harvard University Press.

MATTHEWS, W.
  1899   "The Study of Ethics among the Lower Races." In *Journal of American Folklore* 44: 1–9.
O'BRYAN, AILEEN.
  1956   *The Diné: Origin Myths of the Navaho Indians.* Washington, D. C.: Smithsonian Institution.
REICHARD, GLADYS A.
  1974   *Navaho Religion: A Study of Symbolism.* Second edition. Princeton: Princeton University Press.
SHEPARDSON, MARY, AND HAMMOND, BLODWEN.
  1970   *The Navaho Mountain Community: Social Organization and Kinship Terminology.* Berkeley and Los Angeles: University of California Press.
SPENCER, KATHERINE.
  1957   *Mythology and Values: An Analysis of Navaho Chantway Myths.* Philadelphia: American Folklore Society.
VOGT, EVON Z.
  1951   *Navaho Veterans: A Study of Changing Values.* Papers of the Peabody Museum of Harvard University. Volume 41, No. 1.
WITHERSPOON, GARY.
  1975   *Navaho Kinship and Marriage.* Chicago: University of Chicago Press.
  1977   *Language and Art in the Navaho Universe.* Ann Arbor: University of Michigan Press.
WYMAN, LELAND.
  1950   "The Religion of the Navaho Indians." In *Forgotten Religions.* Vergilius Ferm, ed. New York: Philosophical Library.
  1970   *Blessingway.* Tucson: University of Arizona Press.

7 | Religion and Morality in the Gospel of Matthew

1. INTRODUCTION

In turning to an analysis of practical reasoning in the so-called higher religions, we must, as previously, limit our field of investigation. In the case of Christianity, we shall restrict ourselves to one part of the New Testament. Let us reiterate that we are not attempting an exhaustive examination of any religious tradition, though we hope that our analysis can be applied in an illuminating way to any aspect of a given religious ethical tradition. All we mean to do in this context is to exemplify our approach by applying it, on the basis of more or less accidental selection, to segments of certain religions.

With respect to Christianity, it is not surprising that we attend to New Testament materials since they constitute the putative foundation for much of Christian practical reflection. Moreover, if a selection must be made among the books of the New Testament, there is perhaps some plausibility to choosing the Gospel of Matthew. This book contains much action-guiding language, as well as examples of the variety of practical appeals that Christians have historically employed in taking up their way of life. Of course, in making this selection, we do not imply that we are providing a complete picture of "New Testament ethics," let alone of "Christian ethics."

It is a commonplace that the New Testament, either in part or as a whole, fails to provide a complete, systematic practical code.

While that is true, it should not blind us to Matthew's preoccupation with the regulation of practice. Among the Gospel writers, Matthew is preeminent in the concern to produce correct action, whether in matters of church discipline and law, or in moral and religious behavior. To this end, the author of the Gospel goes some distance, within his lights, toward systematizing what he considers to be the central action-guides of the Christian life, that is, toward generating a specific code of ethics (Grant 1957: 143).

Whatever the historical reasons for Matthew's emphasis on specification and systematization of Christian practice, this book, among the Gospels, provides us with a most promising range of material for comparative ethical analysis. As in the foregoing case study, we shall be concerned to distinguish and relate religious, moral, and legal action-guides, and then to compare Matthew's particular combinations and permutations of the different action-guides with the Navajo and Buddhist materials. The problem of deciding what is religious, moral, and legal about Matthew's teaching pertains to a consideration of both the *content* of the teaching, as well as to the *structure of justification* contained in it. Only when we have concluded our analysis of both content and structure shall we be able to offer a sufficiently complex account of the boundary-lines of, and the system of relations among, the different action-guides.

2. THE CONTENT OF MATTHEW'S PRACTICAL TEACHING

One cannot read the Gospel of Matthew, let alone the New Testament as a whole, without being impressed with the emphasis on a pervasive, powerful sacred authority. Matthew's vision of God and Jesus unmistakably conforms to all of our specifications of what counts as religion. First, God is pictured in a series of authoritative images, as "King," "Judge," "Father," "Master," and "Lord"—as a figure, first of all, who occupies a *specially distinctive* position in the universe. His person, as well as that of his "Son," Jesus, and the "Kingdom" over which they reign supreme, all constitute a scope of reality distinctly apart from everything else in the world, and one that is without any question beyond the volitional control of human beings.

Second, God, and, derivatively, Jesus, as the religious objects of

Matthew's Gospel, are both considered to have *special prominence* in their influence over the generation and distribution of benefit and harm. Whatever the precise status of eschatalogical rewards and punishment, among Matthew's practical appeals, there is no doubt of God's prominent role in controlling and dispensing them.

[Matthew] has more material relating to rewards and punishments than any other evangelist. He offers in vivid if conventional terms both the dangers of heaven and the direst torments of hell (25:31–46). He persistently appends the formula: "there men will weep and gnash their teeth" (8:12; 13:42–50; 22:13; 24:51)—found nowhere else in the Gospels except once in Luke (13:28). He consistently binds commands and exhortations to promises for future assize, giving to sayings which could in themselves easily be read as maxims for present conduct a clear reference to reward or punishment on the Last Day (16:24–6; 16:27; 10:39–42) (Houlden 1973: 52–53).

Moreover, Jesus' miracle-working capacity, which, according to Matthew, manifests his special authority in acts of exorcism and healing, is understood as the power to affect human sickness and misery, which is to say, the power to control physical and psychological benefit and harm.

Thirdly, the utterances and directives of God, and, again derivatively of Jesus, are considered authoritative in being *properly determinative* with respect to the attitudes and behavior of would-be disciples, or members of "the Kingdom." In matters of disposition and deportment, the disciple is enjoined to become a "servant" or "slave," subjugating himself to the will of God and Jesus, going forth to teach "all nations," "to observe all I have commanded you," (28:20).

In its broad outlines, then, the "theology" of Matthew constitutes a cosmology and prescribes a set of attitudes and practices in relation to that cosmology. Beyond that, the outlook suggests answers to our problems of interpretability, as follow: (1) While Matthew shows little inclination to solve theoretical puzzles or inexplicabilities about the relation of God to the universe, he is concerned to provide reassurance in the face of the fears and anxieties of his readers regarding "what you shall eat or what you shall drink, or about your body, what you shall put on. . . . Seek first his kingdom and his righteousness, and all these things shall be yours as well" (6:25,33).

(2) The Gospel of Matthew contains the makings of a theodicy, or an ultimate resolution of the problems of death and suffering, and (3) of the puzzles of human conduct. As Jesus overcomes physical death in his resurrection, so those faithful to him and to "the will of the Father," will inherit eternal life (25:46) and will "shine like the sun in the kingdom of their Father" (13:43). On the other hand, "all causes of sin and all evil-doers" will be removed from the Kingdom and thrown into the furnace of fire" (13:41–42). Similarly, those who suffer "for righteousness' sake" (5:10), "who mourn" (5:4), "who are poor in spirit" (5:3), who endure hatred, rejection, and dislocation "for my name's sake," (10:21–22), their reward will be "great in heaven" (5:12). In other words, suffering and death have a point. There is, consequently, a reason for confidence in face of the distressing discrepancy between virtue and satisfaction "in this age." Neither righteousness and suffering, nor wickedness and prosperity will converge forever.

Matthew's pervasive religious point of view makes difficult the task of rigorously distinguishing and relating religious, moral, and legal action-guides. As several commentators indicate (though often without much critical reflection), religious, moral, and legal matters are all intermingled in Matthew. Take 12:10–12 as an example of the apparent difficulty.

And, behold, there was a man with a withered hand. And they asked him, "Is it lawful to heal on the sabbath?" so that they might accuse him. He said to them, "What man of you, if he has one sheep and it falls into a pit on the sabbath, will not lay hold of it and lift it out? Of how much more value is a man than a sheep! So it is lawful to do good on the sabbath."

On the face of it, the duty to honor the Sabbath by rigidly curtailing everyday activities, might be called a religious duty. The Mosaic tradition, which is modified though not rejected by Matthew, developed Sabbath restrictions on the basis of the Fourth Commandment. Observance of the Sabbath had become a crucially significant "sacramental bond, holding together all adherents of the Jewish religion, for the purpose of worshipping and showing devotion to God" (Moore 1935: vol. II, 38–39). So understood, the message of this passage might be that religious duties "must give way if they stand in the way of real need or moral obligation" (Johnson 1951: 239). Certainly, on our use of terms, giving special

importance to acts affecting the material welfare—or "real need"—
of another, as in the case of the man with the withered hand,
suggests a special emphasis on at least part of what the word *moral*
means.

Still, such a simple distinction between religious and moral
action-guides obscures Matthew's point that, for Jesus, acting so as
to "do good" by improving the welfare of another, is more in line
with the true point of Sabbath observance, of reverence for and
worship of God, than is conventional observance of the Sabbath
laws. In other words, properly understood, religious and moral
action-guides do not conflict. To do the moral thing is preeminently
one's religious duty. Moral considerations simply help to identify
one's religious responsibilities, that is, one's responsibilities to the
sacred authority. Thus, we take note of one facet of the complexity
before us, and we register the fact that, with respect to this and
other passages, we need to make some important distinctions, but we
have not as yet made clear just what these are in relation to
Matthew.

A second facet concerns the role of law or legal action-guides in
relation to the other two. The passage itself raises the question of
whether it is "lawful" to heal on the Sabbath, and concludes that it
is. We might infer, therefore, that since other-impinging or moral
acts (such as healing) are legal or lawful, and since moral acts are
quintessentially religious acts, then what is properly legal is also
both moral and religious. Again, we see the overlap of categories.

But in what sense are we to understand the use of the word *law* in
this context, and, by extension, in Matthew in general? Is Matthew
referring to law in our sense, namely, as "a directive that is taken as
authoritative in that it is officially both legitimate and enforceable."
That is to say, are there designated human officials (such as
members of the Sanhedrin or synagogal courts, or, perhaps, officials
of the Christian church) who are assumed by Matthew to be
authorized to interpret and enforce the law? Are moral and religious
requirements thus legalized by the presence of an official staff? And
does the jurisdiction of the staff apply to all moral and religious
requirements?

Or, does "law" mean something broader, such as "the whole body
of God's commandments and revelations"? (*Webster's New Interna-*

tional Dictionary, 1928: 1222). Has God, as sacred authority, become a kind of "supernatural legal sovereign," a "Divine World Judge" (7:21–23), who himself is authorized to interpret and enforce the law by means of supernatural sanctions, above and beyond the jurisdiction of the human officials?

If it means the latter, two questions emerge. First, what is the connection, if any, between law in our sense, and the broader, more extended sense? That is, what is the relation between apparent references in Matthew to institutional or ecclesiastical law that presupposes an officialdom of some sort, and the broader "law of God"? Second, if we are to understand Matthew to employ law in the latter, extended sense, can we draw any meaningful distinctions at all between law or legal action-guides and moral and religious action-guides? Is not law simply synonymous with what is truly moral and truly religious? If so, then it is no longer a question of the overlapping, but of the collapsing, of categories.

As we indicated earlier, we shall not be able to disentangle the complexities before us completely until we have attended to the structure of justification in Matthew. But in outlining the contents of the practical teaching—the various substantive action-guides, both positive and negative, that are enjoined in Matthew's Gospel—we can make a start. We may begin by focusing our attention on what we loosely called the "moral" emphasis of Matthew, as exemplified in 12:10–12.

Using our definitions of terms, in the kind of acts, both positive and negative, that Matthew recommends, we observe special emphasis on other-impinging or moral attitudes and acts (see Chapter 2, section 2.2). We call this class of acts the *first* of our two senses of other-regardingness. At this point, it is this first sense that is germane to Matthew's practical teaching.

2.1. The Principle of Neighbor-Love.

The relevant summary concept or principle in this context is *agape* in the form of the *second* love commandment (LC_2): "You shall love your neighbor as yourself" (22:39); "So whatever you wish that men would do to you, do so to them; for this is the law and the prophets" (7:12). Whether or not Matthew is quite as consistent as some commentators argue (see Barth 1963; McConnell 1969; Bornkamm

1960: 110) in determining and interpreting his action-guides in relation to the principle of neighbor-love, there is no question that it occupies a central place for him.

Matthew employs the Golden Rule (7:12) to summarize the contents of the Sermon on the Mount (Chaps. 5–7). The clause, "for this is the law and the prophets" (not found in the Lukan or Markan accounts), establishes the centrality of neighbor-love as an organizing principle (McConnell 1969:11–13). Accordingly, much of the specific material on the Sermon on the Mount is structured to show that, as McConnell says, "the intention of many of Jesus' teachings in the Sermon is expressed by the love commandment" (McConnell 1969:12). For example, Chapter 5:12–24, in which the Sixth Commandment against murder is extended to include a prohibition against anger (22a), insult (22b, c) and alienation (23b), broadens the range of moral acts and attitudes that are categorically excluded by true neighbor-love (McConnell 1969: 52–53). But the emphasis is not only negative or prohibitory. Verses 23–24 introduce a positive requirement of active reconciliation as a further entailment of the Sixth Commandment. They are additionally significant in that they identify the priority Matthew assigns to acts of love over conventional sacred-impinging or religious acts (see Chapter 3, section 3). There can be no proper cultic performance unless neighbor-love as reconciliation is attended to first.

Chapter 5:27–8, regarding the extension of the Seventh Commandment against adultery to include lustful intentions and desires, may plausibly be understood as "intensifying" and "inwardizing" the principle of neighbor-love as it applies to marital relations. This is true insofar as adulterous dispositions and acts are assumed to impair the primary bonds of attachment and commitment in marriage.

Even more clearly, verses 38–42 and 42–48 are examples of the application of the principle of neighbor-love. Active and self-sacrificial beneficence toward persecutors (39, 44b), enemies (44a) and the needy (42) is enjoined as a positive requirement of the Christian life. Similarly, all impulses of retaliation against malefactors are to be restrained in favor of active regard for their basic welfare.

Beyond that, the summons to forgiveness (6:14–15), to show mercy (5:7), and the prohibition against judging others (7:1–2) are, again, both positive and negative instances of attitudes and acts that impinge directly on the basic welfare of others. Forgiving, along with not judging, which is but one form of forgiving, and showing mercy, are moral in our sense because they all presuppose that one has a rightful claim against the property or person (the basic material welfare) of an offender, but that, in keeping with the prescription to forgive and to be merciful, one does not make good the claim. Consequently, he contributes to the offender's welfare by so yielding his claims. (On "forgiveness" and "mercy," see Parables, 18:10–14. 25–33.)

The emphasis on the centrality of moral attitudes and acts, as well as of their priority over religious practices, occurs elsewhere in Matthew: 12:10–12, (which we have mentioned already); 9:10–13; 12:1–8; and 23:23. Chapter 15:10–20 can perhaps only be thought of as supplementary to the foregoing material because it does not explicitly refer to neighbor-love (or forgiveness or mercy). Nevertheless, the prohibitions against murder, adultery, fornication, theft, false witness, and slander—to which the purity laws are subordinated—are all of a moral character. Presumably, these prohibitions in no way conflict with Matthew's principle of neighbor-love. Rather, they express its restrictive side.

We ought to stress that the underlying *basic material welfare* component of our notion of moral is present, and strikingly so, in Matthew's understanding of neighbor-love. Along with the teachings already surveyed, there are two main sets of additional evidence. First, there is Chapter 25:31–46.

Then the King will say to those at his right hand, "Come, O blessed of my Father, inherit the kingdom prepared for you from the foundation of the world; for I was hungry and you gave me food, I was thirsty and you gave me drink, I was a stranger and you welcomed me, I was naked and you clothed me, I was sick and you visited me, I was in prison and you came to me." Then the righteous will answer him, "Lord, when did we see thee a stranger and welcome thee, or naked and clothe thee? And when did we see thee sick or in prison and visit thee?" And the King will answer them, "Truly, I say to you, as you did it to one of the least of these my brethren, you did it to me." (25:34–39; cf. 41–43; Luke 10: 20–37)

This account of the Last Judgment identifies as sharply as possible the fundamental characteristics of neighbor-love, and it does so in amazingly "material" terms. Neighbor-love consists, at bottom, in meeting the needs of the hungry, the thirsty, the stranger, the naked, the imprisoned. And individuals will be ultimately judged on the strength of whether or not they acted so as to attend to those in drastic material need. Incidentally, this passage serves as a backdrop for Jesus' injunction to the disciples: "Heal the sick, raise the dead, cleanse lepers, cast out demons" (10:8a).

The second set of evidence is related to the first. It is the events of Jesus' ministry, particularly his miracle working. Chapter 8 and 9, and several other places, record a series of healing incidents, that is, of moral (material welfare-oriented) acts on Jesus' part. (See 4:24; 8:3, 13, 15, 16, 32; 9:7, 22, 29–30, 33, 35; cf 14:13–21; 15:29–31, 32–38; 17:18.) According to Matthew, these acts fulfill Isaiah's prophecy (8:17), and are themselves portentous signs of the dawning kingdom:

Go and tell John what you hear and see: the blind receive their sight and the lame walk, lepers are cleansed, and the deaf hear, and the dead are raised up, and the poor have good news preached to them (11:4b–5).

The connection between the miraculous aspects of Jesus' ministry and Chapter 25:31–46 now becomes unmistakable. This material helps to fill out and to dramatize the meaning of the central concept of neighbor-love in Matthew's Gospel.

When speaking of the content of Matthew's practical teaching, we should add that while there is a certain ambiguity over the range of people upon whom Christian action is enjoined—whether they are exclusively "the lost sheep of the house of Israel" (10:6) or all outsiders, including enemies (5:44, 45b)—there is unquestionably a "universalizing" tendency in Matthew's teaching, as the "great commission" (28:19) makes plain (cf. 21:43; 15:24–28).

Finally, we ought briefly to take note of one action-guide that does not seem in any direct way related to the principle of neighbor-love. It is particularly important for our purposes since it occurs in the midst of the Sermon on the Mount. Chapter 5:33–37, regarding the prohibition against swearing oaths of any kind, is not easily derived from neighbor-love nor does it seem an illustration of the principle. Rather, it has to do with truth-telling and the integrity and reliability of a disciple's word. This prescription neither revises the Mosaic tradition in keeping with neighbor-love (as does for example, 5:38–42), nor does it intensify and inwardize it in conformity with neighbor-love (as do, for example, 5:22 and 5:27–28). It is simply a bald abrogation of the Mosaic tradition (MacArthur 1960: 45–46), and does not appear to fit with the other action-guides.

Outside the Sermon on the Mount, there are two other examples of action-guides whose relation to the principle of neighbor-love is not entirely clear: 15:2–9, honoring parents, and 22:17–21, honoring political authorities. It is likely that the admonition to honor one's parents is taken as an expression of a genuinely loving attitude toward them (Filson 1960: 176–77). Whether this is also true in the case of "Caesar" remains uncertain.

2.2. *Neighbor-Love and the Love and Service of God*

Along with the moral attitudes and acts that are so prominent in Matthew's teaching, as summarized in 22:39, there is a different range of prescribed attitudes and acts, summarized in 22:37, the *first* love commandment (LC_1): "You shall love the Lord your God with all your heart, and with all your soul, and with all your mind."

We can note important similarities as well as differences in the way the same principle, *agape,* is applied in both love commandments. On the one hand, insofar as LC_2 implies attitudes and acts that demonstrate active regard for the welfare of other human beings by promoting their interests, love of God appears to imply a similar impulse. That disciples are expected to "promote the interest of God" comes out most clearly in the Parable of the Talents (25:14–30). To the slothful servant, who buries his talent in the ground, the master declares: "You ought to have invested my money with the bankers, and at my coming, I should have received my own with interest"(27). The same point is made less allegorically at 5:16: "Let your light so shine before men, that they may see your good works and *give glory to your Father who is in heaven"* [our italics].

Moreover, God is depicted as in some sense a moral person and therefore as one who is capable of acting, and in some respects of being treated, according to the conditions of moral behavior. As God's interests can (in a very special way) be promoted, so he is understood to be sensitive to the needs of human beings and to seek to serve those needs (6:8;25–33), to possess a forgiving nature (6:14–15; 18:23–35), and a gracious will (11:26), along with other normal moral attributes. God is, up to a point, a moral agent among moral agents. As in his attitudes and acts he respects and serves the interests of human beings, so he expects to have his interests respected and served in return. As he loves, he expects to be loved.

On the other hand, some aspects of moral action apply to God in only very exceptional ways. God may have "interests" and "welfare," but he could hardly be said to have "material welfare," as human persons do. God does not have basic human needs such as are referred to in 25:31–46, or as are served in the healing ministry of Jesus. In some important respects God is *not* an agent or person in the same way human beings are agents or persons. He is not subject to many of the fundamental conditions and limitations that make human beings human. God is, after all, a "sacred authority," a status that distinguishes him as a special case to be loved in a distinctive, though not altogether divergent, manner from the way fellow human beings are to love one another. Therefore, to put forth two different, though related, love commandments rather than one reflects the fundamental ambiguity in speaking of action toward God as moral action.

The substantive action-guides concerning the attitudes and acts required by LC_1 are centered in chapter 6. They help to specify the contents of the "love of God" in Matthew's Gospel. In the first place, Matthew accepts the legitimacy of certain conventional Jewish "religious acts" (Johnson 1951: 305), such as praying (6:5–13), fasting (6:16–18), and almsgiving (6:2–4).[1] (Compare 5:23–24 for acceptance of conventional Jewish worship activities.) As we noted above, Matthew does not abrogate many of the inherited religious practices of rabbinic Judaism. In some cases, he simply demotes them in relation to moral attitudes and acts.

What is stressed in chapter 6 and elsewhere is the attitude or "spirit" in which the practices ought to be engaged in. For Matthew, Jesus' "primary concern was that men should share his vivid consciousness of the reality, power and omnipresence of God" (Johnson 1951: 305), that, above all, God's name be "hallowed" in the hearts of men (6:9). The hallowing of God's name "may fairly be regarded as the most characteristic feature" of Jewish practical thought (Moore 1935: vol. II, 101), and its centrality in Matthew's Gospel is also beyond doubt. Wilder clarifies its content:

Here . . . it is [a spirit] of reverence that is called for. Here it is the nature of God not in respect of some attribute that has affinity with human virtues, but in its essential and divine quality that is urged: in its majesty, sanctity, hallowedness, glory, power. This aspect of the nature of God . . . lay[s] immense weight on obedience and on reverence and on single-minded devotion to the things of God (Wilder 1950: 123–24; cf. Moore 1935: vol. II, 101–02).

The frequent reference to doing acts "in secret" and therefore from a sense of inner devotion, rather than "in public" to be "praised by men," illustrates this emphasis on an all-consuming *reverential* or *devotional attitude.*

This attitude or spirit implies, in turn, a childlike disposition of "faith" or "trust" in God that signals ultimate dependency on God for all benefits, material and spiritual (6:25–33; 18:1–4) (Barth 1963: 112–16). Finally, the love of God implies a spirit of gratitude to God for his great mercies (18:23 ff.) (see our extended analysis of the Parable of the Unforgiving Servant, section 3.1), as well as a disposition of obedience and dedication to his will (6:24; 7:21).

The complex of attitudinal requirements involved in the love of God is perhaps best summarized as the demand for intense and pervasive *self-subordination* to the sovereign interests of God. That means radical self-denial (10:9–10; 6:19–21; 19:16–26) with respect to one's own material interests and desire for public adulation, but it also means self-denial in the service of God's purposes. It is a decisively other-oriented form of self-subordination, the other self in this case being a sacred authority.

Jesus' voluntary humiliation and lowliness, as a paradigm of discipleship, dramatizes the attitudes and acts required by the notion of love of God (4:8–10; 8:20; 16:21; 26:39; chapter 27). Insofar as discipleship involves the imitation of Jesus, it is the emulation of his self-subordination on behalf of God's purposes: "If any man would follow me, let him deny himself and take up his cross and follow me" (16:24). The image of disciple as "slave" or "servant" naturally comes to mind here (cf. 20:25–28). As McConnell points out, chapter 11:28–30 summarizes the point very well: One who is "gentle and lowly in heart" as Jesus is, is "one who surrenders himself to God's will, who 'fears' Yahweh and seeks righteousness."

Because Jesus bows himself to the will of God, he can give refreshment to those who are bowed down with the burden of the law. If they bear the yoke that he bears—of humility and obedience to God—they will find that this yoke is gentle and light (McConnell 1969: 57).

2.3. The Relations of the Two Love Commandments

We turn now to the relation of LC_1 to LC_2. The relationship may be diagramed as in Figure 7.

Our diagram indicates that there is both overlap and distinctiveness with respect to the attitudes and acts that are appropriate for LC_1 and LC_2. On the one hand, certain attitudes and acts are, in some respects, applicable to both a divine and a human "other." The underlined terms under Appropriate Action-Guides are examples. Some of the underlined terms occur in parentheses—there are two reasons for this. First, they are not explicitly related to LC_2 in the text, though they could conceivably be, as with "honoring superiors" (15:4–6) at category 2.a.i. Second, they can only be inferred from the text to be an appropriate attitude, as with "gratitude" at categories 1.a. and 2.a.i. As we shall see, the Parable of the Unforgiving Servant assumes the applicability of gratitude to both divine and human benefactors. Without much difficulty, gratitude can be related to LC_1 and LC_2, even though that remains an inference.

The case of the prohibition against *blasphemia* [1.b.ii.: "blasphemy against the Holy Spirit" (12:31) and category 2.b.ii.: "slander against one's fellows" (15:19) and uttering "You fool" (5:22)] is interesting. While it is clear that the same concept applies to both human and divine victims (expressly in 12:19 and 15:19), blasphemy against the Holy Spirit is set apart from all transgressions (religious and moral) in that it constitutes the one unforgivable sin (12:32) (Davies 1966a: 239–40). At the same time, slandering another human being by calling him a fool is also a weighty violation (Moore 1935: vol. II, 148–49).

Finally, acts of material self-denial (categories 1.b.i. and 2.b.i.) illustrate the overlapping of acts and attitudes toward God and human beings even though the objectives of material self-denial with respect to each must necessarily be different.

On the other hand, the fact that the interests and character of the divine "other" differ substantially from those of the human "other," entails a set of attitudes and acts that diverge, in some important respects, from the set of attitudes and acts appropriate in relation to human beings. A human person could not intelligibly be enjoined to adopt an attitude of mercy or forgiveness toward God, just as he

Figure 7. Religious and Moral Attitudes and Acts in the Gospel of Matthew

Commandment to love
God and neighbor
requires:

Voluntary self-denial
(physical, psychological)
for the purpose of
promoting the   Appropriate Action-Guides
interests
of
    GOD
    (LC₁)

1. religious attitudes and acts
    a. attitudes of "hallowing":
       of ultimate reverence,
       devotion, *honoring*,
       obedience, faith,
       trust, (*gratitude*)
    b. acts of piety
       i. fasting, prayer,
          worship, sacrifice,
          material self-denial
       ii. prohibition against
          blasphemy (*blasphemia*)

    Direct
    action
    toward
    God

2. moral attitudes and acts
    a. attitudes:
       i. positive: forgiveness,
          mercy, reconciliation,
          (*honoring superiors*),
          (*gratitude*)
       ii. negative: prohibitions
          against brotherly
          anger, lust, etc.

HUMAN
BEINGS
(LC2)

    b. acts
       i. positive: forgiveness,
          mercy, material beneficence,
          material self-denial
       ii. negative: prohibitions
          against murder, adultery,
          theft, retaliation,
          slander (*blasphemia*)

    Direct
    action
    toward
    human
    beings,
    in-
    direct
    action
    toward
    God

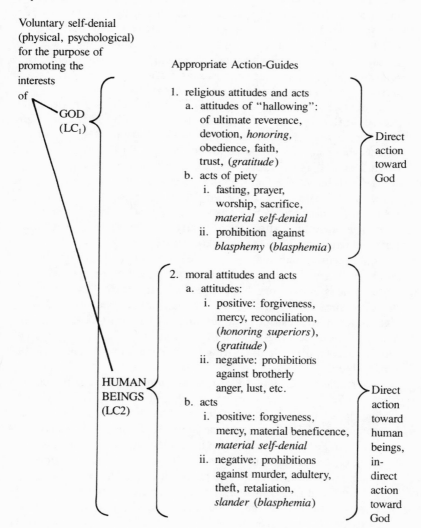

could not lust (in the sense of *epithumeo*) after God. Furthermore, acts of material beneficence or maleficence are hardly relevant to God in the way they are to human beings since God's "welfare" in no way depends on material support. Thus, while acts of material sacrifice to God (category 1.b.i.) are condoned by Matthew (5:23–24), they are devalued in comparison with the service of human need (12:1–7). Acts of murder, adultery, and physical retaliation make no sense in connection with God. Theft might have some figurative relevance,but only figurative, since, as we have pointed out, God's welfare is not material, in the way a human being's is.

In yet one more way, God is a special case. He is a majesterial sacred authority who is believed to be an object of *ultimate* devotion, reverence, obedience, and so on (category 1.a.). He is an object whose name is to be hallowed "among all the nations of the earth," as well as the proper object of acts of piety (category 1.b.). As the Parable of the Unforgiving Servant implies, God is also the object of ultimate or "eternal" gratitude (category 1.a.) because of his overwhelming mercy to mankind. In all cases, the addition of the adjective "ultimate" alters significantly the character of even those terms in category 2.a.i. that overlap with 1.a.

Consequently, our diagram makes clear that action-guides in category 2 are directly pertinent only to human beings, whereas action-guides in category 1 are directly pertinent only to God (with due allowance for the instances of overlap). (The brackets on the far right indicate the respective direct objects of action-guides 1 and 2.) We can see, accordingly, that LC_2 covers *only* the sort of action-guides in category 2, namely those that have human beings as the direct object.

Nevertheless, LC_2 and LC_1 are not symmetrical with respect to the sort of action-guides they cover. LC_1, unlike LC_2, includes *both* action-guides 1 and 2 though category 2 has a different significance in relation to LC_1 than does category 1. Category 1 designates attitudes and acts that are, as we have seen, appropriate to the sort of being God is taken to be. (Incidentally, we must bear in mind the dependent relationship between categories 1.a. and 1.b. Category 1.a.—those attitudes by which the "right spirit" is manifested—is a necessary condition for the proper performance of category 1.b.)

By contrast, the performance of category 2 is of crucial *indirect* significance in complying with LC_1. Several passages demonstrate that acting in accordance with category 2 is a *necessary* though not sufficient *condition* for fulfilling LC_1. Consequently, living up to the requirements of LC_2 affects indirectly one's love of God. According to Bornkamm, neighbor-love becomes a "test" of the love of God (Bornkamm 1960: 110). The most obvious example of this is chapter 5:23–25. With respect to performing acts of piety, it is not simply a question of having the right attitude toward God, though presumably that is assumed. If relevant, an act of brotherly reconciliation is first required before the ceremonial sacrifice may be performed. Chapter 6:12 and 14–15 imply that the right relation between God and human beings is dependent (or conditional) on a forgiving attitude between human beings. Finally, chapter 5:44–45 illustrates the same point. "But I say to you, Love your enemies and pray for those who persecute you, *so that* you may be sons of your Father who is in heaven." In other instances, for example, 12:1–12, acts of piety (category 1.b.i.) are *reinterpreted* in the light of category 2. Thus, doing good by healing on the Sabbath is fully in line with the point of observing the Sabbath.

Accordingly, attitudes and acts in category 2 are generally prior to those in category 1.b.i., either in necessarily preceding, or in serving as a standard by which category 1.b.i. are reinterpreted. But over and above the attitudes and acts in category 2, 1.a. attitudes (and, derivatively category 1.b. acts) constitute the *sufficient condition* for the fulfillment of LC_1.

The logical relations between LC_2 and LC_1, then, are close, if somewhat complex. Our analysis, in which LC_2, or the attitudes and acts in category 2, becomes a necessary condition for the fulfillment of LC_1, while category 1.a. (plus the prohibition against blasphemy) becomes its sufficent condition, rules out the suggestion that LC_2 is not only necessary, but also sufficient for the achievement of LC_1, a suggestion that would collapse LC_1 into LC_2. There is one passage— 25:31–46—that lends weight to this interpretation. No mention is made in this account of the Last Judgment of anything other than the moral attitudes and acts as a criterion for determining the ultimate destiny of individuals. But while such evidence clearly supports the indispensability of LC_2 for carrying out LC_1, it cannot go farther and override the rest of the evidence we have discovered. Throughout Matthew, God has a special character and status that entails a set of attitudes that are, in various ways, distinct from moral attitudes and acts, and are alone sufficient for achieving right relations with God, so long of course as the necessary condition of complying with LC₂ has been met (Bornkamm 1968: 110–11).

Our diagram, then, summarizes the complicated interrelations of the major aspects of the contents of the double love commandment, and clarifies, we hope, the logic of relations between the two commandments.

2.4. The Role of Law.

Earlier, we asked two questions regarding the role of law in Matthew's Gospel, and questioned the relation of law to religious and moral action-guides. The first question regarding the role of law concerns the connection between apparent references in Matthew to institutional or ecclesiastical law, including references to Judaic institutional law, to religious and moral action-guides. In responding to this question, we shall, among other things, have to consider briefly Matthew's attitude toward rabbinic law.

With respect to our definition of law and of legal action-guide, there are two issues we must investigate. First, to what extent does Matthew accept the legitimacy of rabbinic law? Second, to what extent does he support Christian ecclesiastical law?

First-century Judaism had a highly developed official court system for regulating community life (Moore 1935: vol. II, 180 ff.). According to Hare (Hare 1967: 105, fn. 3), during the Diaspora the Jewish courts were primarily synagogal, and their jurisdiction, by Roman sufferance, extended over the inhabitants of the Jewish quarter. The system of courts or "councils" terminated in "the High Council, the Sanhedrin." In Roman times, "this was the highest indigenous governing body in Judea, composed of high priests, elders and scholars (scribes), and meeting under the presidency of the ruling high priest. This body was the ultimate authority not only in religious matters, but in legal and governmental affairs as well, insofar as it did not encroach on the authority of the Roman procurator" (Arndt and Gingrich 1957: 793). Not only did the judicial officialdom adjudicate cases according to established court procedures, but it also meted out punishments, including the death penalty, provided such decisions were confirmed by the Roman procurator (Barrett 1966: 169–72).

Matthew has an ambiguous attitude toward the rabbinic system.

The ambiguity is illustrated by the obvious discrepancy between chapter 5:17–19 and chapter 23:2–3 and much of the rest of the recorded teaching of Jesus. On the one hand, there are traces that Matthew recognized the continuing authority of the rabbinic system over the lives of Christians. The admonitions not to alter "an iota, not a dot" of the law (5:18b) and not to relax "one of the least of these commandments" (5:19a), but to "practice and observe whatever [the Pharisees] tell you" (23:2b), necessarily presupposes the legitimacy of the total rabbinic legal system—its officials, courts, procedures, jurisdiction, and existing legal interpretation. On the other hand, such admonitions conflict with Jesus' revisionary teaching regarding rabbinic judicial law, as, for example, on the issue of divorce (5:31; 19:3–9) (Johnson 1951: 294).

Two passages actually refer to the existing court system. Chapter 5:22, "But I say to you . . . whoever insults his brother *shall be liable to council*" [our italics], is significant, for the words are attributed to Jesus himself as part of a highly authoritative utterance. This passage constitutes one of the most affirmative examples in support of Matthew's belief in the continuing legitimacy of the rabbinic system. Chapter 10:17, "Beware of men; for they will deliver you up to councils, and flog you in their synagogues," is inconclusive. It may seem to suggest the legitimacy of the councils and of their right to impose sanctions on Christians, but that seems unlikely. The passage depicts the councils and synagogues as the wrongful persecutors of Christians. Moreover, the emphasis upon "their" synagogues represents the view that the Jewish Christians are no longer rightfully subject to the jurisdiction of the synagogue (and its courts): "It is an alien institution belonging to an alien people" (Hare 1967: 104).

On the basis of this evidence, the content of the legal action-guides seems only equivocally governed by rabbinic judicial institutions and teaching. Their legitimacy is at best vestigial. This conclusion is perhaps most dramatically supported by the fact that however modified his view is, Matthew conceives of the Christian church as an *eschatological congregation*, living close to the end of history. Therefore, it bears no responsibility for providing and maintaining communitywide social and legal institutions. Klausner makes the point classically, if polemically:

Where there is no call for the enactment of laws, for justice, for national statecraft, where belief in God and the practice of an extreme and one-sided ethic is in itself enough—there we have the negation of national life and of the national state. . . . But it is unquestionable that throughout [Jesus'] entire teaching there is nothing that can serve to the upkeep of the state or serve toward the maintenance of order in the existing world" (Klausner 1925: 374, 376).

In this crucial respect, the early church was a sectarian movement, with typical sectarian indifference to social institutional responsibility. It was thus more analogous to the Dead Sea Sect than to Rabbinic Judaism.

This is not to say that Matthew's Gospel is devoid of significant legal teaching. Perhaps more important than the references to rabbinic legal institutions and teaching are the hints about the development of ecclesiastical law in the Matthean church. Again the references are few and they are hardly less ambiguous than the preceding material. Nevertheless, they may not be overlooked.

Chapter 16:19 and 18:18–20 are the relevant passages. Verse 16:19 concerns the granting of the keys of the Kingdom to Peter, together with the power "to bind and loose" on earth. "And whatever you bind on earth shall be bound in heaven, and whatever you loose on earth shall be loosed in heaven." Verses 18:15–20 propose a means for handling discipline and for overcoming transgressions within the community. If, after several attempts at reconciliation, the offender "refuses to listen even to the church, let him be to you as a Gentile and a tax collector. Truly, I say to you, [repeating 16:19b,c] whatever you bind on earth will be bound in heaven, and whatever you loose on earth will be loosed in heaven."

These are difficult passages. Their sequence suggests that the special legal authority within the church first granted to Peter, is then extended to the church as a whole, or possibly to "the apostles and elders" acting on the church's behalf (cf. Acts 15:6–11,22) (Schweitzer 1961: 53–59; cf. Davies 1966a, 224–25). Scholars are divided regarding the sort of authority involved in "binding and loosing." It probably implies the authority *both* to impose or remove the banning of an offender as a sanction for transgressions, *and* to interpret and decide questions of Christian practice (Strack and Billerbeck 1926: vol. I, 738–39).

The context of verse 18:18 makes clear that more is involved than only interpretation of right action. Verse 18:17b refers to imposing the ban against recalcitrant members, and, consequently, indicates that the Jewish practice of the "synagogue ban" has been taken over by the Matthean church (Strack and Billerbeck 1928). We are dealing here with a matter of incipient "church law"; sanctioning procedures are institutionalized for enforcing what is deemed normative practice.

Of great interest is the fact that whatever is decided "on earth" will be ratified "in heaven." While God will "back up" churchly decisions in the Last Judgment, it is not, in this context, left to him alone to carry out punishment against offenders. Human agents are directly authorized to enforce the law. This state of affairs is undoubtedly related to declining apocalyptic fervor, and to the emergence of an increasingly self-conscious ecclesiastical institution.

As we suggested, the precise character of the emerging legal officialdom is unclear. Certainly, the drift is away from a monarchic pattern, but whether the "apostles and elders" or the church as a whole is invested with the authority to make binding decisions remains an open question. In either case, there is a process of legal institutionalization taking place within the church, and, consequently, a legal officialdom of some sort cannot be far behind. With the waning of eschatological immediacy, the church, as reflected in Matthew's Gospel, is moving more and more toward a self-conscious preoccupation with church order. "It no longer merely proclaims the word but at the same time regulates the common life of its members in a pedagogical and disciplinary temper which requires a new casuistry, managed by experts" (Käsemann 1969: 81; cf. Davies 1966a: 108–14; Davies 1966b: 237).

One of the things that also remains uncertain is just how far the "judicial" function of interpreting and enforcing right practice extends in the church's life. Does the "new casuistry, managed by experts" imply that all the moral and religious action-guides we surveyed earlier are subject to official interpretation as to what is, in specific cases, "forbidden" and "permitted"? Are all of these official determinations then enforceable according to established disciplinary procedures? The evidence will not permit a firm answer, though at 18:21–22, Matthew may suggest a restriction on the legalization of the church's life. Jesus' admonition to forgive an offender "seventy times seven" comes immediately after the discussion of "binding and loosing" (18:15–20). There the disciplinary procedure allows the offender a strictly limited number of chances for forgiveness before he is banned. By contrast, the recommendation in favor of limitless forgiveness undercuts in effect, at least one of the legal functions of the church—the imposition of sanctions against offenders. Which of these conflicting recommendations takes precedence is uncertain, but Matthew's intentional juxtaposition of the two passages lends weight to the above interpretation.

In any case, all we need to say at this point is that to the extent the inchoate legal officialdom is authorized by the Matthean church to interpret and enforce religious and moral teachings, then to that extent the action-guides found in the Gospel of Matthew are legal, as well as being variously religious and moral.[2] In other words, Biblical scholars will have to settle, finally, how "legalized" Matthew's religious and moral prescriptions are. So far as our analysis goes, we are beginning to see some clarity regarding what it means to apply the concept "legal" to the content of Matthew's practical teaching.

The second question regarding the role of law concerns the relation of ecclesiastical law, as we have been discussing it, to a wider notion of law in Matthew's Gospel. We have already indicated that to the extent that Matthew's religious and moral action-guides become regulatory according to our specifications of law, then it makes sense to speak of "religious and moral law." What is religious or moral on other criteria may be, as it happens, also legal.

But that is only one level of the issue. On another level, what sense does the wider notion, "law of God" (15:6), make in connection with institutional law, and in connection with religious and moral practices in the Matthean community? As a self-evident minimum, we may understand the words *law of God* to mean the body of commandments uttered and enforced by God. So understood, we can see immediately that the notion of a law of God is only partially consonant with our definition of legal action-guide. The similarity, as well as the divergence, is significant.

On the one hand, there is an assumed agent who is accepted as a "legitimate official" (a Judge and sovereign Legislator) with the authority to adjudicate and enforce his prescriptions. On the other hand, the agent is not a human being (which is one condition of our definition). God is a "supernatural legal sovereign." Therefore, the law of God is only partly law in our sense. In the Matthean materials, God occupies a position that makes him in some important respects *like* a human legal sovereign, but he is like no other legal sovereign. Consequently, when speaking of the law of God, it is indispensible, for the sake of precision, to employ a modifier like "holy," as, for example Käsemann does in his essay, "Sentences of Holy Law in the New Testament" (Käsemann: 1969). God's law is law, but only in a special mode, for it consists of the directives of a "holy" (or sacred) authority.

Let us clarify this point by amplifying slightly Käsemann's thesis. Käsemann argues that there exists in the New Testament vestigial evidence of a primitive form of legal utterance—an expression of "the eschatological *jus talionis*," which is taken to be a direct, unmediated kind of divine law. Examples from Matthew are 10:32–33:

So everyone who acknowledges me before men, I will also acknowledge before my Father who is in heaven; but who ever denies me before men, I also will deny before my Father who is in heaven;

and 6:14–15:

For if you forgive men their trespasses, your heavenly Father also will forgive you; but if you do not forgive men their trespasses, neither will your Father forgive your trespasses.

(Cf. 6:12 and 5:7: "Blessed are the merciful for they shall obtain mercy"). Now these are "sentences of *holy* law," in part because they presuppose no official human intermediary who is charged with interpreting and enforcing the law by means of material or physical sanctions. There do exist charismatic figures who announce the decrees of God, but they do not institute them in our sense. These individuals may be the law's "instruments but not its executors" (Käsemann 1969: 81). In this early or pristine form, there is "in very real terms a law which has to be observed in the community, *although it has almost nothing to do with the forms of law which we assume and administer*" [our italics] (Käsemann 1969: 72).

Käsemann goes on to contend that this primitve legal form gave way in Christian experience to the gradual institutionalization of the authority-structure in the church in response to the functional imperatives of organizational life.

Only at this early point in history was it possible to do without the formation of a law of Church organization in the sense of administrative, disciplinary and canon law *in order that rewards and punishments might be left solely to the universal Judge himself;* only at this point did the Church see in Jesus the returning Son of Man; only at this point did a battle rage round the continuing validity of the Mosaic law in all its parts. In the measure in which the organization of the Church grew more fixed, and the expectation of an imminent end lost burning inspiration, the ground was cut from under the feet of that *eschatological divine law* of which we have been speaking (Käsemann 1969: 78) [our italics].

Our main point, then, is confirmed by Käsemann's convincing analysis. The law of God in Matthew is, in important ways, both similar and dissimilar to the pattern of ecclesiastical law present in the Gospel. It earns the right to be called law, up to a point, since it manifests some of the characteristics of legal action-guides. But it is so only up to a point; it is *holy* law. The crucial element of human officialdom is excluded. The law is understood to be directly administered by the sacred authority himself, in self-conscious contrast to human, institutional law.

In the case of Matthew, and perhaps elsewhere, this thesis needs to be extended. It is a mistake to restrict the notion of holy law to a certain primitive sentential form. For instance, the form of expression attributed to Jesus in 28:20—teaching them to observe *all that I have commanded you* [our italics]"—parallels the Deuteronomic utterances of Moses, who is regarded as the instrument or transmitter of God's law at Sinai. Correspondingly, "Jesus is portrayed [in Matthew] as the God-sent proclaimer of God's will, the revealer of the New Torah" (McConnell 1969: 96–100; cf. Bacon 1930). In other words, Jesus, in some ways analogous to Moses, is regarded, in Käsemann's terms, as a charismatic or direct instrument of God's holy law. This same role shines through in Jesus' utterances in the Sermon on the Mount: "You have heard . . . , but I say to you. . . ." Moreover, 7:21–23 and 25:31–46 are additional examples of an extended notion of holy law in Matthew.

We may now conclude our discussion of the role of law in the contents of Matthew's practical teaching. We can see that the sort of overlap we discovered among religious, moral, and legal action-guides, on the level of institutional or ecclesiastical law, also applies to holy law—if anything more completely. In Matthew the law of God encompasses the religious and moral action-guides we have examined. All these prescriptions, even including mercy and forgiveness (5:7; 6:14–15; 18:23–35, esp. 35), are cast in a legal form: They are decreed by an authoritative official who has the right to command, interpret, and enforce his decrees, and who will do precisely that "on the Last Day." What is religious or moral also becomes legal (or legal-like) when it is cast in the above form.

At the same time, all these action-guides are legal only in a special sense. They must be described as part of holy law, or law that is directly associated with the sacred authority and therefore crucially "beyond the volitional control of human beings." It is, then, in all of these rather complex ways that we distinguish and relate religious, moral, and legal action-guides, so far as the contents of Matthew's practical teaching is concerned.

3. THE STRUCTURE OF
MATTHEW'S PRACTICAL TEACHING

We have reserved our final verdict regarding the place of religion, morality, and law in Matthew's practical teaching until we could address the question of *justification,* or the system or structure of validating and vindicating reasons given in support of the contents of the teaching.

As we have tried to show, certain meaningful distinctions can be made among religious, moral, and legal terms simply by identifying the *content* of a given action-guide, namely, who the relevant agent and the direct recipient of the prescribed act are and, in some instances, how the act affects the recipient. But beyond this, religious, moral, and legal action-guides must still be justified, and we are interested in distinguishing religious from moral justificatory reasons in relation to the content of Matthew's practical teaching.

As we suggested in Part I, a moral action-guide—for example, "Love your enemies" (5:44a)—may be justified by moral reasons. If it is, it then becomes a moral action-guide (see Chapter 2, section 2). On the other hand, such a moral action-guide might be justified by religious reasons—that is, as part of system based on a belief in a sacred authority (see Chapter 3, section 3.1). In that event, it becomes, in our terminology, a religious-moral action-guide. Recall that the same applies in reverse to a religious action-guide such as, "When you pray, go into your room and shut the door" (6:5b). If it is justified religiously, it becomes fully a religious action-guide. If justified morally, it becomes a moral-religious action-guide. The general question before us, then, is which pattern(s) of justification does Matthew employ in providing defense for his practical teaching.

3.1. Patterns of Validation

There are, in Matthew, two basic patterns of validation, which, though mutually exclusive from a logical point of view, are nevertheless intertwined in the text. The reader is never sure which is the preferred pattern; indeed, it is doubtful that the author himself was ever aware of the difference.

The two patterns are our two types of deontological appeal: the *authoritarian* and the *formalistic*. The one is paradigmatically a religious validating system: A personalized sacred authority is assumed to be a supreme commander whose will is, by definition, right and obligatory. That means that the will of the supreme commander is itself the basic norm, the standard of validity, according to which religious, moral, and legal action-guides are themselves finally validated. The second, the formalistic pattern, presupposes a moral principle that is, in Matthew's case, a combination of versions of the law of reciprocity. That principle becomes the basic norm, the standard of validity, according to which substantive religious, moral, and legal action-guides are validated in the second system.

This is to state the alternative patterns in their starkest and simplest terms. In the Gospel of Matthew each has complexities and variations that we must endeavor to sort out and clarify.

There are two related though distinguishable manifestations of the authoritarian pattern. The first, according to which God is the supreme commander, is basic. The second, in which Jesus is a charismatic commander, is a derivative of the first, in that Jesus' authority is delegated by God.

There are five defining characteristics of the authoritarian pattern: (1) the commander is assumed to be practically competent in a way that is superior to his "subordinates"; (2) he communicates in terms of comprehensible and practicable commands; (3) the commands are *justified by origin,* that is, by having originated in his will; (4) a self-subordinating and obedient disposition on the part of the subordinates is emphasized as a cardinal virtue; (5) the supreme commander is authorized to impose sanctions though the sanctions have a logically secondary function: They simply enforce what is held to be right on other grounds (that is, on grounds of the commander's will).

What G. F. Moore described as the fundamental (though not exclusive) characteristic of Judaic practical reasoning conforms to these five defining characteristics of authoritarianism, and it seems clear that the same pattern also had an important effect upon "the Gospel of the Christian rabbi." Moore's description is essential for understanding the background of Matthew's authoritarianism; therefore we quote from him at some length.

What are called Jewish ethics are in substance and form more exactly described as preceptive morals; *they are the morals of a religion, and their obligation lies not in the reason and conscience of men but in the authority of the sovereign Lawgiver* [our italics] (Moore 1935: vol. II, 81–82).

That it is the will of [the] Father in heaven is *the all-sufficient reason* [our italics] and motive for abstaining from what he forbids (Moore 1935: vol. II, 205).

God "hallows his name" (makes it holy), therefore, by doing things that lead or constrain men to acknowledge him as God. And as it is God's supreme end that all mankind shall ultimately own and serve him as the true God, so it is the chief end of Israel, to whom he has in a unique manner revealed himself, to hallow his name by living so that men shall see and say that the God of Israel is the true God. *This is the meaning of Kiddush he-Shem, the hallowing of the Name, as the supreme principle and motive of moral conduct in Judaism* [our italics] Moore 1935: vol. II, 103).

God punishes sin and rewards obedience. This is the constant teaching of Scripture. From the simple notion that God was well-pleased with those who did his will and showed them favor in return, while he was angry with those who ignored or defied his commands and made them feel his displeasure, there had grown, under the influence of prophetic teaching, a doctrine of retribution in which God's justice was committed to requite men strictly according to their deeds (Moore 1935: vol. II, 89).

[But] however legitimate the motive of reward may be, there is a higher obedience than that which is rendered from this motive: . . . "Be not like slaves who serve their master in the expectation of receiving a gratuity; but be like slaves who serve their master in no expectation of receiving a gratuity; and let the fear [or reverence] of Heaven be upon you" [Antigonus of Socho] . . . That the law of God and every commandment in it should be "kept for its own sake" [because it *is* the law], not for any advantage to be gained by it among men or with God, is frequently emphasized . . . "Whoever does a commandment not for its own sake . . . , it were better for him that he had never been created" (Raba) (Moore 1935: vol. II, 95, 97).

All five of our defining characteristics are instantiated in these descriptions of the bases of Judaic practical thought. None calls for special comment except that regarding the role of sanctions. Moore shows two things: first, that rewards and punishments have nothing logically to do with the grounds of justification in Judaism. A given act will be rewarded because it is already considered to be right by the determination of God's will. It is not considered right because it will be rewarded. Thus, we have the "logically secondary function" of sanctions that is expected by our definition. Second, sanctions appear to operate as *motivating rather than as justifying reasons*. But even here the achievement of reward or the avoidance of punishment is not the highest motive from which to act. "It was better to lead a man to obey the law of God from an inferior motive than that he should not obey it; and, as is frequently observed, if he is diligent in keeping the law from a lower motive he may come to do it from a higher" (Moore 1935: vol. II, 90).

Matthew employs various images to characterize God as a supreme commander, understood against this Judaic background. He is referred to as a "Father" (for example, ch. 6), a "King" (5:35; 18:23; 22:2), a "Master" (for example, 6:24); a "Lord" (for example, 4:7,10), a "householder" (or "lord of an estate") (13:27; 20:1; 21:33). Not all the images possess corresponding descriptives for human subordinates—but "Father" does: "So that you may be *sons* of your Father" (5:45), as does "Master," and "Lord" or "householder": "The *servants* (*slaves*) of the householder came and said to him. . . ." (18:23–35).

Probably because of the strong authoritarian orientation of Judaic practical thinking, Matthew could simply assume, without defending or elaborating, the existence of a sovereign, or supreme authority. God is conceived by Matthew to be superior to human beings in many ways, including his special competence in practical matters, his right to communicate in the form of absolutely binding commands, his entitlement to self-subordinating reverence and obedience on the part of his subordinates, and his right to enforce his commands.

With respect to validation, there are two ways the basic form of Judaic and Matthean authoritarianism might be represented: by a *definist position* (Frankena 1973) or by a *position of proprietary entitlement* (Brody 1974). The definist position simply postulates a basic norm in the terms of a definition: Whatever God wills=what is right, obligatory. The implications of such a position are as follows:

Premise 1: (Basic norm.) Whatever God wills=what is right, obligatory.

Premise 2: God wills attitudes x and acts y.

Conclusion: x and y are right, obligatory.

The position of proprietary authority comes to the same conclusion though its structure is different from the definist position in one interesting way:

Premise 1: (Basic norm.) Owners have ultimate authority to do with their property as they please (with respect to their property, whatever is directed by owners=what is right, obligatory).

Premise 2: All the world, including human beings, is God's property.

Premise 3: God commands that human beings adopt attitudes x and perform acts y.

Conclusion: x and y are right, obligatory.

Unlike the definist alternative which, so to speak, writes authoritarianism into the major premise, authoritarianism in the position of proprietary entitlement is derived from a combination of a prior and general prescriptive premise (premise 1) with a particular empirical belief about God and his role as owner of all the world (premise 2). Theoretically, the first premise applies to every owner; however, God alone is believed to own everything, including all human beings. Therefore, God alone is supreme authority over everything, including all human beings. There is no definitive way to settle which of these positions best characterizes Matthew's authoritarianism, though several parables and passages suggest the position of proprietary entitlement. Summarizing, in part, Chapters 20:1–16 and 25:14–30, Bornkamm remarks:

God is lord and man is his servant.... For the servant is his master's property, his slave whose body and life belong to him.... The master is entitled to claim his servant completely. To 'serve two masters' (6:24) is therefore an absurdity. The master can entrust his servant with money and goods, as he pleases (25:14 ff.), and he can claim it back from him when he pleases (18:23–35). As far as the slave is concerned, however, the field to which he has been sent to work is not his own, the goods entrusted to him do not belong to him, and the services which he is obliged to render do not rest with him [are not determined by him]. *He is therefore required to be faithful, faithful in the face of his master's strange, superior will* [our italics] (Bornkamm 1960: 138).

Elsewhere, Bornkamm reenforces this interpretation, speaking of God's "sovereign rights" (Bornkamm 1960: 110), and indicating that in the New Testament, "What is [morally] good or evil is stated by the law of God, and by nothing else" (Bornkamm 1970: 80).

At this point, we can reconstruct the relation of God as a supreme commander to the content of Matthean practical teaching as analyzed in section 2 of this chapter, working under the assumption that the position of proprietary entitlement best expresses the sort of authoritarianism at work here. Bearing in mind that this is a reconstruction, though we hope a plausible one, we enlarge on the earlier syllogism and deal, first, with the validation of religious and moral action-guides. After that, we examine the validation of legal action-guides.

Premise 1: (Basic norm.) With respect to their property, whatever is directed by owners=what is right, obligatory.

Premise 2: All the world, including human beings, is God's property (human beings=God's servants).

Premise 3: God commands that human beings obey the double love commandment LC_1 and LC_2.

Premise 4: The content and relations of LC_1 and LC_2 are as represented on pages 167–72.

Conclusion: LC_1 and LC_2 (as stipulated in Premise 4) is right, obligatory.

This type of authoritarianism is a paradigmatic form of religious validation. Together, premise 1 and premise 2 establish the ultimate authority of the sacred authority, who is God. In turn, all action-guides are then validated insofar as they are determined by God's will. *There is nothing necessarily moral about such a pattern of validation.* On our definition of moral, some expression of "other-regarding consideration" (strictly understood) is constitutive of a moral basic norm. Premise 1, however, is logically unrestrictive with respect to what might be commanded. It is purely a contingent or empirical matter that God dictates the double love commandment (premise 3), which happens to include moral content (category 2, Figure 7). God might not have so commanded for, according to premise 1, God may, as owner, "do as he pleases." Consequently, we may conclude that the religious action-guides (category 1, Figure 7) and the moral action-guides (category 2, Figure 7) are all validated religiously on this system. That is, they are authenticated by the will of the sacred authority. This yields what we call a *religious-moral system*. (See Chapter 5, section 5.2.)

We ought to stress that if there is nothing in this type of authoritarianism that is necessarily moral in character, *as a matter of fact* the will of God does lay on emphasis on moral attitudes and acts, in LC_2. And insofar as LC_2 occupies the significant place it does in expressing the will of God, moral matters (at least on the level of content) are not ignored. But again that is, finally, "at the pleasure of God." It need not be so.

Though remarks about the relation of this pattern of validation to institutional legal action-guides are best reserved until after we have considered the special authority of Jesus, we call attention here to the relation of this pattern to expressions of what we called God's "holy law." The relation is straightforward.

Premise 1: (Basic norm.) With respect to their property, whatever is directed by owners=what is right, obligatory.

Premise 2: All the world, including human beings, is God's property (human beings=God's servants).

Premise 3: God's communications with his servants take *legal form in a special sense* (that is, God as a sacred authority takes on judicial characteristics, and his "holy law" is enforced by sanctions).

Premise 4: The content of God's law is the double love commandment.

Conclusion: The double love commandment, as God's holy law, is right, obligatory (and will be enforced).

As to Jesus as God's regent, according to Matthew, Jesus is granted a "staggering" (McConnell 1969: 99) degree of authority by God (see, for example, 11:27: "All things have been delivered to me by my Father"; 24:35: "Heaven and earth will pass away, but my words will not pass away"; 28:18: "All authority in heaven and on earth has been given to me"). In comparison with all preceding human authorities, Jesus is unquestionably in a class by himself. He possesses the rightful power to perform, in the name of God, all his functions as supreme commander. Thus, Jesus is "King" (26:34), "Divine World Judge" (7:21–23, where "the will of my Father" is equated with "these words of mine," and the last Judgment is determined accordingly), and "Lord" or "Master" (12:8; 17:15; 21:3; 23:10, and so on).

At the same time, there is no question this extensive authority is *delegated* to Jesus by God (11:27: "delivered to me"; 28:18; "given to me"). The other images applied to Jesus also make this clear: he is the "Son" of the Father (11:27), and of God (16:16; 27:54); he is also a "servant" or "slave" (20:27–28). In short, Jesus is the appointed official, or regent of God.

As such, he is authorized to act as supreme commander on behalf of God. In McConnell's words:

Jesus has the supreme and divine right to command obedience and faithfulness to God and to God's will, and, at the same time, to himself. The Old Testament Law, of course, directed obedience to God himself and not to itself, but this is not the case with Jesus for whom obedience and loyalty to himself were one with obedience and loyalty to God; this presupposes his unique relationship with the Father. (5:21–22; 27–28; 33–34; 38–39; 43–45) (McConnell 1969: 95).

It is in that light that the antitheses and other authoritative deliverances of Jesus must be viewed. "That Jesus annuls what he believes no longer expresses God's will shows that he is not bound to the Old Testament law but rather free from it. The right to decide what in the old law is valid, and what is not valid in the present age is Jesus' right alone" (McConnell 1969: 96; cf. 93 ff.).

It is obvious that Jesus takes on, along with the other functions of the supreme commander, a judicial and law-giving role, and in that role he shares directly in the interpretation, administration, and enforcement of God's holy law. But beyond that, it is Jesus as God's regent who delegates legal authority (now in the human, institutional sense) to the church (16:16–19; 18:15–20). "For where two or three are gathered together in my name there I am in the midst of them" (18:20) means that the institutional church, in interpreting and enforcing the law, is vicariously carrying out Jesus' supreme authority. What remains unclear, as we pointed out, is just how far the church's vicarious legal authority extends.

Let us reconstruct the various forms of authoritarian argument in the light of Jesus' special authority. Again, we shall deal first with the validation of the religious and moral action-guides, and then consider the legal action-guides.

Premise 1: (Basic norm.) With respect to their property, whatever is directed by owners=what is right, obligatory.

Premise 2: All the world, including human beings, is God's property (human beings=God's servants).

Premise 3: God delegates to Jesus the supreme right to command in his name.

Premise 4: Jesus commands the double love commandment (see premise 4, page 184).

Conclusion: The double love commandment is right, obligatory.

Premise 1: (Basic norm.) With respect to their property, whatever is directed by owners=what is right, obligatory.

Premise 2: All the world, including human beings, is God's property (human beings=God's servants).

Premise 3: God's communications with his servants take legal form in a special sense (see premise 3, page 185).

Premise 4: God delegates to Jesus the supreme right to interpret and enforce his holy law.

Premise 5: Jesus' legal deliverances are summarized in the double love commandment.

Conclusion: The double love commandment is right, obligatory.

Premise 1: (Basic norm.) With respect to their property, whatever is directed by owners=what is right, obligatory.

Premise 2: All the world, including human beings, is God's property (human beings=God's servants).

Premise 3: God's communications with his servants take legal form in a special sense (see premise 3, page 185).

Premise 4: God delegates to Jesus the supreme right to interpret and enforce his holy law.

Premise 5:   Jesus delegates to the church vicarious (institutional) legal authority to "bind and loose."

Conclusion: Whatever the church (duly constituted) "binds and
looses"=what is right, obligatory.

An authoritarian pattern easily lends itself to a *mode of direct
deduction.* Ideally, in a given situation, the only relevant question is:
Has the supreme commander issued a commandment that directly
covers the situation or that can be applied by direct deduction to it?
The assumption is that the commands are comprehensible, readily
practicable, complete, and free of contradiction. The greatest obsta-
cle is taken to be weakness of will in putting the commands into
practice, rather than weakness of understanding or interpretation.

This is Matthew's emphasis. What must be combatted is hypocri-
sy and backsliding in relation to the clear and compelling commands
of Jesus. How simple a task Matthew assumes the discernment of
the appropriate command to be is illustrated in the admonition to
"Turn and become like little children" (18:3). Granted there are
references to the disciples' lack of understanding, including their
inability in some cases to grasp the practical point of a parable or an
event (for example, 15:15–20; cf. 16:8–12), but the references
invariably express surprise, if not rebuke, for the disciples'
shortcomings.

There is always a strong probability that the directives of an
authoritarian system are not in fact as comprehensible, readily
practicable, complete, and free of contradiction as they are assumed
to be. It is possible that the development of a "new casuistry,
managed by experts," hinted at in 16:9 and 18:18–20, is the tribute
the Matthean church had to pay to this hard reality. If the
deliverances of the supernatural lawgiver lose clarity, the next
natural step is to turn to human authorities, in the hope that what
they declare to be permitted or forbidden on earth will be so in
heaven.

The uncertainty we registered about the extent of the legalization
of religious and moral teachings in the Matthean community is
relevant in determining the mode of validation. To the extent that
there are recognized officers and procedures for interpreting and
enforcing the commands of Jesus, to that extent the mode of direct
deduction is supplemented by a *mode of interpretation,* defined in
terms of the offices and procedures according to which definitive

judgments of what is right and obligatory are made. If an interpretation goes through the proper channels, it is right and obligatory. Actually, it is probable that the mode of direct deduction and the mode of (legal) interpretation were both operative in some sort of complementary relation to each other, but the evidence is too sketchy to be sure.

As we noted, one of the conditions for an authoritarian system is that, while the supreme commander is authorized to impose sanctions, the sanctions have a "logically secondary function" in relation to validation. That an act will be sanctioned (positively or negatively) does not determine the rightness or wrongness of the act, as certain forms of teleological reasoning might hold. In an authoritarian system, sanctions may supply, at most, a motivating reason for complying with the commands of the supreme authority. We noticed in connection with Judaic authoritarianism, however, that appealing to a person's desire for reward or aversion to punishment is an inferior appeal, though it is tolerated.

This perspective on rewards and punishments is essentially Matthew's. There is no evidence of a teleological justification of attitudes and acts according to their capacity to produce good or ill results. Matthew does, though, make extensive reference to rewards and punishments apparently as a motivating reason for complying with God's commandments. But frequently the appropriateness of appealing to sanctions in relation to doing God's will is called into question. The Parable of the Laborers in the Vineyard (20:1–16) stresses that the sovereign proprietor possesses discretionary authority to compensate the laborers in whatever way he pleases, including open disregard for accepted standards of fair compensation.

This theme is, of course, completely consonant with the form of authoritarianism we called "proprietary entitlement," and in fact helps to illustrate it. A master-servant relationship implies that the servant, as the master's property, does what he is told *because* he is the master's property, and not because of the reward or punishment he is likely to receive as the result. This does not mean rewards and punishments are excluded, but they are nothing more than tokens of the proprietor's discretionary favor or disfavor. In this view, the servant properly seeks to please the master as an end in itself, and not as a way of achieving rewards or avoiding punishments (Bornkamm 1970: 69–92, cf. 1960: 137–43). Furthermore, chapter 25:37–

39, significantly emphasizes the element of surprise, or total lack of calculation, with respect to the results of performing or not performing the will of God.

Whereas the authoritarian pattern in Matthew is characterized by a self-authenticating supreme will or by proprietary entitlement, the formalistic pattern is characterized by a basic practical principle whose form sets the standard for validating lower-order action-guides and judgments. It is, logically speaking, of a very different order from the authoritarian pattern, even though it is often interwoven empirically and historically with other patterns in various religious traditions.

The clearest and most important example of the formalistic pattern appears in the Parable of the Unforgiving Servant (18:23–41). Much of this section is devoted to a careful analysis of that parable, and we attempt to show why it is such a salient instance of practical reasoning in relation to the rest of Matthew's practical teaching.

But it is important to note first that the "moral" of the parable is an example of the law of reciprocity (LR) in Matthew's Gospel, a "law" or principle of the greatest significance in Matthean practical reasoning. The law of reciprocity, at its most abstract, may be formulated: *Insofar as possible, there ought to be an equivalence between others' treatment of one and one's treatment of others.* It is interesting, but not sufficiently appreciated, that there are at least four different versions of LR in Matthew. These versions reveal a number of notable variations and complexities.

Versions of the Law of Reciprocity (LR)

LR$_1$. One ought to be treated as one has treated others. Examples are 6:14–15: "For if you forgive men their trespasses, your heavenly father also will forgive you"; 7:2: "For with the judgment you give will be the measure you get back" (cf. 5:7; 6:14). In these examples, the equivalence is *strict*—one's treatment of others is precisely the treatment he will receive. Furthermore, examples in this version exhibit both *recompensatory* (benefit for benefit) and *retributive* (injury for injury) possibilities. A somewhat similar example is 5:10: "Blessed are those who are persecuted for righteousness' sake, for theirs is the kingdom of heaven" (cf. 5:21–22,27–30; 25:31–46). Here the equivalence is *extended*—one does not receive exactly the same form of treatment one has employed toward others, though good treatment is still repaid by some kind of benefit, and, correspondingly, bad treatment is repaid by some kind of injury. Again, with this type of example, there are both recompensatory and retributive examples. In both sets of examples, the "others" are unspecified, which means that a good or bad done to anyone ought to be duly repaid, though not necessarily by the recipient of the deed.

LR₂. One ought to treat others as he has been treated. Whereas LR_1 presupposes that the self is the initiating agent, and the recipient or patient the one who responds, LR_2 presupposes the other as the initiating agent to whom the self responds. As in LR_1 the others are unspecified—a variety of others may conceivably be the recipients of the self's due response, not just the individual who instigated the act in the first place. For example, 10:8b: "You received without pay, give without pay," which, in the context, means that the disciple, having "received, without deserving and without paying for it, the gift of forgiveness and the power to heal, [is obligated] to give the message and healing to others without payment" (Filson 1960: 130). What the disciple has received from an other (God), he is obligated to extend to many different others—the sick, the lepers, and so on (10:8a). In the context of 10:7–15 the equivalence is clearly extended, and this example is applied only in a recompensatory way. Verse 18:33: "Should not you have had mercy on your fellow servant, as I had mercy on you" is also an example of recompensatory behavior that involves unspecified others, though the equivalence is strict.

Incidentally, there are no examples in Matthew of a retributive application of LR_2 (unlike for LR_1). As long as the others remain unspecified, this is not surprising. A retributive application hardly seems sensible. It would go something like this: If someone has injured you, an innocent, you are entitled to commit injuries of the same sort against similarly situated innocents! There is evidence of no such application in Matthew.

LR₃. One ought to treat those who have treated him, in the same way they have treated him. Unlike LR_1 and LR_2, this version specifies as others those particular individuals who have acted in a certain way toward one. With respect to the examples, we ought to make a distinction. Chapter 10:32–33 exemplifies this version with respect to *divine-human relations,* namely, in the relations between Jesus and human beings: "So everyone who acknowledges me before men, I will also acknowledge before my Father who is in heaven; but whoever denies me before men, I will also deny before my Father who is in heaven." Here the equivalence is strict, and it exhibits both a recompensatory and a retributive possibility, depending on the performance of a given human being.

On the other hand, at the level of *human relations,* there is one possible example of a recompensatory application (18:23 ff., see below), but no examples of a retributive application. Indeed, the relevant examples are all aimed against a retributive application— 5:38–39: "You have heard that it was said, 'An eye for an eye and a tooth for a tooth.' [The *lex talionis* is a remarkable expression of a retributive application of LR_3.] But I say to you . . . if anyone strikes you on the right cheek, turn to him the other also" (cf. 5:44). In short, if another person has mistreated one, one is *not* entitled, according to the teaching of Jesus, to retaliate by returning like for like. There appears, then, to be a common asymmetry between a recompensatory and a retributive application of LR in both LR_2 and LR_3. Though retributive reciprocity makes sense in the case of LR_3, Matthew displays a disposition against it, at least on the human level.

LR_4. The Golden Rule: One ought to treat others, who are in similar circumstances, as it is loving to be treated. The Golden Rule has not received sufficient philosophical attention, especially not in relation to the other versions of LR as we have sketched them (Singer 1971: 16–17, 344; Sidgwick 1874: 380–85; Hare 1965: 106, 108). Yet enough has been said to show that 7:12: "So whatever you wish that men would do to you, do so to them" is, as an expression of LR, anything but clear or precise. Much might follow from it that would run counter to Matthew's basic practical message. For example, as Sidgwick points out, "One might wish for another's cooperation in sin and be willing to reciprocate it" (Sidgwick 1874: 358), because the possibility of wishing for a "sinful objective" is not excluded by the "whatever" in 7:12. All that can be wrung from the sentence as it stands is a restriction in favor of universalizing practical judgments: "We cannot . . . judge it right for A to treat B in a manner in which, under precisely similar circumstances, it would be wrong for B to treat A" (Sidgwick 1874: 358–59).

Nevertheless, 7:12 should not be interpreted by itself. Matthew consciously links it to Chapter 22:36–40, the double love commandment. He does that by adding the words, "the law and the prophets" (7:12b; 22:40), in both instances. Thus, the Golden Rule "is to be understood in its Matthean usage as another way of expressing the commandment to love one's neighbor (McConnell 1969: 111–12). So interpreted, 7:12 is not as open-ended as it first appears. It presupposes a particular standard of good treatment, namely LC_2. And, as we know, LC_2 means for Matthew, "voluntary self-denial for the purpose of promoting the interests of other human beings," a principle specified according to the attitudes and acts mentioned in category 2, Figure 7. Of special interest in this context is the emphasis in category 2 on the benevolent attitudes and acts of forgiveness, mercy, reconciliation, and the prohibition against retaliation. This emphasis explains the explicit exclusion, at least on the human level, of a retributive application of LR_3.

When verses 7:12 and 22:39 are combined in this way, it is clear that Matthew's understanding of LR_4 rests on two assumptions: first, that every person considers it good to be treated in a forgiving, merciful, and reconciling way—in short, "to be loved" (as Matthew conceives the notion). That is what everyone "wish[es] that men would do to [him] . . ." Second, according to the principle of universalizability encased in both 7:12 and 22:39, one cannot judge that it is good for himself to be treated mercifully, and so forth, and, under similar circumstances, deny the same treatment to others. With respect to both assumptions, the reciprocal equivalence appears to be extended, in that love might be variously expressed within certain broad limits. Also, the stress is on a recompensatory application of LR: One considers it good to be treated lovingly (that is, mercifully, and so on), but not vengefully. Therefore, according to LR_4, one ought to treat others lovingly, but not vengefully. Retribution (on the human level) is conceptually excluded.

Two general conclusions can be drawn about the relations among the four versions of LR. First, in certain respects, LR_4 occupies a superordinate position, at least in relation to LR_2 and LR_3. Thanks to LR_4 we can understand Matthew's bias in favor of recompensatory and against retributive treatment in LR_3 and probably LR_2, even though, on strictly logical grounds, a retributive application is conceivable. At the same time, there is a deep tension between the exclusively positive or recompensatory emphasis in LR_4 and (on the human level) in LR_3, and the inclusion of a negative or retributive form of reciprocity in LR_1 and (on the divine-human level) in LR_3. In other words, reciprocity is applied to divine-human relations in a way that is generally excluded in human relations.

Second, LR_2 and LR_3 especially, as they are applied by Matthew, add some important stipulations to LR_4. According to LR_2, when one has in fact been well-treated by a particular other in a particular way, that simply strengthens one's obligation to treat (unspecified) others well in return. According to 10:8b, the fact that one has been well-treated by God's gracious act, provides additional prompting to treat all others in like circumstances in a similar way: "You received without pay, give without pay." In LR_3 the fact that one has received benefits at the hands of a specific benefactor implies a strong obligation to return the favor to that specific benefactor, as well as a strong obligation to treat others, in similar circumstances, as one has been treated (18:23–35). In our discussion of the Parable of the Unforgiving Servant we shall explore the way LR_2 and LR_3 strengthen and specify the obligation implied in LR_4.

By this survey of versions of the law of reciprocity, we have sought to suggest how pervasive and basic LR is in Matthew's practical thinking, and thereby to set the stage for our analysis of the Parable of the Unforgiving Servant, which combines the different versions of LR in a most remarkable and significant way. In so doing, the parable is a clear example of the formalistic pattern of validation.

The Parable of the Unforgiving Servant (18:23–35).

The general context in which Matthew sets the parable is important. The parable is intended both to provide backing for 18:21–22 (on forgiving "seventy times seven"), and to indicate, in line with LR_1, what will happen to those who fail to comply with the "moral" of the story (18:34–35). In describing the basic conditions for entrance into the Kingdom, it is a parable of the Last Judgment.

The relationship of the king to the first servant is significant. The king entrusted the servant with responsibility over a large amount of his wealth that he then called due. When the king heard that the servant was unable to pay, he acted within his rights as sovereign proprietor and laid claim to everything the servant owned—his person, his family, and his property—and then threatened to sell all of this as partial payment of the debt. The servant was now bereft of all claim to call anything his own. The only thing he had left was the king's gracious (discretionary) mercy, a condition the servant acknowledged, temporarily at least, by the tone of his fervent entreaty. The king's subsequent act of forgiveness (verse 27b), in which he released the servant from imprisonment and cancelled his debt completely, had the effect of returning to the servant his very selfhood, along with his family and possessions.

It is in this restored capacity that "the same servant" (verse 28a) encountered a second servant, one who owed him a debt that was quite insignificant in comparison with the one he had just been forgiven. In circumstances that are relevantly similar—a fact underscored by the repetition of almost exactly the same words used by the first servant toward the king (verses 26b, 29b)—the first servant treats the second servant in a fashion that contradicts the treatment he received at the hands of the king. He is then hauled before the king, harshly blamed, and then condemned to what appears to be everlasting punishment (Filson 1960: 204).

The crucial words in the parable, which we attempt to analyze in detail, are verses 32–34a: "Then his lord summoned him and said to him, 'You wicked servant! I forgave you all that debt because you besought me; and should not you have had mercy on your fellow servant, as I had mercy on you?' And in anger his lord delivered him to the jailers." First, the appeal here is *not* authoritarian. The argument does not run, "I am a supreme commander, and I command you to forgive others, and because you did not do what I said, I hereby condemn you." Nor does the argument go, "As I am king and you servant, I have proprietary rights over you according to which I command you to forgive others. Because you have not done so, I hereby condemn you." On the contrary, the appeal is clearly to some version, or combination of versions, of LR. Insofar as proprietary rights play a role in the parable, as they do in the opening encounter between king and servant, it is in a logically subordinate role. The appeal to proprietary rights in no way establishes the principle at verse 33: "You should have had mercy on others, as I did on you." Rather, instead of supporting the unique and absolute authority of the king over the servant, *verse 33 puts the king and the servant, and the rights and obligations they have in relation to others, on a comparable footing.* If not identical, the two cases, the one involving the king and the first servant, and the other involving the first and the second servant, are similar enough to be governed by *exactly the same prior principle.*

Second, it is immediately obvious that, in context, verse 33 expresses our reconstruction of the Golden Rule (LR$_4$:) "One ought to treat others, who are in similar circumstances, as it is loving to be treated." One assumption of this parable is that the first servant does wish to be treated lovingly (that is, mercifully, forgivingly), and particularly so when such treatment involves recovering his very selfhood or personhood, including control over his own welfare and property, which he would be denied in bondage and in prison. Clearly the servant enjoys, and proceeds to trade on, the benefits extended to him by the king's benevolent act. The other assumption is that the servant cannot acceptably prefer loving treatment as good for himself, and refuse, under similar circumstances, to apply it to others. Incidentally, at least up to verse 34, the application of LR is only recompensatory, and the implied equivalence is strict ("forgive your debtors, as your debts have been forgiven," to alter 6:12 somewhat). The others who are eligible for similar treatment are unspecified.

Third, verse 33 also exemplifies LR$_2$: "One ought to treat others as he has been treated," and, as such, *strengthens* the obligation to treat others as it is loving to be treated. In other words, a further assumption is made in the parable that to have been treated mercifully by the king, especially on such a large scale, increases the servant's moral indebtedness. Literally, the translation of verse 33 should read: *"Were you not bound by the compulsion of duty (ouk edei)* [see Arndt and Gingrich 1957: 171, entry 2] to have had mercy on your fellow servant, *as I had mercy* [our italics] on you?" The accomplished fact of the king's merciful behavior towards the servant, together with the servant's ready acceptance of it, creates what Kant would have called a "perfect duty" on the part of the servant: "I understand by a perfect duty one that admits no exception in favor of inclination" (Kant 1949: 39, fn. 9). In other words, a perfect duty for Kant can rightly be claimed from and held against the individual who owes it in such a way that he is blameworthy, and sanctionable, if he defaults. That means that a strong claim against the servant may be made that he act in a reciprocally equivalent way toward (unspecified) others. If he does not, he is properly liable for condemnation and punishment, a consideration that makes sense of the way the king treats the first servant in verse 34. The strength of this requirement springs from the fact that a transaction between king and servant has already taken place, a transaction somewhat analogous to a loan or promise made in the past. As in the case of those outstanding obligations, the resultant reciprocal obligation upon the servant is not optional or discretionary, but strict and enforceable.

Fourth, there is in verse 33 a clear, though never explicit, assumption of LR_3: "One ought to treat those who have treated him, in the same way they have treated him." *The Expositor's Greek Testament* speaks here of "an appeal to gratitude" for the "magnificent generosity of the king" (vol. I, 243). Thus, an obligation of gratitude on the part of the first servant directly to the king can be inferred from the parable. Insofar as the king, by his self-sacrificial act, freely restores to the servant his selfhood, and thereby his capacity to act at all, the servant is obligated to acknowledge his debt to the king by freely sacrificing, reciprocally, his own interests in the service of the king. Moreover, there is surely the added assumption that as a result of the magnitude of the king's generosity, the servant's gratitude is correspondingly limitless.

It seems implied in the parable that one way (though by no means the only way) the servant has of demonstrating his gratitude to the king is by being ready to replicate in his behavior toward others the sort of benevolence the king showed toward him. Filson captures the point well: "Having received forgiveness the servant should have been not merely grateful but forgiving. In fact, had he been really grateful he would have been forgiving" (Filson 1967: 204). But, *The Expositor's Greek Testament* goes on, "Ungenerous himself, he was incapable of conceiving and therefore appreciating such magnificent generosity" (vol. I, 243).

Accordingly, in addition to assuming LR_2, verse 33 appears also to assume LR_3. The servant is strongly obligated to be merciful to others for *two* reasons: first, simply because he has been so treated and, according to the requirements of LR_2, is obligated to replicate toward others in similar circumstances the sort of treatment he has received; and, second, because, according to the requirements of LR_3, he is obligated to demonstrate his gratitude to the king, his benefactor. In this way, LR_2 combines with LR_3 to strengthen and specify the servant's reciprocal obligation.

Finally, verses 34–35 make clear that at least divine-human

relations are ultimately governed by LR_1: "One ought to be treated as one has treated others," a version of LR which is in Matthew applied in a retributive as well as a recompensatory way. Indeed, verses 34–35 obviously restate, in part, Chapter 6:14–15 ("For if you forgive men their trespasses . . ."), one of our leading illustrations of LR_1. Moreover, it is an example of strict equivalency: Forgive and one will be forgiven; do not and one will not be forgiven.

By converting the characters of the parable into the figures they are intended to represent, we can now reconstruct in syllogistic form the essential practical argument implied in the Parable of the Unforgiving Servant and thereby demonstrate how our second pattern of validation—the formalistic one—works in relation to the rest of Matthew's practical teaching.

Premise 1: (Basic norm.) Given that there ought to be equivalence, so far as possible, in reciprocal action (LR), and that one ought to treat others in similar circumstances as it is loving to be treated (LR_4), one is strongly obligated both to treat others lovingly, if one has been treated lovingly (LR_2), and to treat those who have treated one lovingly in a similarly loving way (LR_3), where "strongly obligated" means that noncompliance is met with retribution and compliance with recompensation (LR_1).

Premise 2: God has treated one in an extraordinarily loving way.

Conclusion: One is strongly obligated both to treat others lovingly (LC_2), and to treat God in an extraordinarily loving way (LC_1), and recompensation and retribution is determined in respect to compliance or noncompliance with LC_1–LC_2.

Premise 1, the basic norm in this instance, is a *formalistic deontological moral principle.* It is a formalistic deontological principle because if lower-order rules and judgments conform to the relevant constitutitive parts (the form) of the principle, without reference to consequences and regardless of who happens to espouse the principle, then those lower-order rules and judgments are right and obligatory. According to our syllogism, both LC_1 and LC_2 are validated that way; the various attitudes and acts that make up LC_1 and LC_2 (categories 1 and 2 in Figure 7) are similarly validated, as are all judgments that consistently apply these action-guides to concrete cases.

It is a *moral* principle because, along with meeting the other conditions of our definition of moral (prescriptivity, superiority, and the general conditions of legitimacy), it also includes human, other-regarding consideration (our special condition of moral legitimacy) as an essential feature. An act could correctly conform to the principle only if the agent of the act grasped and undertook to put into practice the implications of the principle for the treatment of other human beings. Strictly speaking, the principle is not "understood" if its human other-regarding implications are ignored, which is surely the central point of the Parable of the Unforgiving Servant. In this respect, LC_2 is validated as being a necessary condition for acting in a loving way. According to the principle, one could not conceivably act in a loving way and disregard the loving treatment of other human beings.

The obligation of gratitude, discussed in connection with LR_3, locates the basis within the principle for validating LC_1. Clearly, reciprocal equivalence applies to the relations between God and human beings, but, as we saw above, and as premise 2 indicates, this sort of equivalence is quite special. God (represented by the king and by his exceptional beneficence toward the servant) has, as premise 2 states, "treated one in an *extraordinarily* loving way." Thus, according to LR_3, one owes God (a specified other) a debt of gratitude, and the sort of debt owed is determined in relation to the "extraordinary" character of God's gift. The magnitude of God's gift is extraordinary in large degree because God himself is an extraordinary being, possessed of superhuman traits and capable of superhuman activities. Therefore, the recipient of God's beneficence owes a special reciprocal debt in two senses. First, because of God's "magnificent generosity," the claim on the recipient is of equivalent magnitude, at least from his human point of view: "You shall love the Lord your God with all your heart, and with all your soul, and with all your mind" (22:37). In other words, the attitudes of *ultimate* reverence, honor, gratitude, and so on (category 1.a, Figure 7) are a fitting recompensation to God for his generosity. This recompensation would not be appropriate in relation to a human benefactor because none is conceivably capable of bestowing the sort of gift God did.

Second, because God is not human, but only, in some respects,

humanlike, certain attitudes and acts that are appropriate in relation to human beings are not appropriate in relation to him.
Conversely, certain attitudes and acts (such as in category 1.b,
Figure 7), are for the most part appropriately performed only in
relation to God. Consequently, the distinctions, as well as the
similarities and overlaps between categories 1 and 2 in Figure 7 are
justified by this validating scheme. Since all the religious and moral
action-guides are validated by a moral principle, this is a *moral-
religious system.*

The system bears directly on legal matters insofar as law, in part,
has to do with the enforcement of action-guides by the authorized
imposition of sanctions. The notion of "strongly obligated," as
involved in LR_2 and LR_3, entails the enforceability of $LC_1–LC_2$,
that is, the imposition of recompensation or retribution according to
compliance or noncompliance with the double love commandment.
The double love commandment becomes the standard on the basis of
which the law is applied. This seems exactly what is meant by 22:40:
"On these two commandments depend all the law and the prophets." And it provides a clear rationale for passages like 6:12 and
6:14–15. As a result, God's law (or the holy law) is defined and
applied with reference to the double love commandment, and, by
implication, whatever human, institutional law is authorized in the
Matthean church must be applied according to the same standard.

But there is still the question of how this validating system
accounts for the fact that God is authorized as legal authority. Why
is he entitled, on this scheme, to "stand in judgment" as the
interpreter and enforcer of the law, as well as to delegate legal
authority to others. That is not made clear in our syllogism as it
stands.

The reason, as far as we can tell, centers in an additional
assumption deducible from LR_1 that *only the offended party, never
the offender, may properly impose retribution.* Since God is understood as the offended party and is inconceivable as the offender, and
since man is the offender, only God possesses the right to reciprocate punitively. This appears to be one of the points made in 7:1–2:
"Judge not, that you be not judged. For with the judgment you
pronounce you will be judged, and the measure you give will be the
measure you get." Whatever else the words mean, the lesson against
self-righteousness that is drawn from verses 3–5 suggests that only

those who are themselves free of guilt are entitled to pass judgment on others. Only the injured innocent may injure in return. Since God alone has been injured without ever injuring others, he alone may "stand in judgment."

We may, therefore, extend our syllogism as follows:

Premise 1:   (Basic norm.) Given that there ought to be equivalence, so far as possible, in reciprocal action (LR), and that one ought to treat others in similar circumstances as it is loving to be treated (LR_4), one is strongly obligated both to treat others lovingly, if one has been treated lovingly (LR_2), and to treat those who have treated one lovingly in a similarly loving way (LR_3), where "strongly obligated" means that noncompliance is met with retribution and compliance with recompensation (LR_1).

Premise 2:   God has treated one in an extraordinarily loving way.

Premise 3:   One is strongly obligated both to treat others lovingly (LC_2), and to treat God in an extraordinarily loving way (LC_1), and recompensation and retribution is determined in respect to compliance or noncompliance with LC_1–LC_2.

Premise 4:   Only those who have themselves been injured by the standard of the double love commandment and have not injured others, are entitled to "stand in judgment" (to interpret and enforce the law).

Premise 5:   God is the only one who qualifies.

Conclusion: God alone may stand in judgment (be a legal official).

The same pattern of reasoning applies to the authorization of Jesus as a legal authority and further to the authorization of church officials as legal authorities, to the extent that exists in Matthew. In the latter case, however, we can readily understand, on this system, the basis for the ambiguity over church, institutional law that is signaled in the discrepancy between verses 18:18 and 18:22. Since human beings are regarded as inevitably guilty of some form of offense, even the duly authorized ought to stand in judgment only most reluctantly.

As to the mode of validation in the formalistic pattern, it is difficult to form any firm conviction because the evidence is so sketchy. Nevertheless, there is reason to think, at least with respect to a certain range of substantive action-guides within the Gospel of Matthew, that the mode assumed is either *direct deduction* or *interpretation*. The pertinent range of action-guides is that set of action-guides dealt with in sections 2.1 and 2.2 in this chapter, which are understood as expressions or specifications of LC_2 and LC_1.

Insofar as neighbor-love requires and excludes, respectively, the attitudes and acts contained under category 2 (Figure 7), and love-of-God requires and excludes, respectively, the attitudes and acts contained under category 1 (Figure 7), all such attitudes and acts appear to be directly deducible from the complex form of the basic prescriptive premise. If "love" means, as we suggested, "voluntary self-denial (physical and psychological) for the purpose of promoting the interests of the other (human beings or God)," and if it is reciprocally required in the ways indicated in the basic prescriptive premise, then all the attitudes and acts in categories 1 and 2 seem to *enact* love in various ways.

It is of course impossible to tell from Matthew's text how the notorious task of assigning priorities among conflicting duties to love would be handled. Can such priorities be directly deduced when, say, a disciple attempts to satisfy mutually exclusive, yet strongly compelling, needs or obligations? It is apparently assumed either that when the time comes, the appropriate deductions can be made, or that the disciple (or possibly the church in some official capacity) has a discretionary capability to decide "hard cases." In the latter event, we have the makings of the mode of interpretation, which allows for a range of discretionary application.

3.2. Patterns of Vindication

Matthew makes remarkably little attempt to argue for the sort of beliefs that provide convincing backing for either the authoritarian or the formalistic validating patterns. Naturally, a number of important assumptions are made about the nature of the universe and the nature of man that serve to make the two basic validating norms we uncovered plausible and intelligible. But these beliefs are simply assumed. No case is made for them. There is, it is true, extensive reference to a set of "motivating reasons" for adopting the recommended code of conduct, but again, these references assume, as well as trade on, motivations that are believed to be part of universal human nature.

Up to a point, the same general set of cosmological and anthropological beliefs goes for both the authoritarian and the formalistic patterns. The universe is fundamentally pictured in legal-political images, or, more precisely, in regal images. A personalized divine ruler and lawgiver is assumed to exist, who is author and controller of the universe, as well as the proper authority over all human subjects. In this universe the characteristics normally associated with human agency are central.

On the one hand, the divine ruler is depicted, in many respects, as a humanlike actor with the attributes of intelligence, consciousness, purposiveness, and a capacity for volition—although all in superhuman measure. His way of acting is understood on the model of human rulership: He organizes a "kingdom" around a basic law; he plans, issues decrees, punishes, rewards, affirms, protects and extends his kingdom, and provides for the welfare of his subjects, all in keeping with the basic law of his kingdom.

On the other hand, human beings are understood as political subjects, or as citizens. Again, the Gospel of Matthew emphasizes the centrality of human agency in a political and legal mode. An individual is conceived of as essentially an actor expected to submit himself to the "kingdom of God." He (or she) is expected to organize his action in keeping with the law of God, to understand his welfare in terms of that law, and to anticipate ultimate punishment and reward in proportion to the degree of compliance with the requirements of the kingdom.

In the ideal or eschatological kingdom, the divine ruler's authority is finally and completely honored and implemented, both, presumably, as between the subjects and the ruler and among the subjects or citizens themselves. In other words, in the Gospel of Matthew, normative human nature is pictured in terms of a collectivity of cooperative, yet discrete, human actors, who willingly submit themselves in all their actions to the authority of the ruler and the law of his kingdom, and thereby achieve their welfare as well as the welfare of their ruler.

The set of human motivations assumed in the Gospel of Matthew conforms to this general description. That is, human beings are taken as subject to the ordinary physical and psychological inclinations toward achieving satisfaction and avoiding pain, where satisfaction and pain are depicted in "material" terms, such as aversion to illness, hunger and thirst, and psychic distress. The kingdom of God will not negate these ordinary inclinations, but provide for them in abundance, a belief that signals the centrality of the "material" dimension of human action in the Gospel of Matthew.

Moreover, the Gospel-writer plays on these motives in attempting to stimulate his readers to seek the kingdom of God. It is assumed that everyone will naturally desire to achieve rewards and avoid punishment, and all the more when rewards and punishments are "eternal." Thus, the writer appeals especially to the fear of punishment of his readers in trying to motivate them to Christian discipleship. He seems to feel no need to prove the reality of the coming judgment and the attendant liabilities for those found wanting, but takes his audience's anxieties along those lines for granted.

This is not to say, of course, that Matthew's appeal to ordinary motives, such as fear of punishment, illustrates anything more than his use of "exciting reasons" in prompting a quest for righteousness. There is, as we argued, no evidence whatsoever that the law of God is validated in reference to some calculus of individual pleasure and pain. On the contrary, there is some evidence that an appeal to such motives is out of keeping with a full or mature understanding of the grounds and character of God's righteousness.

In any case, there is no confidence that, left to their own motives and interests, human beings can readily achieve right understanding and right practice. The Gospel of Matthew does assume in many places that human beings as agents are responsible for their actions, and thus properly deserve the rewards or penalties they receive, but there is also much stress upon God's discretionary revelation as the means of true righteousness. A good example is Chapter 11:25–26 (cf. Chapter 13):

At that time Jesus declared, "I thank thee, Father, Lord of heaven and earth, that thou hast hidden these things from the wise and understanding and revealed them to babes; yea, Father, for such was thy gracious will."

As background considerations, all this applies equally to the authoritarian and the formalistic patterns. Both patterns, as they exhibit themselves in the Gospel of Matthew, assume a "regal universe," constituted cosmologically and anthropologically along the lines we have sketched out. Indeed, it will be remembered that despite the significant differences between them, both patterns are deontological in character. They are both examples of command ethics or ethics of duty, as opposed to consequential or results-oriented ethics. They belong to the same family, and are understandably backed by similar vindicatory beliefs.

Nonetheless, the differences are also important. In the case of the formalistic pattern, the universe is assumed to be governed by a moral law composed of various versions of the law of reciprocity. Whatever its origins, and they are not discussed by Matthew, this moral law governs and limits the activities of God, as well as of human beings. It is because God acted in accordance with the law of reciprocity that man is beholden to God, though in ways that are, in turn, specified and restricted by the law of reciprocity. Politically speaking, the image here is of a constitutional monarch. God, like man, is under the law.

Moreover, the governing law is "moral" in that the universe is so constructed that other-regardingness (in our material welfare-oriented sense) is constitutive of right practice. Put another way, right practice is unintelligible apart from other-regardingness. This is one way of construing the general image of normative human nature we described above, including a belief in the continuing existence of independent, though cooperative—or mutually regarding—actors.

There is, as we have seen, an explicit set of religious beliefs relevant to this pattern, along with an attendant set of religious action-guides. But the religious realm is, so to speak, circumscribed by the moral realm. God, the sacred authority, is superhuman in a variety of ways but most importantly in moral capability. Unlike human beings he is morally perfect and thus able and ready to perform deeds of the highest purity and rectitude, such as his act of "magnificent generosity" suggested by the Parable of the Unforgiving Servant. His sacredness and transcendence are, on this pattern, authenticated by his demonstrated moral perfection, as are the religious action-guides required in response to him by the disciple. In short, the religious is measured and determined according to the moral.

In the case of the authoritarian pattern, whether of the definist or the proprietary sort, the universe, as well as human nature and the directives for human conduct, are comparatively much less determinate. Since on this pattern God is entitled to do with the world and human beings "as he pleases" because "his word is law," discipleship consists in honoring and obeying whatever may be commanded by God, regardless of content. Here there are no necessary controls on God's will. Neither his sacred authority nor religious acts toward him are authenticated according to assumed standards of moral perfection, as in the case of the formalistic pattern. Here God's sacred authority is warranted by definition or by proprietary entitlement.

Because his sacred authority is independent of and prior to any moral standard, the moral action-guides dictated by his will (love, or mutual other-regarding concern) are also contingent upon God's will. That is, the requirements of LC_2 are binding only so long as God continues to authorize and enforce them, although from the perspective of the Gospel-writer, such requirements do, at present, very much happen to be God's will.

We can see in the Gospel of Matthew, then, the roots of a long-standing ambivalence in the Christian tradition regarding the grounds of Christian action. "Is something right because God wills it, or does he will it because it is right?" turns out to be a dilemma springing directly from the Gospel of Matthew itself, and from the competing patterns of justification contained in that book. Both patterns, though with their different emphases and implications, are at home in, and sustained by, a similar set of cosmological and anthropological beliefs.

NOTES

1. Although almsgiving is here conceived of as a religious act—an instance of practicing piety (6:1–2)—it can be distinguished from prayer and fasting in that it contains a direct other-impinging feature. To give alms is, after all, to contribute gratuitously to the material support of deprived human beings. The notions of prayer and fasting bear no such direct reference, even though prayers *may* be offered for the material benefit of others. In our terms, prayer and fasting are primarily sacred-impinging acts, while almsgiving is an example of the overlapping moral and religious categories. Almsgiving is an other-impinging act that is, at the same time, understood as a sacred-impinging act.

2. Something religious or moral may or may not also be legal, depending on whether the conditions of a legal action-guide are met. Thus, we have made sense of the possible overlap of action-guide categories in Matthew.

REFERENCES

ARNDT, WILLIAM F., AND GINGRICH, F. WILBUR.
1957   *A Greek-English Lexicon of the New Testament and Other Early Christian Literature.* Chicago and Cambridge: University of Chicago and Cambridge University Press.

BACON, BENJAMIN W.
1930   *Studies in Matthew.* New York: Henry Holt & Co.

BARRETT, C. K.
1966   *The New Testament Background: Selected Documents.* New York: Harper & Row.

BARTH, GERHARD.
1963   "Matthew's Understanding of the Law." In *Tradition and Interpretation in Matthew,* pp. 58–164. Günther Bornkamm et al., eds. Philadelphia: Westminster Press.

BORNKAMM, GÜNTHER.
1960   *Jesus of Nazareth.* Irene McLuskey, Fraser McLuskey, and James M. Robinson, trans. New York: Harper & Row.
1968   "Das Doppelgebot der Liebe." In *Geschichte und Glaube,* pp. 37–45. Munich: Kaiser Verlag.
1970   "Der Lohngedanke im Neuen Testament." In *Studien zu Antike und Urchristentum,* pp. 69–92. Munich: Kaiser Verlag.

BRODY, BARUCH A.
1974   "Morality and Religion Reconsidered." In *Readings in the Philosophy of Religion,* pp. 592–603. Baruch A. Brody, ed. Englewood Cliffs, N.J.: Prentice-Hall.

DAVIES, W. D.
1966a   *The Setting of the Sermon on the Mount.* Cambridge: Cambridge University Press.
1966b   *The Sermon on the Mount.* Cambridge: Cambridge University Press.

THE EXPOSITOR'S GREEK TESTAMENT.
         Vol. I by A.B. Bruce. London: Hodder and Stoughton.

FILSON, FLOYD V.
1960   *Commentary on the Gospel according to St. Matthew.* London: Adam & Charles Black.

208 APPLICATION

FRANKENA, WILLIAM K.
 1973 "Is Morality Logically Dependent on Religion?" In *Religion and Morality,* Gene Outka and John P. Reeder, eds. Garden City, New York: Doubleday & Co., pp. 295–317. Anchor Press.

GRANT, F. C.
 1957 *The Gospels: Their Origin and their Growth.* New York: Harper & Row.

HARE, DOUGLAS R. A.
 1967 *The Theme of Jewish Persecution of the Christians in the Gospel according to St. Matthew.* Cambridge: Cambridge University Press.

HARE, R. M.
 1965 *Freedom and Reason.* New York: Oxford University Press.

HOULDEN, J. L.
 1973 *Ethics and the New Testament.* London: Penguin Books.

JOHNSON, S. E.
 1951 "Matthew: Introduction." In *The Interpreter's Bible.* Volume VII, pp. 231–50. George Arthur Buttrick, Walter Russell Bowie, John Knox et al., eds. New York: Abingdon Press.

KANT, IMMANUEL.
 1949 *Fundamental Principles of the Metaphysic of Morals.* New York: The Liberal Arts Press.

KÄSEMANN, ERNST.
 1969 "Sentences of Holy Law in the New Testament." pp. 66–81, in *New Testament Questions of Today.* Philadelphia: Fortress Press.

KLAUSNER, JOSEPH.
 1925 *Jesus of Nazareth.* New York: Macmillan Co.

MacARTHUR, HARVEY K.
 1960 *Understanding the Sermon on the Mount.* New York: Harper & Row.

McCONNELL, RICHARD S.
 1969 *Law and Prophecy in Matthew's Gospel.* Basel: Friedrich Reinhardt Kommisionsverlag.

MOORE, GEORGE FOOT.
 1935 *Judaism.* Cambridge, Mass.: Harvard University Press. 3 volumes.

THE NEW OXFORD ANNOTATED BIBLE
 1977 Revised Standard Version. Herbert G. May and Bruce M. Metzger, eds. New York: Oxford University Press.

SCHWEITZER, EDUARD.
 1961 *Church Order in the New Testament.* London: SCM Press.

SIDGWICK, HENRY.
1874 *Methods of Ethics.* London: Macmillan & Co.
SINGER, MARCUS G.
1971 *Generalization in Ethics.* New York: Atheneum.
STRACK, HERMANN L., AND BILLERBECK, PAUL.
1926 *Das Evangelium nach Mättaus.* Munich: C. H. Beck'sche Verlagsbuchhandlung. 2 volumes.
1928 "Der Synagogenbann." In *Excurse zu Einselnen Stellen des Neuen Testaments,* pp. 291–333. Munich: C. H. Beck'sche Verlagsbuchhandlung.
WEBSTER'S NEW INTERNATIONAL DICTIONARY.
1928 Springfield, Mass.: G. & C. Merriam Co.
WILDER, AMOS.
1950 *Eschatology and Ethics in The Teaching of Jesus.* New York: Harper & Row.

8 Religion and Morality in Theravada Buddhism

1. INTRODUCTION

1.1. The Theravada Tradition

Buddhism represents a distinctive contrast to Christianity. But, of the possible versions of Buddhism, the Theravadin tradition is an especially illuminating version for comparison. For our purposes, the distinction between Theravada and the other schools of Hinayana and Mahayana Buddhism is simply canonical. It is a question of which of the discourses of the Buddha are taken as authentic. The Theravadin canon was probably compiled around the third century B.C. and includes five collections of discourses that are still available today. These sets of discourses form the basis for Theravadin scriptural commentaries and doctrinal interpretation.

No one discourse combines and epitomizes the central Theravadin beliefs and practical teachings, and thus corresponds to the Gospel of Matthew within Christian literature. For that reason, it is not possible to dwell in depth on only one of the books of that tradition. Rather, it is necessary to reconstruct the practical system from among many of the discourses included in the Theravadin canon. Also, while we tried to keep reliance on the commentaries at a minimum, we have had to make reference to them occasionally, particularly in respect to the discussion of sublime attitudes.

1.2. Some Key Doctrines in Buddhist Ideology

Although Theravadins have their own sacred literature that distinguishes them from the rest of Buddhism, they do share certain central beliefs with other Buddhists—albeit providing their own unique interpretation and emphasis at important points.

The central objective of all forms of Buddhism is escape or release from suffering. The means of escape, as described in the teachings of the Buddha, is summarized in the so-called Eightfold Path or the Middle Way of Self-Conquest, which may be organized as follows: correct conduct, including right speech, right action, right livelihood; correct effort for concentration, including right effort, right mindfulness, and right concentration; and wisdom, including right thought and right understanding (Saddhatissa 1970: 70–74).

In discussing some key doctrines of Buddhism, we shall focus on the sort of "right understanding" that is requisite for wisdom, giving some attention to the role of concentration in the cultivation of wisdom and ultimate enlightenment. Right understanding is, basically, to know the world of appearance for what it is: impermanent, fraught with suffering, and bound up with an ultimately illusory belief in the existence of discrete, independent selves. Of these three considerations, the last—the so-called *anatta,* or "no-self" doctrine—is of particular interest. According to this doctrine, a belief in the existence of selves, so characteristic of unenlightened thinking, is the root of suffering. The belief in the existence of a durable self leads to a desire for long-lasting happiness, which is fundamentally unattainable. This belief thus involves individuals in frustration and suffering. Consequently, the dissolution of suffering depends on the dissolution of the concept of the self.

This dissolution takes place when the proper form of wisdom and insight is achieved, namely the realization that selves are, in the ultimate sense, artificial constructs that can be reduced to more basic independent elements (*skandhas*). To the extent that these elements are synthesized by an observer so as to appear to him as perduring individual selves, a fiction or illusion is said to have been created. True enlightenment sees through such syntheses.

On the other hand (and somewhat mystifying to the outsider), selves are regarded as fictitious only "in the ultimate sense." Theravadins do grant some provisional reality to empirical selves. It is believed that the world of appearance is governed by a set of inexorable conditions or laws of cause and effect—the laws of karma. With respect to human action, these laws control the "cycle of rebirths" to which individual selves are subject, so long as they have not fully escaped the world of appearance. Good acts beget good results (relatively increased happiness) and bad acts beget bad results (relatively increased suffering)—both in relation to future rebirths. On this understanding, selves are to some degree "responsible" for their actions, so that the social, economic, or spiritual advantages or disadvantages of given individuals at given times are considered the "just deserts" of action taken by them in a previous incarnation. Accordingly, "Deeds are one's own . . . beings are heirs to deeds" (MLS: Vol. III, 249).

Right understanding, then, enables one to grasp the conditions of cause and effect that govern the destiny of individual selves, but at a more profound level it enables an individual to see beyond the provisional reality of selves. It allows the individual to penetrate beyond the world of karma and its repetitive sufferings of birth, aging, sickness, and death to a condition beyond suffering and individuality—to nirvana. Western readers should always remember that the value of the undifferentiated, quiet, and peaceful state of nirvana comes from the fact that it is the only escape from the sufferings of an otherwise closed circle of repeated births and deaths. Nirvana is "the state of transcendent attainment; release from the limitations of existence and rebirth; the ultimate goal" (Hamilton 1952: 181). Or, in the words of the Sutta-Nipata: "Where there is no-thing, where naught is grasped, this is the Isle of No-beyond. Nirvana do I call it—the utter extinction of ageing and dying" (Conze 1964: 93).

With respect to the doctrine of nirvana, we need to bring out an important distinction in Theravada understanding between the *attainment* and the *realization* of nirvana, a distinction we shall presuppose below. Attainment is the final "entry" into nirvana in which the ultimate goal of insight and wisdom is achieved. It is believed to take place upon the physical death of a fully liberated individual. Realization is a temporary experience of nirvana, and of the appropriate insight and wisdom, during an individual's life. After the experience, the individual—for example, the Buddha himself—continues in physical existence, albeit with a drastically altered perspective on the world of appearance. There are, in turn, grades of realization, that depend on the profundity of insight with regard to the nature of the changing phenomena and the nature of that which is beyond change, namely, nirvana. Realization is achieved through observing action-guides and performing a set of graded practices and techniques of meditation, elaborately developed and exposited in the Theravada tradition.

2. CONTENT OF THERAVADIN PRACTICAL TEACHING

The long-standing debate over whether Buddhism constitutes a "religion" or not turns, of course, on how religion is defined. On our understanding of the term, there can be no question that Buddhism qualifies. It readily conforms to each of our defining characteristics.

To begin with, it posits a sacred authority—nirvana—which is understood as a *specially distinctive* scope of reality systematically set apart from "this world." In the words of Edward Conze:

Buddhism, like most religions, distinguishes two sets of facts, or two "worlds." In the one everything bears the three marks, is impermanent, ill [fraught with suffering], not self; in the other, which is "unborn, not become, not made, uncompounded," all is permanence, bliss, in full possession of itself. The impermanent, etc. facts are actual, the permanent, etc. are ideal (Conze 1970: 43–44).

And, interestingly, this same distinction applies to the categorization of human beings:

The Buddhists introduce what might be called an "existentialist" distinction between two qualitatively different kinds of persons, the "holy persons" and the ordinary people. What a man's knowledge can encompass depends on what he is. Holy men and ordinary people occupy two distinct planes of existence, the "worldly" and the "supramundane." A person becomes "supramundane" on "entering the Path," i.e., when he has detached himself from conditioned things to such an extent that he can effectively turn to the Path which leads to Nirvana (Conze 1970: 57).

This supramundane world is decidedly beyond the volitional control of human beings. In fact, the very concept of a human being as a discrete, self-conscious actor or agent is ultimately an illusion. The ultimate objective of insight or enlightenment is "the cessation of individuality" in the immortal nirvana (Aronson 1975: 288). Consequently, far from controlling or manipulating the sacred realm of nirvana, human selves lose their identity in relation to it, and are, in a radical and total sense, subject to it.

Secondly, nirvana is taken as *specially prominent* with respect to benefit and harm. It is regarded as "the highest happiness" (Hamilton 1952: 80), "the supreme goal of the higher life" (MLS: 169), "the highest end" (Hamilton 1952: 95), and so on. In other words, nirvana is the standard of ultimate value against which good and evil is measured.

Thirdly, nirvana, the sacred authority, is taken as *properly determinative* in respect to dispositions, attitudes, and acts. As we shall see, the whole Theravada Buddhist practical system is ultimately justified in relation to a belief in nirvana. For example, the Eightfold Path is warranted in that it enables the practitioner to "reach the quiet place" (nirvana). Indeed, Theravada Buddhism is a religiously grounded system par excellence.

Finally, the Buddhist sacred authority "functions to resolve the 'ontological' problems of interpretability," such as the inexplicabilities of the natural world, suffering and death, and the ambiguities and puzzles of human conduct.

It is the preoccupying concern of Buddhism to "resolve" the problems of suffering and death by showing them to be problems caused by misunderstanding and ignorance of the true character of reality. For example, the famous doctrine of the Four Noble Truths makes this point clear: (1) Life is subject to suffering; (2) this suffering is caused by ignorance, which results in desire (attachment); (3) suffering can be eliminated by the elimination of desire (through the elimination of ignorance); (4) the path to accomplish this is the Eightfold Path.

As for the puzzles of human conduct—the prospering of the wicked and the suffering of the righteous—there are two aspects to the Buddhist solution. First, as far as action in the phenomenal world goes, the law of karma provides a thoroughly consistent explanation of advantage and deprivation on the basis of performance in previous incarnations. Second, however, even this symmetrical vision is transcended in the realization of nirvanic experience, in comparison to which the puzzles and ambiguities of human conduct lose their significance.

Given the centrality and preeminence of this view of sacred

authority in Theravada thought, it is not surprising that the Theravada practical system turns out to be, in our terms, a thoroughgoing religious system. Properly understood, all action-guides have as their object nirvanic attainment, a condition that ultimately transcends morality by disallowing the concepts of "self" and "other," concepts necessary, in our usage, for the existence of morality. In the last analysis, all of this rests on the question of how the action-guides are justified. The reasons given for legitimating the various action-guides are religious, a matter we shall take up when we turn to the structure of the system.

But before that, we can, in a preliminary way, sort out the content of the various action-guides with respect to the *character* of the acts that are prohibited, enjoined, and permitted, identifying especially the recipients of those acts and the *condition* of the actor. It seems clear that the character of all prescribed and proscribed acts is ultimately defined in reference to "self-conquest" (DB: vol. I, 31) or the overcoming of those "hinderances"—including an attachment to the self—that blind one to the nature of things. Accordingly, the system of action-guides is hierarchic and progressive. Acts appear to be arranged, understood, and evaluated in reference to a pattern of increasing and cumulative efficacy for realizing self-conquest. (It is, of course possible to break through to insight at any stage of the system. It is not necessary to pass through every stage.)

At the most elementary stage in the practical system, there is a proscribed set of acts called "mere morality" (*sila*), which is binding on householders and holy persons alike, though in different ways. This stage includes the so-called five precepts (DB, vol. I, 3–5):

1. Avoid taking life (animal or human).
2. Avoid stealing (taking what is not offered).
3. Avoid illicit sexual relations.
4. Avoid lying.
5. Avoid intoxicants.

Precepts 1–4 include, though they are not restricted to, other-impinging acts. To the extent such acts are implied, they are moral in one sense of our usage. It is true that in the case of precept 1, the prohibition against taking life, the class of victims or recipients extends to all "living beings," which is to say to all "sentient beings" (*pana*). "Let [one] not kill, nor cause to be killed any living being, nor let him approve of others killing, after having refrained from hurting all creatures, both those that are strong and those that tremble in the world" (SN-SBE: 65).

Nevertheless, there is the assumption in the systematic treatise on monastic discipline *The Book of Discipline* (see pages 222–26 for a fuller treatment) that killing or injuring human beings is a graver offense than killing or injuring subhuman creatures. And, according to Saddhatissa, this assumption that "the extent of moral guilt in killing depends [in part] on the physical and mental development of the being killed" (Saddhatissa 1970: 88) is explicitly elaborated in the later commentary material. Consequently, the protection of the physical welfare of human beings occupies an especially important place in the fundamental practical beliefs of the Theravadins.

This condition also applies to precept 2, the prohibition against stealing, and to precept 4, the prohibition against lying. In both cases, human beings are the potential recipients of the interdicted acts. "Let [the disciple] abstain from (taking) anything in any place that has not been given (to him), knowing (it to belong to another), let him not cause anyone to take, nor approve of those that take, let him avoid all (sort of theft)" (SN-SBE: 65). "Let no one speak falsely in the hall of justice or in the hall of the assembly, let him not cause (anyone) to speak (falsely), nor approve of those that speak (falsely), let him avoid all (sort of) untruth" (SN-SBE: 65). Lying is apparently understood as deliberately misleading others (see Saddhatissa 1970: 106–07).

Precept 3, the prohibition against illicit sexual relations, seems to lay special emphasis on the gravity of adultery, at least so far as the householder is concerned. At verse 246 in the *Dhammapada* (D-SBE: 61), the four precepts are summarized in this way: "He who destroys life, who speaks untruth, who in this world takes what is not given to him, *who goes to another man's wife* [is] . . . in a bad state." Of course, ideally, total sexual abstinence is preferable (see below), but for those householders "not being able to live a life of [total] chastity, let him not transgress with another man's wife" (D-SBE: 65).

The evidence is inconclusive as to whether other forms of sexual incontinence, such as bestiality, are as grave as adultery for the householder. (See our discussion of *The Book of Discipline*, beginning at page 222.) If bestiality were as grave an offense, then the centrality of the human other-impinging feature would be modified to a degree. Nevertheless, whatever qualifications may be appropriate with respect to the precept against illicit sexual relations, the human other-impinging feature is undeniably central and significant, in this case as in the other three.

It is important to add here that in the dialogue materials, the character of an act, even at this elementary stage in the system, is crucially affected by *the condition of the agent*, namely by his intentions, motives, and awareness. For example, violations of the first four precepts, called, at one point, "the four vices in conduct" (DB: vol. III, 174), are "done from motives of partiality, enmity, stupidity and fear. But [the passage continues] inasmuch as [a disciple] is not led away by these motives, he through them does no evil deed." Though extensive reflection on the relation of motives and intentions to acts is not available except in the *The Book of Discipline*, it is implicit in this passage that the condition of the agent is indispensable in assessing practical behavior. "Slaughter of life, theft, adultery, and lying" are thought to occur as evil acts only if they are perpetrated from any or all of the motives mentioned.

This emphasis on the general importance of motives and intentions in Theravada practical life is reaffirmed in the *Discourse with Upali* (MLS: vol. II, 36–54). There the Buddha takes issue with an avowed Jain conviction that external action itself is most significant in evaluating an act. "I lay down that deed of mind is the more blamable in the effecting of an evil deed, in the rolling of an evil deed" (MLS: vol. II, 38). In support of this, the Buddha proceeds to show that the Jains themselves cannot avoid assessing the blameworthiness of an act according to whether the act was intentional or accidental.[1]

In respect to the precept materials, it appears that there is a distinction to be drawn between the moral acts (precepts 1–4) and what we may call "acts of personal discipline," a set of acts of the greatest importance in Theravada Buddhism. Precept 5, against the use of intoxicants, is a primary example of this latter. The act of imbibing intoxicants does not, on the face of it, seem as immediately other-impinging as the acts prohibited in precepts 1–4. Whereas life-taking, stealing, illicit sexual relations, and lying necessarily and directly involve others (with the appropriate modifications in the case of sexual relations discussed above), imbibing appears directly to involve only the agent. But while there is something in this distinction, which we shall want to make use of later on, it must not be drawn too sharply. In the dialogue materials, intoxication is understood to produce—"necessarily and directly," we may almost say—other-impinging effects. "Let the householder who approves of this [teaching], not give himself to intoxicating drinks, nor approve of those that drink, *knowing it to end in madness* [cf. GS: vol. IV, 169]. For through intoxication *the stupid commit sins and make other people intoxicated*; let him avoid *this seat of sin, this madness,* this folly, delightful to the stupid [our italics]" (SN-SBE: 66). And, in the *Sigalovada Suttanta* (DB: vol. III, 175), one of the "six dangers" of violating the fifth precept is the "increase of quarrels."[2]

In the same family as the prohibition against intoxicants are three additional precepts: (6) abstaining from "untimely food" (that is, after noontime); (7) abstaining from worldly amusements such as sports, gambling, dancing, singing, music, watching mime shows, and from using perfumes, garlands, cosmetics, and personal adornments; (8) avoiding the use of luxurious seats and beds. As far as the householder goes, these additional acts of personal discipline are to be kept periodically "on the fourteenth, fifteenth, and eighth days of the half (lunar) month" (SN-SBE: 66). Also, during these periods of special abstinence, several of the first five precepts are to be more rigorously applied: Non-killing is extended to rule out all but a vegetarian diet, and sexual restraint is interpreted as total sexual abstinence. The holy person, as well as the particulary pious householder, is required to abide by the more rigorous application of precepts 1 and 3, and to follow permanently precepts 6 through 8.[3] Finally, the holy person is required permanently to observe a prohibition against handling gold and silver (9).[4]

As with the precept against using intoxicants (5), the other acts of personal discipline apparently have a twofold objective of minimizing preoccupation with the self's own desires and inclinations, as well as of producing harmonious relations with others. For example, one of the "perils" of gambling (prohibited in precept 7) is that "it begets hatred" (DB: vol. III, 175); other perils are loss of wealth, of credibility, and so on. Precepts 5 through 9 do have an other-impinging effect, if a more indirect one than precepts 1 through 4.

There is still another set of ten precepts that is relevant in varying degrees of rigor to both the householder and the holy person. This list includes attitudes and acts that are both directly and indirectly other-impinging. Prohibitions 1, 2, 3, 4, 5, 6, and 9—respectively against taking life, theft, unchastity, lying, abuse, slander, and malevolence—proscribe other-impinging attitudes and acts. Prohibitions 7, 8, and 10—against idle talk, covetousness, and holding wrong views—are a mixture of attitudes and acts of personal discipline that, to varying degrees, may indirectly have other-impinging effects.

Over and above the formal lists of prohibitions, there are here and there unsystematic references to various kinds of attitudes and acts. For example, the extensive elaboration of the proposition, "Not by birth does one become an outcast ... by deeds one becomes an outcast" (SN-SBE: ch. 7, 20–24) restates and supplements particularly precepts 1–4 and 6–10. Several of the supplements and additions are worth noting: Avoid defaulting on debts in general and on debts of gratitude in particular; avoid bearing false witness, or covering up misdeeds.

2.1. *Duties of the Householder*

Another class of prescriptions describes the role requirements of, particularly, a householder. These prescriptions presuppose the relevant prohibitions just dealt with, but they go beyond them to outline positive requirements. The respective roles are depicted as the "six quarters":

The following should be looked upon as the six quarters: parents as the east, teachers as the south, wife and children as the west, friends and companions as the north, servants and work people as the nadir, religious teachers and Brahmins as the zenith. (DB: vol. III, 180 ff.).

Each direction has special significance in regard to the various duties of each role.

As for the eastern direction (parents-children), "eastern" in Pali is *puratthima*, which includes the word *pura*, meaning "before." Because of parental deeds done "before" for the children, certain duties are owed in return: "Once supported by them I will now be their support; I will perform duties incumbent on them; I will keep the lineage and tradition of my family; I will make myself worthy of my heritage" (DB: vol. III, 180). Parental obligations to children are as follows: "They restrain him from vice, they exhort him to virtue, they train him to a profession, they contract a suitable marriage for him, and in due time they hand over his inheritance."

In the case of the southern direction (teachers-pupils), the Pali word *dakkhina*, as adjective, means "south," and as a feminine noun (with a different etymology) it means "gift." Thus, teachers are worthy of gifts: "Pupils should minister to their teachers by rising (from their seat in salutation), by waiting upon them, by eagerness to learn, by personal service, and by attention when receiving their teaching." Similarly, teachers are givers of gifts: "They train [the pupil] in that wherein he has been well trained; they make him hold fast that which is well held; they thoroughly instruct him in the love of every art; they speak well of him among his friends and companions. They provide for his safety in every quarter" (DB: vol. III, 181).

Wife and children are the western direction, as *pacchima* ("west") has the sense of "last" or "hind part," and the wife and children "follow in back." "In five ways should a wife . . be ministered to by her husband: by respect, by courtesy, by faithfulness, by handing over authority to her, by providing her with adornment. In these five ways does the wife . . . love [her husband]: her duties are well performed, by hospitality to the kin of both, by faithfulness, by watching over the goods he brings, and by skill and industry in discharging all her business" (DB: vol. III, 181–82).

With respect to the northern direction (friends and companions), the word for "northern" (*uttara*) is related to the *uttarati*, meaning "crosses." As it is said, one "crosses" various sufferings through relying on friends and companions. "In five ways should a clansman minister to his friends and familiars . . . by generosity and benevolence, by treating them as he treats himself, and by being as good as his word. In these five ways thus ministered to . . . his friends and familiars love him: they protect him when he is off his guard, and on such occasions guard his property; they become a refuge in danger, they do not forsake him in his troubles, and they show consideration for his family" (DB: vol. III, 182).

Special and extended attention is given to the duties of friendship, probably because the model of friendship, duly reinterpreted, becomes important in shaping the requisite attitudes at "higher" levels in the practical system. From the additional guidance given to friends, we may single out the following: "The friend who is a helper is to be reckoned as sound at heart ... when you have tasks to perform he provides a double supply [of what you may need]"; "The friend who sympathizes is to be reckoned as sound at heart" (DB: vol. III, 178–79).

The friend who is a helpmate, and the friend
Of bright days and of dark, and he who shows
What 't is you need, and he who throbs for you
With sympathy [literally "one who vibrates because
of"]—these four the wise should know
As friends, and should devote himself to them
As mother to her own, her bosom's child (DB: vol. II, 179).

As to the nadir, servants and employees are those who stay at one's feet, and are thus considered in an inferior position. "In five ways does a ... master minister to his servants and employees ... by supplying them with food and wages; by tending them in sickness; by sharing with them unusual delicacies; by granting leave at times. In these ways ... servants and employees love their master ... they rise before him, they lie down to rest after him; they are content with what is given to them; they do their work well; and they carry about his praise and good fame" (DB: vol. III, 182).

Finally, the relations between the householder and the recluses and brahmins are regarded as the zenith because the recluses and brahmins stand in a spiritually superior position. "In five ways should the clansman minister to recluses and brahmins ... by affection in act and speech and mind; by keeping open house to them, by supplying their temporal needs. Thus ministered to ..., recluses and brahmins show their love for the clansmen in six ways: they restrain him from evil, they exhort him to good, they love him with kindly thoughts; they teach him what he had not heard, they correct and purify what he has heard, they reveal to him the way to heaven" (DB: vol. III, 183).

We hasten to add that while the role requirements of the various directions are positively enjoined, they are, with the exception of the recluse-householder relationship, regarded as of *inferior significance* in the general practical system. This is true because, even at its best, the life of the householder, made up as it is of his involvements with friends, family, and business associates, only reenforces his attachment to the world of self and others, the world of affection and frustration.

In him who has intercourse (with others) affections arise, (and then) the pain which follows affection; considering the misery that originates in affection let one wander alone like a rhinoceros.

He who has compassion on his friends and confidential (companions) loses (his own) advantage, having a fettered mind; seeing this danger in friendship let one wander alone like a rhinoceros.

Just as a large bamboo tree (with its branches) entangled (in each other, such is) the care one has with children and wife; (but) like the shoot of a bamboo not clinging (to anything) let one wander alone like a rhinoceros.

The sensual pleasures indeed, which are various, sweet, and charming, under their different shapes agitate the mind; seeing the misery (originating) in sensual pleasures, let one wander alone like a rhinoceros.

Having left son and wife, father and mother, wealth and corn, and relatives, the different objects of desire, let one wander alone like a rhinoceros.

Removing the characteristics of a (householder), like a Parikhatta tree whose leaves are cut off, clothed in a yellow robe after wandering away (from his house), let one wander alone like a rhinoceros (SN-SBE: 6–10).

The recommended form of life is not quite as hermitic as it sounds, for this section of the *Sutta-Nipata* goes on to urge new associations, obviously with other holy people: "Let one cultivate (the society of) a friend who is learned and keeps the Dhamma, who is magnanimous and wise; know the meaning (of things and) subduing his doubts, let one wander alone like a rhinoceros" (SN-SBE: 9). Moreover, associations with householders, when engaged in from the right motive are also acceptable. Holy persons, however, must be cautious when they teach or accept alms that they are not motivated by selfish interests, which would enmesh them in regressive relationships. Worldly contacts are always fraught with danger in this respect.

2.2. Duties of Holy Persons

While it may invite some modification,[5] Conze's assertion seems generally sound:

The core of the Buddhist movement consisted of monks. A monastic life alone will normally provide the conditions favourable to a spiritual life bent on the highest good (Conze 1959: 53).

It is fitting at this point to give some special attention to the code of conduct prescribed for holy persons themselves in the monastic *Book of Discipline.*[6]

The first major part of *The Book of Discipline* delineates five classes of offense. The first consists of the gravest offenses a holy person can commit, those that result in the severest of sanctions, "defeat" or expulsion from the monastic order. Even in this class, however, allowance is made for diminished responsibility, and therefore for reduced punishment, depending on the circumstances. The second through the fifth classes consist of decreasingly grave offenses, as designated by gradually less serious sanctions. The second class of offenses warrants a collective judgment by a formal meeting of the order, according to which a guilty offender may, for example, be placed on probation, required to start his novitiate all over again, subjected to a special discipline. (See *Discipline:* Vol. I, 196–97). The third class requires "expiation involving forfeiture," entailing the return of an illicitly acquired object; the fourth class requires (unspecified) expiation; and the fifth, expiation in the form of confession.

It is interesting that the first class is made up of violations of the first four precepts, though the first, third, and fourth have here a specified application. (In *The Book of Discipline,* the third precept, prohibiting sexual incontinence, is treated first; the second, against stealing, comes second; the first, against life-taking, comes third; and the fourth, against lying, comes fourth.) The first precept is limited to the acts of causing directly and intentionally the death of another human being, or of deliberately inciting another human being to commit suicide. All other forms of life-taking are relegated to classes of less grave offense.

With respect to taking the life of another person, the following three instances highlight the significant features according to which the degree of offense is assessed and the appropriate sanction applied; they provide a good illustration of the refinements in practical reasoning characteristic of monastic discipline.

At one time while a certain monk was eating, some meat stuck in his throat. A certain monk gave a blow to that monk's neck; the meat fell out with blood, and that monk died. [The second monk] was remorseful ... "There is no offence, monk, as you did not mean to cause his death."

At one time while a certain monk was eating, some meat stuck in his throat. A certain monk, meaning to cause his death, gave a blow to that monk's neck; the meat fell out with blood, and that monk died. [The second monk] was remorseful. ["There is an offense involving] defeat."

At one time while a certain monk was eating, some meat stuck in his throat. A certain monk, meaning to cause his death, gave a blow to that monk's neck. The meat fell out with blood, but that monk did not die. [The second monk] was remorseful ... "There is no offence involving defeat, monk; there is a grave offence" (*Discipline:* Vol. I, 139–40).

The second instance provides a model of the gravest form of violation against the first precept: (1) An agent, (2) intends the death of, (3) another human being, and (4) undertakes directly to cause the death, and (5) the death occurs. All five conditions must be satisfied for the gravest form of life-taking to happen. Variations from the model diminish the degree of gravity and of responsibility although the conditions are not equally salient. If, as in third instance, condition 2 is present, but condition 5 is not, the offense is relatively graver than if condition 5 is present and condition 2 is not, as in the first instance. As we commented earlier, intentionality is indispensable in Theravada thought for assessing responsibility, though it is not all-important. Whether or not death actually results from a malicious act influences the assessment of the offense. In other instances, negligent (unintentional but avoidable) homocide is considered to be of diminished culpability.[7]

Incitement to suicide is explicitly linked to murder, and the same model of five conditions obtains in assessing the gravity of the offense.[8]

Whatever monk should intentionally deprive a human being of life or should look about so as to be his knife-bringer, or should praise the beauty of death, or should incite (anyone) to death, saying, "Hullo there, my man, of what use to you is this evil, difficult life? Death is better for you than life," or you should deliberately and purposefully in various ways praise the beauty of death or should incite (anyone) to death: he is one who is defeated, he is not in the communion (*Discipline:* Vol. I, 125–26).

For those who, upon their death, do not attain nirvana, suicide is not a genuine remedy. Because of rebirth, such individuals still face a future of suffering. Furthermore, insofar as suicide is motivated by ignorance, it leads to a painful rebirth.

The severest violations of the second precept, against stealing, including the conditions for determining degree of gravity and responsibility, are well-exemplified in the following passage.

There is an offence involving defeat through appropriating in five ways what is not given: it is the possession of another, and known to be the possession of another, and it is important, and it is a requisite to the value of five or more *masakas,* and there is present the intention to steal. If he touches it, there is an offence of wrong-doing. If he makes it quiver, there is a grave offence. If he removes it from the place, there is an offence involving defeat (*Discipline:* Vol. I, 90–91).

The following examples are also interesting with respect to the importance of intentions in assessing action.

At one time a certain monk out of compassion released a pig trapped in a snare. He was remorseful . . . "Of what were you thinking, monk?" "I acted from a compassionate motive, lord," he said. "There is no offence, monk, since you acted from a compassionate motive."

At one time a certain monk released a pig trapped in a snare, intending to steal it "before the owners see it." He was remorseful. ["There is an offence involving] defeat." (*Discipline:* Vol. I, 105).

The gravest violations of the third precept, against sexual incontinence, are against sexual intercourse or manipulation with other human beings and animals, with undecomposed dead human beings, and against a few forms of self-manipulation. Sexual relations with "practically decomposed bodies" are less grave violations (*Discipline:* Vol. I, 57). Masturbation is normally a less serious or second-class offense, or one that involves a formal meeting of the order to pass sentence, though one form of acrobatic self-manipulation does require expulsion from the order (*Discipline:* Vol. I, 55).

The same sort of conditions that applied to the first two precepts, also apply here.

Now at one time a certain monk was lying down, having gone into the Great Wood at Vesali for the day-sojourn. A certain woman seeing him, sat down on him, and having taken her pleasure, stood laughing near by. The monk, waking up, spoke thus to the woman: "Have you done this?" "Yes, I have," she said. On account of this he was remorseful . . .
"Monk, did you consent?"
"I did not know, lord."
"Monk, there is no offence as you did not know" (*Discipline:* Vol. I, 59).

The gravest violation against the fourth precept, prohibiting lying, is restricted to the deliberate misrepresentation by a holy person of spiritual insight and accomplishment. Other forms of lying are designated as class-three offenses, warranting only expiation.

Whatever monk should boast, with reference to himself of a state of further-men, sufficient . . . knowledge and insight, though not knowing it fully, and saying: "This I know, this I see," then if later on, he, being pressed or not being pressed, fallen, should desire to be purified, and should say: "Your reverence, I said that I know what I do not know, see what I do not see, I spoke idly, falsely, vainly," apart from the undue estimate of himself, he also is one who is defeated, he is not in communion *(Discipline:* Vol. I, 159).

The reason for restricting the fourth precept to misrepresentation of the spiritual life, and dwelling at length on it, is undoubtedly that such misrepresentation impedes the essential point of the monastic life; namely, to direct others, by veridical teaching and exemplification, toward enlightenment.

Moreover, this application of the fourth precept brings out a pervasive emphasis throughout *The Book of Discipline*: that one of the chief purposes of maintaining monastic discipline is to exemplify, for the benefit of the householders, the path of enlightenment. If transgressions of any sort occur among those responsible for pointing the way, the recipients of guidance will themselves be mislead. Again and again, Buddha upbraids monastic offenders: "[What you do] is not, foolish man, for the benefit of unbelievers, nor for the increase in the number of believers, but, foolish man, it is to the detriment of both unbelievers and believers, and it causes wavering in some" (Discipline: vol. I, 37).

The classes of less grave offenses consist, as was suggested in several above examples, of many of the less serious transgressions of the first four precepts, of violations of some of the additional precepts (see pages 215–19), including the duties of personal discipline, and of the directives for sleeping, eating, rising, and so forth.

The action-guides enumerated in *The Book of Discipline* have legal characteristics, in our sense. Whatever else they are, these are all directives that are "taken as authoritative in that [they are] officially both legitimate and enforceable." The local monastic order, gathered in concert, constitutes the disciplinary agency or "staff." It is invested with the authority to interpret and pass judgment on the alleged violations of the members. "Should any member of the Order have committed, in the opinion of any other member, any breach of one of the regulations, the latter could bring forward, at the next meeting of the Chapter, a resolution on the subject" (Rhys Davids 1916: 714).

In contrast, there is little reference to any official enforcement of the practical code against householders. According to Rhys Davids, there is only one allusion to punitive measures against offending householders, and that did not gain widerspread acceptance (Rhys Davids 1916: 714).

2.3. Dana

The notion of giving (*dana*), or "liberality" or "generosity," which is, as we saw, of special importance in respect to the duties owed friends and companions and also in respect to the duties owed holy people, has a much broader significance in the Theravada system. Although there is generally little emphasis on simple material beneficence to the needy beyond the obligations for friends and holy people, there is an occasional reference to it.

Say of what folk by day and night
For ever doth the merit grow?
In righteousness and virtuous might
What folk from earth to heaven go?
Planters of groves and fruitful trees,
And they who build causeway and dam,
And wells construct and watering-sheds
And [to the homeless] shelter give:
Of such as these by day and night
For ever doeth the merit grow.
In righteousness and virtue's might
Such folk from earth to heaven go (KS: vol. III, 45).

But generally speaking, the character of an act of giving is determined more by the spiritual state of the recipient than by the degree of his material need. For example, in one account Buddha ascertains the worth of a gift of food according to the level of spiritual advancement of the one who receives the food.

For, though brahman Velama gave that very rich gift, greater would have been the fruit thereof, had he fed one person of the right view [rather than

just anyone].... Or though he fed a hundred persons of right view, greater
would have been the fruit thereof, had he fed on Once-returner ... Or
though he fed a hundred Once-returners, greater would have been the fruit
thereof, had he fed one Non-returner ... though he fed a hundred Non-
returners, greater would have been the fruit thereof, had he fed one
Arahant ... though he fed a hundred Arahants, greater would have been
the fruit thereof, had he fed one silent Buddha ... though he fed a hundred
silent Buddhas, greater would have been the fruit thereof, had he fed one
Tathagata, arahant, fully awake ... though he fed the Order of monks,
with the Buddha at their head, greater would have been the fruit thereof,
had he built a monastery for the use of the monks of the Order of the
surrounding country (GS: vol. IV, 264–65).

In our terms, many of the prescribed acts of giving, such as
supplying the temporal needs of holy people, friends and companions, and "the needy," are other-impinging in two ways. These acts
clearly impinge in an important way on the material welfare of the
recipient, whether he is a high-status holy person, a friend, or simply
one who is homeless. Accordingly, they are moral acts. Secondly,
the enjoined acts are conceived in such a way as to require on the
part of the giver some positive consideration of the welfare of the
recipient; in other words, the acts involve moral attitudes.

Monks, these five are a good man's gifts; What five? He gives a gift in faith,
with deference, in time, with unconstrained heart, [and] *he gives a gift
without hurt to self or others* (GS: vol. III, 130, italics supplied).

The fact that the spiritual position of the recipient affects the worth
of the gift in no way lessens with the importance of considering the
material welfare of the recipient, or eliminates the significance of
acts of material beneficence to different sorts of people.

Still, the phrase "He gives a gift without hurt to self or others"
suggests an important distinction between *material* and *spiritual*
welfare that will soon become obvious. The commentary (rather
tersely, to be sure) construes this pregnant utterance to require
giving so as not to "hurt the virtue" of self or others. If that
plausible construction is admitted, then we may infer that no gift is
permissible that in any way violates the basic precepts of the
Theravada system (precepts 1–5), or where relevant, any of the
additional precepts (for example, 6–8, or 6–10). If an agent offered
a gift that would cause the death of the recipient, the agent would
clearly "hurt his own virtue" by depriving the victim of material

existence. Or if he offered a gift that would cause the recipient to violate precepts 2–4 or any of the acts of personal discipline, the gift would "hurt [the virtue of] self and others." In this way, the agent is required to consider not only the material effects of a gift (where relevant), but also the "spiritual effects," that is, whether a gift retards or advances the spiritual achievement of the recipient.

Further, the phrase about giving so as not to hurt self and others entails an intermingling of other-regarding concerns with concerns for personal discipline. Presumably, it is as wrong to disregard the other's material and spiritual welfare as it is to disregard one's own.

This discussion of giving leads us naturally to a pivotal subject in the Theravada practical code: the meaning and role of the virtue of sympathy (*anukampa*) and simple compassion, which are virtually synonymous. Here we draw shamelessly on the work of Aronson 1975. Aronson demonstrates that in the dialogues and commentaries sympathy is conceptually distinct from any of the meditative attitudes, the so-called sublime attitudes: love, compassion, sympathetic joy, and equanimity. Indeed, as we shall see, it has a somewhat different objective and character from these.

Sympathy implies both attitudes and acts of an other-regarding sort. According to the dialogues, the Buddha was motivated to concern himself with the "welfare and happiness of gods and men," and to engage in benevolent action, out of an attitude of sympathy.

Monks, there is one individual who arose and came to be for the welfare of the multitudes, for the happiness of the multitudes, out of sympathy for the world, for the profit, welfare, and happiness of gods and men. Who is that one individual? The Harmonious One, the Worthy One, the Perfectly Enlightened One (Aronson 1975: 120).

The sort of action implied can apparently include concern for the material well-being of a friend, companion, or needy person, as we already noted. At one point, the Buddha cites the case of removing a sharp object from the mouth of a child. He points out that the nurse will remove the object, even though the operation may be painful to the child.

Monks, it is done in this way out of sympathy. The nurse desires [the child's] profit, wishes for [his] welfare and is sympathetic (Aronson 1975: 137).

And surely we may continue to assume, as we did in the case of gift-giving, that no attitude or action that violated the prohibitions protecting the material well-being of others (precepts 1–4 and, indirectly, the acts of personal discipline) could be considered sympathetic.

But undoubtedly of greatest valence among those acts that manifest sympathy is *spiritual instruction,* or revealing the way to higher rebirth or nirvana. As Aronson notes: "The fact that no other action is mentioned as frequently in connection with sympathy as teaching, can lead us to infer that according to the discourses the most highly regarded form of sympathy was helpful instruction" (Aronson 1975: 131).

Monks, go and travel around for the welfare of the multitudes, for the happiness of the multitudes, out of sympathy for the world, for the profit, welfare, and happiness of gods and men. Two should not go on one [path]. Monks teach the dharma which is beneficial at the start, beneficial in the middle and beneficial at the end (Aronson 1975: 150).

So understood, instruction, as the most important manifestation of sympathy, is the special province of holy people. Only monastics and particularly pious householders are in a position to exhibit the virtue of sympathy in its fullest form, for they alone are sufficiently enlightened to instruct others.

Two other important expressions of sympathy, besides instruction, are related to the holy person's exalted spiritual status: exemplification of the way to nirvara and the reception of alms (Aronson 1975: 138–140).

Although concern for both the material and spiritual welfare of specified others is recognized, either implicitly or explicitly, in relation to sympathy, it is obvious that regard for *spiritual* welfare is paramount. The essence of sympathy is the communication of spiritual enlightenment, for the welfare of the multitudes is most fully improved by such enlightenment.

This point is unmistakable when the commentaries interpret the meaning of "welfare" and "profit":

For when, *for the profit,* is said, for the sake of the ultimate truth, for the sake of nirvana, is meant. When, *for the welfare,* is said, for the sake of the path which leads to it [nirvana], is meant. For there is no higher benefit than the path which leads to nirvana (Aronson 1975: 129–30).

Moreover, the dialogues and commentaries stress that Buddha

himself, exhibiting the ideal form of sympathy, "was not taken over by his sympathy and bound by it which is the case with worldly individuals" (Aronson 1975: 132). And when the Buddha is tempted by Mara, the evil deity, to forsake teaching from sympathy because it produces bonds of personal affection, the Buddha answered:

The Harmonious One is sympathetic to others' welfare. He is enlightened. When he teaches he is liberated from satisfaction and dissatisfaction (Aronson 1975: 132–33).

In expressing sympathy for the suffering of others, the Buddha displays a sympathy that is permeated with balance. It precludes any emotional entanglement, as well as any of the "tainted" attitudes of greed or aversion, for his sympathy arose within the context of his belief that in the ultimate sense there is no sentient being, and thus no one with whom attachment would make any sense. Spiritual enlightenment, then, drastically, recasts the ordinary attitude of sympathy, and, beyond that, introduces a somewhat paradoxical element. While holding that in the ultimate sense there are no selves and others, the Buddha provisionally accepts the existence of selves with individual material and spiritual identity, and he proceeds to alleviate their suffering through teaching and exemplification.

Hence, sympathy, as discussed, presupposes the experience of suffering by individual persons, and, therefore, the intelligibility of a provisional concern by one actor for the welfare, or decrease of suffering, of another. So understood, we can make sense of the role of other-regarding considerations that are attached to the notion of sympathy, even though these considerations must, in the final analysis, dissolve along with the dissolution of the concepts of self and others.

This provisional emphasis on other-regarding considerations is relatively much greater in respect to the notion of sympathy than in respect to the sublime attitudes, with which sympathy must, to some degree, be contrasted.[9] The sublime attitudes—love, compassion, sympathetic joy, and equanimity—are essentially *meditative techniques or practices*. They have as their objective liberating the meditator's mind from all aversive attitudes: enmity or anger, harmfulness, displeasure, and lust, thus preparing him for ultimate insight, or the realization of nirvana. They are, in our terms, techniques of personal discipline. They appear to be distinguished, in the dialogues and commentaries, from the attitude of sympathy, which is other-regarding or "social" in a more direct and active sense than they are.

The . . . attitudes love, compassion, sympathetic joy and equanimity culti-vated as a group according to the method of the fourfold instructions are never discussed in terms of fraternal activities. The sublime [attitudes] are discussed in terms of the benefits they bring to the meditator. Thus, though we may feel that every discussion of social attitudes entails a discussion of the social activities which flow from these attitudes, the Theravada dis-courses and commentaries do not accept this premise (Aronson 1975: 372).

The effects of these practices [of the sublime attitudes] is to be sought in the practitioner, not in the other. The fact that the criteria for judging the success of these practices are internal criteria gives these practices a unique flavor. The approach . . . can be contrasted with the approach of a recipient oriented fraternalism which would judge itself by its effects on others (Aronson 1975: 355).

It is never said that a meditator's practice should be judged by the effects it produces in others. The criteria for success in the cultivation of love, compassion, sympathetic joy and equanimity would be the meditator's skill in entering and sustaining absorption, and his skill in abandoning the respective opposites of love and so forth (Aronson 1975: 357).

"The teachings concerning social *activity* occur in the discussions on the social attitudes sympathy and simple compassion . . . but not in the discussions of [the sublime attitudes]" (Aronson 1975: 370–71). Thus, sympathy, appears to stand, to some degree, on its own so far as implying direct other-regarding attitudes and acts. Moreover, it is clear that the cultivation of the sublime attitudes is not necessary in order to engage in "fraternal activities."

This is unusual because the first three sublime attitudes at least appear "social" or other-regarding in character. According to the commentaries, "love" (*metta*) is "the wish for others' welfare"; "compassion" (*karuna*) is "the wish that others be free from suffering"; and "sympathetic joy" (*mudita*) is "joy in others' success." For example, the *Mettasutta* describes love as follows:

Let no one deceive another, let him not despise (another) in any place, let him not out of anger or resentment wish harm to another. As a mother at the risk of her life watches over her own child, her only child, so also let everyone cultivate a boundless (friendly) mind towards all beings. And let him cultivate goodwill towards all the world, a boundless (friendly) mind, above and below and across, unobstructed, without hatred, without enmity (SN–SBE: 25).

Social implications might seem to follow from the cultivation of such an attitude, and it is true that love may have certain benefits in regard to human beings and others,[10] namely, that other human beings may regard the meditator "more dearly," and that he might successfully protect himself and others by the force of a loving mind (Aronson 1975: 231).

However, these are decidedly side effects, and they do not necessarily happen. *Above all, they do not constitute the point of the cultivation of love.* Rather, as Aronson's words indicate, the most important point of the cultivation of love and the other sublime attitudes is to develop "absorption" through stages of deepening mental concentration, and thereby to prepare the way for the highest insight—the realization of nirvana (Aronson 1975: 222–24). In that realization, as we would expect, there comes the temporary dissolution of the concept of the self and the other such that "love in its usual [other-regarding] sense cannot occur" (Aronson 1975: 194). The direct object of one's concentration, nirvana, presupposes the dissolution of the concept of the self. Thus, the most important use of love is to serve as a basis for overcoming the belief in the existence of the self and the other through the techniques of meditation. Of course, since the notion of the "realization of nirvana" implies only a temporary awareness, one returns subsequent to the experience to a provisional acknowledgement of self and others, and carries on as though they truly existed. Strictly speaking, one's relation to oneself and others is qualified by the conviction that ultimately one does not exist.

The same description applies to the sublime attitudes of compassion and sympathetic joy. They are putatively other-regarding. But they have as their ultimate objective the cultivation, by meditative means, of that level of absorption necessary to the realization of the highest insight in which other-regardingness is unintelligible, because there are no persons of whom to be aware.

There are several distinct forms of equanimity in Theravada Buddhism, one of which is the sublime attitude equanimity. The sublime attitude, like the other forms of equanimity, consists of "constituential balance" or the proper balancing of the constituents of a wholesome mind. Any truly virtuous attitude or act will require equanimity in this sense as a necessary condition.

Of special interest to us is equanimity as a sublime attitude and as a "limb of enlightenment." As a sublime attitude, equanimity means "balance with regard to sentient beings" (Aronson 1975: 268). But the sublime attitude equanimity, in which a mind of "balanced detachment" exists, can occur only *after* the other three sublime attitudes have been fully developed, and then transcended. "There is danger in love and sympathetic joy in that the practitioner may become attracted or attached to the other's well-being. There is danger in compassion in that the practitioner may develop dislike for certain conditions and experience the mental grief associated with aversion" (Aronson 1975: 269). In other words, the first three sublime attitudes, which are constituted so as to be instrumental in the final dissolution of the concept of the self and others, as well as in the elimination of all desire and aversion associated with those notions, appear after all to be too congenial to the notions of self and other, and too readily attached to another's well-being.

The sublime attitude equanimity purges all such debilitating tendencies from the other sublime attitudes and is, accordingly, most conducive to the development of the "limb of enlightenment" equanimity, the balance of mind necessary for the realization of nirvana.[11] We emphasize that in developing both the sublime attitude equanimity, and the limb of enlightenment equanimity, use is made of the contemplation that *"in the ultimate sense there is no sentient being."* This contemplation is conducive to creating balance with regard to provisionally accepted sentient beings, balance constitutive of the sublime attitude equanimity. At a still more profound level, it is conducive to creating balance with regard to the realization of nirvana—which is the fullest realization that in the ultimate sense there is no sentient being. This realization constitutes the fulfillment of the meditative objective.

Before turning to the matter of justification and the structure of the code, we must comment directly on the religious and moral character of the content of the action-guides, and on their relation to the legal aspects we identified in our discussion of *The Book of Discipline.*

We have seen that the Theravada practical system places considerable emphasis on prescriptions and prohibitions of an other-impinging nature. The dialogues explicitly prefer "moral" attitudes and acts to certain kinds of "religious" acts, namely, the observance of conventional ascetic and ritualistic practices. According to the *Sutta-Nipata,* what purifies is not "the flesh of fish, nor fasting, nor nakedness, nor tonsure, . . . nor the worshipping of the fire, nor the many immortal penances in the world, nor hymns, nor oblations, nor sacrifices" (SN–SBE: 41; cf. D–SBE: 38–39).

Destroying living beings, killing, cutting, binding, stealing, speaking false-hood, fraud and deception, worthless reading, intercourse with another's wife; . . . this is [defiling], but not the eating of flesh (SN–SBE; 40).

This persistent preference appears to lend plausibility to the frequent assertion that "the religion of the Buddha *is* morality" (cited in King 1964: 3). On one level at least Theravada Buddhism does encourage the cultivation of certain social attitudes and acts, attitudes and acts that reflect a regard for the material integrity and welfare of others. No enlightened Theravidin might ever, at any stage of his development, violate the basic other-protecting precepts of the system. Moreover, even the "acts of personal discipline"—those acts (and attitudes) that are putatively less "social"—are also seen to have indirect social effects.

Finally, the central role assigned to the virtues of sympathy and generosity underlines the moral or other-impinging side of the system. The benevolent concern for the suffering of others displayed in Buddha's teachings and life is premised on the principles of noninjury, nonaggressiveness and forthrightness in dealing with the lives and property of others.

Nevertheless, with all the importance of these features, there can be no doubt that the content of the action-guides, when systematically analyzed, is, in the last analysis, religious in character (according to our usage). All moral attitudes and acts are consistently modified by a belief in a sacred authority (nirvana) that not only drastically subordinates the material welfare of others in favor of their spiritual enlightenment, but also, and even more importantly, disallows the ultimate reality of selves and others.

We noted that a sympathic commitment to relieve the suffering of others was *provisional* within Theravada thought. It is provisional, we conclude, because that commitment is, like all the action-guides, understood in relation to the sacred authority, nirvana, whose attainment renders all considerations of self and other unintelligible. The conception of sacred authority systematically conditions the character of each and every action-guide, even though considerable provisional room is made for moral attitudes and acts.

There is nothing complicated about the relation of this system of religious action-guides to legal action-guides. *The Book of Discipline* makes clear that a particular application of the practical system takes on a legal character insofar as it is the subject of institutionalized interpretation and enforcement.

3. THE STRUCTURE OF THERAVADIN PRACTICAL TEACHING

3.1. *Patterns of Validation*

There appear to be three disjunctive patterns of validation in the Theravada system. They are logical possibilities given the dialogue and commentary materials. They are not all of equal importance, however, though the presence of all three may cause some strain in the tradition.

We call the first a pattern of *qualified intrapersonal teleology (or transpersonal teleology 1)*; the second, a pattern of *qualified extrapersonal teleology (or transpersonal teleology 2);* and the third, a pattern of *unqualified intrapersonal teleology.*

Theravada Buddhism manifests a teleological bias with respect to practical justification. In the three various ways mentioned, the *effects* or *consequences* of attitudes and acts determine practical goodness and badness, rightness and wrongness. We have encountered no evidence of deontological reasoning. But among the three types, the *kind* of effects vary, as does the *point of reference:* good or bad consequences for whom? In the first two types, the concept of nirvana directly qualifies the kinds of consequences taken to be desirable. In the third type, the notion of desirable consequences is independent of the concept of nirvana.

As to reference points, for the first type (at least to begin with) and for the third type it is the self and its own individual good: for the second type it is "the good and happiness of the great multitudes." We remain finally uncertain whether the first type constitutes an independent pattern of justification, or whether it ought to be subsumed under, and modified by, the second type of justification. Since we are uncertain, it seems best both to sketch the first type as an independent pattern, and also to indicate a possible way of subsuming the first under the second type of justification.

Throughout the dialogues one occasionally encounters references such as the following:

Be zealous, I beseech you, Anada, in your own behalf! Devote yourselves to your own good! Be earnest, be zealous, be intent on your own good! (DB: vol. II, 154).

If it is the case, first, that one's own good excludes the good of others to an imporant degree, that one can attain "the highest happiness," the realization of nirvana, without directly benefitting any beside the self, and second, that one is encouraged so to do, then we have the makings of an intrapersonal validating pattern. In relation to the content of the Theravada code, discussed in section 2, it looks something like this:

Premise 1: (Basic norm.) Each person ought to maximize his own happiness (minimize his own suffering).

Premise 2: The happiness of each person is maximized (suffering minimized) in the realization of nirvana.

Premise 3: Nirvana is realized by adopting and developing the teachings and practices of Buddha (see section 2).

Conclusion: Each person ought to adopt and develop Buddha's teachings and practices (see section 2).

To bring out the "qualified" character of this intrapersonal pattern of justification, we must add one more premise:

Premise 1: (Basic norm.) Each person ought to maximize his own happiness (minimize his own suffering).

Premise 2: The happiness of each person is maximized (suffering minimized) in the realization of nirvana.

Premise 3: Nirvana is only realized in the awareness of the dissolution of the concept of the person ("self-conquest").

Premise 4: Nirvana is realized by adopting and developing the teachings and practices of Buddha. (see section 2).

Conclusion: Each person ought to adopt and develop the teachings and practices of Buddha, according to which the concept of the person dissolves.

Several things must be noted about the second version of the pattern. First, insofar as nirvana constitutes a sacred authority and is thus a part of a religious position (see pages 213–14), this appeal is religiously qualified. And insofar as moral attitudes and acts are justified by this pattern, this is a *religious-moral system.*

Second, this pattern appears to provide a warrant for certain features of the sublime attitudes that we noted. The point of reference from which to evaluate the effects of cultivating the sublime attitudes was expressly the good of the meditator himself, and not the good of others who may have been contemplated in the meditative exercise. In addition, there is an explicit reference in the dialogues to the instrumental value that contemplating the good of others has for the achievement of one's own absorption (GS: vol. III, 137–40; cf. Aronson 1975: 246–52). Such a reference subordinates other-regardingness to intrapersonal or self-oriented concerns, just as the practice of the sublime attitudes appears to do.

Were this the pervasive and predominant pattern within Theravada Buddhism, all other-impinging attitudes and acts would similarly become instrumental to the achievement of the self's own good. For example, when the *Dhammapada* states, "The sages who injure nobody, and who always control their body, . . . will go to the unchangeable place (nirvana), where, if they have gone, they will suffer no more" (D-SBE: 58), then the prohibition against injury would be justified in respect to helping *the sage himself* attain nirvana.

Though the positive injunction to liberality is in fact frequently justified by an appeal to self-interest, the same cannot generally be said of appeals to sympathy. Thus, it would be a mistake to leave the impression that the pattern of qualified intrapersonal teleology is actually the pervasive and predominant pattern in the tradition. It appears to be in tension with the other two patterns, and it may even be subsumable under the second. Some evidence does exist, however, in favor of designating this as an independent pattern. Also, it does account for certain important emphases in the Theravada practical system.

Qualified extrapersonal teleology (transpersonal teleology 2) is the second apparent validating pattern in Theravada Buddhism. In his discussion of the concept sympathy, Aronson makes the following important observation:

It is interesting to note that it is not said in the discourses that the meditations on love, etc., precede sympathy. Nor for that matter is it said that the meditations on love, etc., precede a devotion to others' welfare, etc. The impression conveyed in the discourses is that sympathy and the words and phrases associated with it were easily understood and accepted as proper motivations for religious activity. The Buddha is shown appealing to others' sympathy in the discourses. However he is not in turn shown justifying sympathy. Sympathy, it appears, needs no justification. It was apparently easily experienced and accepted as a valid motivation for fraternal activity by the populace described in the discourses (Aronson 1975: 125).

Several things require comment. First, "sympathy" is to be understood as "devotion to others' welfare" or somewhat more specifically as *devotion to maximizing the welfare (minimizing the suffering) of others, including all human beings.*[13] The principle is "extrapersonal" (as defined in Part I, Chap. 5, 3.1) in that, to begin with, it presupposes the provisional existence of selves capable of experiencing both satisfaction and suffering, and it commits one to acting so as to increase their satisfaction and decrease their suffering. The principle is also teleological since it presupposes that attitudes and actions are justified with reference to maximizing satisfaction and minimizing suffering.

Second, this principle is simply accepted as valid. It needed no justification but, in our terms, it is itself a basic norm. As an example of this principle we may recall Buddha's injunction to the monks, quoted earlier:

Monks, go and travel around for the welfare of the multitudes, for the happiness of the multitudes, out of sympathy for the world, for the profit, welfare, and happiness of gods and men. Two should not go on one [path]. Monks teach the dharma which is beneficial at the start, beneficial in the middle and beneficial at the end (quoted in Aronson 1975: 150).

There are other formulations, among them the refrain repeated throughout portions of the *Maha Parinibbana Suttanta:*

Therefore, O brethren—ye to whom the truths I have perceived have been made known by me—having thoroughly made yourselves masters of them, practise them, meditate upon them, and spread them abroad; in order that pure religion may last long and be perpetuated, in order that it may continue to be for the good and happiness of the great multitudes, out of pity for the world, to the good and gain and the weal of gods and men! (DB: vol. II, 127).

And in the *Sutta-Nipata* it states:

As in a clump of trees with their tops in bloom in the first heat of the hot month, so (Buddha) taught the excellent Dhamma leading to Nibbana to the greatest benefit (for all). This excellent jewel (is found) in Buddha, by this truth may there be salvation (SN-SBE:39).

These passages not only exemplify a basic extrapersonal teleological principle, but also help to identify in what way the principle is "qualified." "The excellent Dhamma leading to Nibbana," which ought to be made available to all through teaching and exemplification, has the effect of maximizing the "good and happiness of the great multitudes" precisely by revealing the illusion of the concept of personhood. Thus, one maximally promotes the happiness (relieves the suffering) of all persons by revealing, through instruction and practical exemplification, the ultimate nonexistence of all persons. Given this basic Theravadin belief, the basic norm, as we have described it, can reflect a commitment to "extrapersonal welfare" *only in a highly qualified and rather paradoxical sense.* Nevertheless, such a commitment is present and important in the Theravadin tradition.

Furthermore, as was the case in the first pattern, the kind of qualification is a religious one, since the qualifying concept, the notion of nirvana, constitutes a sacred authority and is thus part of a religious position. The whole point of the practical system is to realize a religious objective: nirvana. A representative syllogism, composed so as to bring out the religious qualification of the basic norm, would work as follows:

Premise 1: (Basic norm.) To maximize welfare (minimize suffering) of all others, including all human persons, is right and ought to be done.

Premise 2: The welfare of all human persons is maximized by means of the full adoption and development (in belief and practice) of Buddha's doctrines.

Premise 3: The doctrines of Buddha ("religious" by definition) contain a fundamental belief in the ultimate unreality of human persons.

Premise 4: The doctrines of Buddha are best made available for adoption and development by teaching and exemplifying them.

Conclusion: One ought to adopt and develop Buddha's doctrines and, by teaching and exemplification, make them available to human persons, doctrines ("religious" by definition) that contain a fundamental belief in the ultimate unreality of human persons.

Again, as was the case for the first pattern, and for the very same reasons, this is a *religious-moral system.*

According to this pattern, it is understood that each individual is finally responsible to appropriate for himself the doctrines of Buddha and thereby find his own way toward nirvana. Indeed, it is implicit in premise 2 and premise 4 that all one person can do for another is make the doctrines available by teaching and exemplification. "The pure and impure stand and fall by themselves, no one can purify another" (D-SBE: 46). "You yourself must make an effort. The Tathagathas (Buddhas) are only preachers" (D-SBE: 67).

However, an enlightened individual, to the extent he can, is bound on this pattern to help others find enlightenment and, consequently, happiness (release from suffering), *out of concern for the welfare of others.* Despite the one reference we cited (see page 237), few passages suggest that an individual ought to help others because he will thereby improve his own chances for the realization of nirvana. On the contrary, as the words from Aronson indicate, there is remarkably little interest in the dialogues in justifying the principle of sympathy at all. It appears to stand by itself.

Moreover, the principle of sympathy appears to justify Buddha's own mission:

I shall not die . . . until the brethren and sisters of the Order, and until the lay-disciples of either sex shall have become true hearers, wise and well-trained, ready and learned, carrying the doctrinal books in their memory, masters of the lesser corollaries that follow from the larger doctrine, correct in life, walking according to the precepts—until they, having thus themselves learned the doctrine, shall be able to tell others of it, preach it, make it known, establish it, open it, minutely explain it and make it clear—until they, when others start vain doctrine easy to be refuted by the truth, shall be able in refuting it, to spread the wonder-working truth abroad! (DB: vol. II, 112).

Were this pattern the predominant and pervasive one within Theravada Buddhism, then all self-oriented concern for achieving happiness through living an upright life and cultivating sucessful meditative techniques would be justified with respect to the general good—that is, the maximization of the happiness of the greatest number of others, including human persons. All efforts at self-development—a virtuous life, attaining the highest levels of absorption, and the ultimate realization of nirvana—would all, presumably, be undertaken because they were believed to contribute to "the good and happiness of the great multitudes."

There are problems, however, in arguing that this pattern is the predominant and pervasive one. We have seen that the cultivation of the sublime attitudes explicitly *does not* have an extrapersonal objective. The meditator is instructed to "use" contemplation of the welfare of others self-consciously for the achievement of *the meditator's own* ultimate enlightenment. Moreover, since an important goal of achieving enlightenment in the Theravada system is to experience the dissolution of the concepts of self and other, it is hard to see—on one level, at least—the grounds for a thoroughgoing other-regarding or extrapersonal commitment.

On the other hand, it is possible that for the Theravadin tradition all acts of self-purification, including meditation unto the realization of nirvana, are conceived of as other-regarding as well as self-regarding, in that they *exemplify* the path of enlightenment for others—with "others" understood in our provisional and qualified sense. The Buddha's own example, along with many scriptural references, gives support to this understanding. If this interpretation is correct, then the apparently intrapersonal evidence advanced in support of the first pattern could be subsumed under this second type.

We are not competent to settle the question as to whether the tension between the two types of transpersonal teleology is finally resolvable within the Theravada system. At this stage, we prefer simply to identify and elucidate what seem to be two discrete types of justifying pattern, and to provide reasons for suggesting a strain between them.

Unqualified intrapersonal teleology is the third apparent validating pattern in Theravada Buddhism.

Throughout the dialogues Buddha makes recurrent allusion to the karmic consequences—the accumulations of "merit" or "demerit"—that result from good or bad action.

Alvaka said: "How does one obtain understanding? how does one acquire wealth? how does one obtain fame? how does one bind friends (to himself)? how does one not grieve passing away from this world to the other?"

[Buddha] said: "He who believes in the Dhamma of the venerable ones as to the acquisition of Nibbana, will obtain understanding from his desire to hear, being zealous and discerning.

He who does what is proper, who takes the yoke (upon him and) exerts himself, will acquire wealth, by truth he will obtain fame, and being charitable he will bind friends (to himself) . . . [that person] does not grieve when passing away."

Or, again:

Monks, there are these eight rebirths due to making gifts. What eight?

Herein monks, a man makes a gift to a recluse or godly man in the shape of food, drink, raiment, a vehicle, flowers, scent, ointment, bedding, dwelling and lights. He gives hoping for a return. He sees wealthy nobles, brahmans, and householders surrounded by, attended by, enjoying the five strands of sensuous pleasure, and thinks: "Ah, if only I can be reborn among them, on the breaking up of the body after death!" And he fixes his mind on this thought, directs his attention to it and makes the thought become . . . and he is reborn after death among the wealthy . . . And I say this of the virtuous, not of the vicious. Monks, the mental aspiration of the virtuous prospers because of its purity, (GS: vol. IV, 163–64).

In other words, with reference to this pattern, there is a fixed calculus of consequences applicable to those individuals who are still enmeshed in the karmic cycle of rebirth. For them, the action-guides set forth in section 2 are justified by their utility for maximizing the well-being of the actor, whether on earth in the next birth, or in "heaven." Violation of those action-guides, of course, produces disutility with respect to the same end, either in the next birth, or in "hell." Syllogistically, the pattern is simple:

Premise 1:   (Basic norm.) Each person ought to maximize his own happiness (minimize his own suffering).

Premise 2:   Happiness and suffering are defined with reference to an experiencing person.

Premise 3:   Adopting and developing the doctrines of Buddha will maximize (material, spiritual) happiness (minimize suffering), according to the calculus of karmic consequences.

Conclusion: Each person ought to adopt and develop the doctrines of Buddha.

Notice that this pattern is "unqualified" in that the person or agent remains in tact as the subject of satisfaction/suffering, whether his satisfaction/suffering is of a material or spiritual sort. Within the karmic realm, one acts "as if" there existed perduring individual centers or units of desire/aversion—divine, human, and sub-human—centers that are "driven," so to speak, by a pleasure principle, a principle of intrapersonal utility.

However, from the point of view of the dialogues, this is decidedly a secondary or subsidiary pattern of validation. After all, the avowed and consistent objective of the system is to escape from the realm of desire and aversion, the realm governed by a principle of intrapersonal utility. "There is no satisfying lusts, even by a shower of gold pieces; he who knows that lusts have a short taste and cause pain, he is wise; even in heavenly pleasures he finds no satisfaction; the disciple who is fully awakened delights only in the destruction of all desires" (D-SBE: 51).

While it is true, then, that this pattern is present, and is appealed to, we must assume that it is employed as a concession to spiritually retarded individuals. However real the karmic realm may appear, it is ultimately "seen through" by enlightened individuals.

We have not discovered much direct evidence in the dialogues concerning the mode of validation employed in Theravada Buddhism. It seems obvious, however, that the *mode of interpretation* would be the appropriate type in all cases. Only a restricted class of individuals, of course, is eligible to make authoritative pronouncements on practical matters, namely, that class of individuals advanced in achieving the virtues of the Eightfold Path. The most advanced—the Buddha himself—would naturally be the most authoritative, and thus his teachings constitute the foundation of all practical guidance. Thereafter, the authority of practical utterances would be calculated according to the degree of spiritual achievement manifested by the utterer. It would be assumed that those of low spiritual estate would not themselves be sufficiently enlightened to provide reliable guidance for themselves or others. In face of practical difficulties or uncertainties, born as they are of ignorance, it follows that those who possess clarity of vision and special insight, would alone be able to determine satisfactory solutions.

While there is room, then, for discretionary interpretation on the part of "spiritual experts," spiritual expertise is itself determinable according to commonly available standards of enlightenment and rectitude manifested in the life and teachings of the Buddha. In other words, there exist, as there must so far as the mode of interpretation is concerned, general standards and restrictions within which and on the basis of which all practical application must proceed. The action-guides we analysed in section 2 constitute these general standards and restrictions.

3.2. Patterns of Vindication

Behind the three validating patterns is a relatively unified set of vindicating cosmological and anthropological beliefs. The beliefs apply to all three validating systems, although, particularly in the case of unqualified intrapersonal teleology, certain aspects of the belief system are emphasized more than others.

The set of cosmological and anthropological beliefs is perhaps best organized around the complex concept of "dharma." Buddhists themselves use the word *dharma* to describe what outsiders call "Buddhism." The concept involves a number of different denotations (see Conze 1970: 92–96), several of which are of direct relevance to our inquiry. Ontologically understood, it means both "the order of the law of the universe, immanent, eternal, uncreated," and "a transcendental reality which is real in absolute truth and in the ultimate sense" (Conze 1970: 93). The "supreme dharma" or "the object of supreme knowledge" is of course nirvana, in relation to which the phenomenal world is understood as evanescent and unreliable.

In addition, dharma refers to the basic law of conduct. To live in harmony with dharma, to be a *dharmika,* is to orient one's life and character toward "the supreme dharma," nirvana, and to cultivate those practices, dispositions, and meditative abilities that eventually produce the attainment of nirvana, which is total conformity with the requirements of dharma.

So far as the Theravadin view of normative human nature goes, this understanding entails *a radical depersonalization of humanity.* As we have seen, this is accomplished by coming to understand that the ordinary notion of human self or personality is in actuality a reified construct mistakenly imposed on the five *skandhas* or constituents, which are form, feelings, perceptions, impulses, and consciousness. In other words, to comprehend dharma is to perceive the unreality of the concept "self," by reducing all putative selves to their more basic elementary constituents. This belief in the ultimate unreality of the concept of human self comprises, as we have stressed, the *annatta,* or "no-self" doctrine.

While the dissolution of the concept of self is unquestionably the overarching belief that "qualifies" all reflection on human nature, there is an accompanying (and, as we have pointed out, somewhat puzzling) belief in the provisional reality of conventionally understood human selves. Such a conviction is required in order to make sense of the commitment to sympathy as one validating standard (transpersonal teleology[2]). According to that standard, the aspiration to achieve happiness and avoid suffering of ordinary sentient selves is acknowledged and respected by teaching and exemplifying enlightenment in the world. Such activities are explicitly undertaken by the Buddha and recommended to his followers "for the welfare of the multitudes, . . . [for] the profit, welfare and happiness of gods and men."

As far as we can determine, there is no expressed reflection or "vindicative" elaboration of the crucial assumptions that underlie this commitment to relieve the suffering of ultimately nonexistent beings. Without such assumptions, the worthwhileness of delaying the attainment of nirvana in favor of serving the needs of human beings, as the Buddha did, would not make sense.

Let us reemphasize that there is one special feature of the cosmological and anthropological beliefs held by the Theravadins that renders this system, finally, a religious-moral one. The commitment to serve the aspirations of conventionally understood human selves is qualified by a belief in a sacred authority (nirvana, "the supreme dharma") according to which the concept of the self (and other) is, dissolved. The commitment to sympathy is religiously qualified in that the notion of welfare is defined in reference to a sacred authority whose character precludes, in the last analysis, understanding welfare in a material, other-regarding sense.

Nevertheless, there is the provisional acknowledgment of individual selves (and others), together with their desire for happiness and their aversion to suffering. This acknowledgment includes provisional legitimation of the ordinary human inclinations to material self-protection (body, wealth, wards), and accordingly Theravada Buddhism prescribes moral rules concerning other-impinging attitudes and acts. At the same time, these moral rules are clearly justified from a religious point of view when the appropriate qualifications are taken into account. Fundamentally, morality, while present and important in Theravadin thought, is there provisionally at best. "In the ultimate sense," which is to say when looked at in respect to "the supreme dharma," discussion of morality is inappropriate because the notion of morality presupposes persons, or at least intentions normally associated with persons, and these are not found in nirvana. This sketch of basic cosmological and anthropological beliefs supports both types of the transpersonal teleological validating pattern.

The vindicatory beliefs of special relevance to the third validating pattern (unqualified intrapersonal teleology) concern the laws of karma which are still another aspect of the encompassing notion of dharma. For our purposes, the brief account of karma contained on pages 211–12 will suffice. We may simply add that karma applies to the conventionally accepted but provisional realities such as the existence of selves, and it is taken as (provisionally) governing their behavior as indicated in our analysis on pages 211–12. It follows, of course, that those spiritually successful in attaining nirvana are no longer subject to the laws of karma.

NOTES

1. See MLS: vol. II, 41–42. The issue is complicated in the dialogue when the Buddha goes on later to contend that "acts of mind" are causally more potent in producing external damage than are external acts (cf. 42–43). He thus shifts the

debate from the assessment of the *importance* of the mental and physical constituents of an act to the assessment of the *causal efficacy* of mind and body.

2. The other "dangers" are more directly self-regarding though, again, we cannot be hard and fast: "actual loss of wealth," "susceptibility to disease," "loss of good character," "indecent exposure," "impaired intelligence."

3. See the story of Ugga of Vesali, an especially pious householder who, having embraced the "rules of training of the godly life," surrenders his wife to another man: "Yet I was not a whit discomfited at parting with my wife." (GS: vol. III, 144).

4. Precept 7 is sometimes separated into two precepts: (7) avoid worldy amusements, etc.; (8) avoid perfumes, etc. The prohibition against handling gold and silver is then treated as precept 10.

5. There are some examples of exceptionally pious householders instructing monks. K.S.: vol. 3, 203–6; G.S.: vol. 4, 144.

6. *The Book of Discipline* is divided into three major parts; the first part enumerates some 227 prescriptions and is of special interest to us. We shall not examine the other two sections. See Saddhatissa 1970: 75–76, for summaries of these other sections.

7. See Discipline, vol. I, 142–43 for a case of throwing stones in fun, which results in the accidental death of a bystander.

8. Two accounts of what is apparently the same incident depict the Buddha as tolerating, if not encouraging, suicide by a sick monk. But this appears to be an exceptional case, since the monk obtains arahatship upon his death. (KS: vol. III, 104–05).

9. *Sublime attitudes*, is the term used now by Aronson. They are also sometimes called "Blessed Dispositions." Aronson calls them "sublime ways of living" in his thesis. (Aronson 1975).

10. There is some promise of physical protection for the meditator against snakebites, fire, weapons, and poison, and more peaceful relations with deities and nonhuman creatures (Aronson 1975: 234; for other benefits: 216–17).

11. See "Aronson 1975: 282; and cf. 276–82 for other practices conducive to the "limb of enlightenment."

12. The translator of this material compares the section from which these passages come to Matthew 15:10: "Listen to this, and grasp it! It is not what goes into a man's mouth that pollutes him; it is what comes out of his mouth that pollutes a man."

13. As we have noted, "others" extends beyond human beings to include spiritual and subhuman beings as well. We need not go into the concern for the welfare of nonhuman beings. We simply emphasize that *all human beings* are included in this principle.

REFERENCES

Primary materials

Dialogues of the Buddha (DB). Trans. by T. W. Rhys Davids and C. A. F. Rhys Davids. I, 1899; reprinted 1956. II, 4th ed. 1959. III, 1920; reprinted, London: Pali Text Society, 1957.

The Book of the Gradual Sayings (GS). Trans. by F. L. Woodward. I, 1932; reprinted, 1970. II, 1933; reprinted, 1973. Trans. by E. M. Hare. III, 1934; reprinted, 1973. IV, 1935; reprinted 1965. V, 1936; reprinted London: Pali Text Society, 1972.

The Book of Kindred Sayings (KS). Trans. by C. A. F. Rhys Davids, I, 1917; reprinted, 1971. II, 1917; reprinted, 1971. Trans. by F. L. Woodward. III, 1925; reprinted, 1954. IV, 1927; reprinted, 1972. V. 1930; reprinted London: Pali Text Society, 1965.

The Middle Length Sayings (MLS). Trans. by I. B. Horner. I, 1954; reprinted, 1967. II, 1957; reprinted, 1970. III, 1959; reprinted London: Pali Text Society, 1967.

Dhammapada (D-SBE). In *Sacred Books of the East*. Volume X, pp. 3–89. Max Muller, ed. Delhi: Motilal Banarsidass, 1965.

Sutta-Nipata (SN-SBE). In *Sacred Books of the East*. Volume X, pp. 1–43. Max Muller, ed. Delhi: Motilal Banarsidass, 1965.

Book of Discipline (Discipline). Trans. by I. B. Horner. I, 1970; II, 1969; III, 1969.

A Discourse of the Buddha on the Path to God (PG). Trans. by T. W. Rhys Davids and Paul Debes. Kandy, Ceylon, Kandy, Sri-Lanka: Buddhist Publication Society, 1963.

Secondary Materials

ARONSON, HARVEY BEAR.
  1975 "Love, Compassion, Sympathetic Joy and Equanimity in Theravada Buddhism." Unpublished Ph.D. dissertation. University of Wisconsin (Madison) Ann Arbor, Mich.: University Microfilms.
  1978 "Equanimity in Theravada Buddhism." In A.K. Narain, ed., *Studies in Pali and Buddhism*. Delhi: D.K. Publishers.

CONZE, EDWARD.
  1959 *Buddhism: Its Essence and Development*. New York: Harper & Row.
  1964 *Buddhist Texts Through the Ages*. Edward Conze, ed. New York: Harper & Row.
  1970 *Buddhist Thought in India*. Ann Arbor: University of Michigan Press.

DANTO, ARTHUR C.
  1972 *Mysticism and Morality*. New York: Basic Books.

HAMILTON, CLARENCE H.
  1952 *Buddhism: A Religion of Infinite Compassion*. Indianapolis: Bobbs-Merrill Co.

KING, WINSTON L.
  1964   *In the Hope of Nibbana: An Essay on Theravada Buddhist Ethics.* LaSalle, Ill.: Open Court.
RHYS DAVIDS, T. W.
  1916   "Discipline (Buddhist)." In *Hastings Encyclopedia of Religion and Ethics.* Volume IV, pp. 214–15. James Hastings, ed. New York: Charles Scribner's Sons.
SADDHATISSA, H.
  1970   *Buddhist Ethics: Essence of Buddhism.* New York: George Braziller.

Conclusion

Considering all that has been undertaken in the name of comparative religious ethics, our study, while admittedly ambitious, is limited in scope. We have confined ourselves to the preliminary, though controversial and important task of providing definitions for morality and religion, and, tangentially, for law. We have seen fit to propose a method for conducting cross-cultural comparative analysis, where these notions overlap. Our method centers on practical justification, since we are convinced that whatever else we ought to know about morality, religion, and law, we would have missed something essential if we did not take sufficient account of their function in offering reasons for action. If we have succeeded in substantiating that claim, and in demonstrating with some precision the distinctions and relationships among moral, religious, and legal reasons in the process of guiding action, we will have accomplished our purpose.

In the emerging and as yet ill-defined area of the comparative study of religious ethics, there is, of course, much more to be investigated. We are aware that, for comprehensive understanding, it is not enough to analyze a few selected texts from various traditions, as we have done in the case of Christianity and Buddhism, or to examine only the more or less official accounts of nonliterate practical beliefs, as we have done in the case of the Navajo. So far as this study is concerned, our use of these materials is an illustration of the utility of our definitions and method. But apart from the obvious need to test our proposals against a broader range of materials, particularly in respect to Christianity and

Buddhism, there is the need to compare the normative practical teaching of groups like the Christians, Theravadins, and Navajo with the lived teaching in those traditions. It is a truism in the study of the history of religions that there is likely to be a discrepancy between the ideal beliefs of a tradition and the day-by-day operational beliefs of practitioners. We have made no contribution to studying that discrepancy, since we have explicitly restricted ourselves to the normative traditions.

It is important, we believe, to begin to get the normative tradition straight before we trace points of deviation, let alone study those deviations carefully. It is our contention that existing secondary literature respecting each of the traditions we have taken up does not, for one reason or another, satisfactorily explicate the Christian, Theravadin, or Navajo traditions as systems of practical justification. As to the Navajo practical code, Ladd's conclusions (1957), although the most systematically derived and still significant in their own right, stand in need of the revisions we have advanced. Not only did we find his account of Navajo validating and vindicating beliefs deficient in the moral sphere; we discovered that in order to understand fully Navajo practical convictions, we must make more room for religious beliefs than Ladd does. We were greatly aided by recent anthropological work, although even there we had to interpret and appropriate the results for our own purposes.

In the case of early Christianity and Theravada Buddhism, the secondary literature needs to be supplemented by the sort of systematic analysis we have conducted. We have tried to demonstrate that primary texts are susceptible to such analysis. Moreover, it seems to us that our framework can illuminate important features of the texts, and can elucidate the way the minds of the authors work, so to speak.

Consequently, the comparativist on our model has a distinctive contribution to make at three points. First, even though the comparativist may not have mastered the languages and scholarship of individual traditions, he or she can provide a perspective and a way of analyzing a tradition that otherwise does not occur to the specialists. Second, the comparativist can advance the work of religious ethicists by broadening their horizons. Third, the comparativist who does the sort of thing we recommend can contribute to a much neglected aspect of the study of the history of religions, namely, the systematic examination of religion and morality in various cultures. We trust our claims at this point will be assessed by those who are experts in the various traditions.

Our experience in producing the case studies in Part II goes some way toward removing the sting of the epithet that haunts all comparative work: "dilettantes compare." The reaction of experts whom we have consulted, particularly to the chapter on Theravada Buddhism, has been encouraging in this regard. In the studies of the Navajo and the Gospel of Matthew, we feel confident that the conclusions are at least respectable in relation to contemporary scholarship. This is not to say that our arguments and conclusions are uncontroversial.

There are other things in the field of comparative religious ethics that are worthy of attention, but which we have not considered. We have not, for example, addressed the full range of social scientific concerns in this area. If scientific inquiry, including social science, may be thought of as involving definitions and classification of data first, and then the explanation of that data, our study concerns primarily the first aspect, and the second only in part. We give extended attention to the identification and analysis of moral, religious, and (to a lesser extent) legal phenomena, as well as to the structure and dynamics of their interrelationship in selected traditions. In addition, insofar as the reconstruction of the logical relations or the internal structure of cultural values amounts to an exercise in explanation, we do explain the data. We do not, of course, offer the standard sort of social scientific explanations, namely, economic, sociological, or psychological accounts as to why particular moral and religious beliefs take the shape they do in given traditions (cf. Smart, 1973a: 43–44; 1973b: 132–138).

We neither disparage nor are indifferent to this second kind of explanation. But given many of the attempts at standard social scientific explanation of moral, religious, and legal matters, we feel it is important first to clarify exactly what it is we mean to explain, as well as to supply explanations on the level of meaning, before proceeding to the still more involved task of developing full-fledged scientific theories, to the extent that they are possible.

Within the scope of our concern, it is appropriate to make some general concluding observations about our study.

1. Our working definitions of morality and religion (moral action-

guide and religious action-guide) are useful for investigating materials from three highly disparate traditions. (The definition of law [legal action-guide] was not applied to all these cases, though it was indispensable in analyzing the Matthean materials.) The distinction between other-regardingness, in the material human welfare oriented sense, and sacred-regardingness, has proved to have great utility in differentiating and relating moral and religious action-guides in particular traditions.

While matters of definition will remain debatable, there is something intuitively obvious about this distinction as we have explicated it. Given the physical and emotional makeup of human beings, together with the generalized conditions of scarcity, competition, and conflict over primary goods, it is understandable that human groups would generate authoritative prescriptions built up around other-impinging considerations, i.e., those attitudes and acts that bear directly and dramatically on the basic material welfare of other human beings. This is one way of saying that other-impinging attitudes and acts are of central importance in human experience, no matter what circumstantial variations may exist among cultures in their articulation.

Similarly, given that the problems of interpretability (as we defined them) are unavoidable and significant in human experience, the widespread tendency of human beings to posit, in one form or another, a sacred realm, and to regard that realm as the source of solutions to those problems, as well as the source of authoritative prescriptions, is not surprising.

There is no doubt that both these emphases are present in the three traditions we examined. Nor is there any doubt that the various attempts to harmonize and integrate these emphases lie at the center of practical reflection among the Navajo, early Christians, and Theravada Buddhists.

2. Our scheme for analyzing practical justification in different religious ethical systems appears to have utility. We had no difficulty reconstructing the respective patterns of justification according to our categories, and we were able to show the specific relevance of legal reasoning to moral and religious justification in the Matthean materials.

We recognize that in employing our scheme for comparing types of practical justification or practical reasoning in different cultures we are charting a course through troubled waters. There is considerable debate these days over the cross-cultural comparability of beliefs and patterns of reasoning. As between those who hold that certain basic criteria of rationality are universal (Lukes 1970: 208), thus making cross-cultural comparisons of beliefs possible, and those who do not (Winch 1970: 78–111), we stand with the former group. On the basis of our investigations (which are admittedly limited), we see no cause to doubt the applicability of our general scheme of practical justification to radically divergent traditions. We conclude that our own specific applications demonstrate the comparability of moral and religious materials that have emerged from very different settings. We are not dogmatic about this. We will be eager to see whether our applications hold up under scholarly scrutiny. There is always the danger in a work such as this that the comparativist will force his or her terminology and method, and thereby distort the beliefs of the subjects under study. Presumably, if distortions occur, they can and will be detected by experts.

3. Finally, we call attention to the diversity of types of justification that float, so to speak, within each of the three traditions. This is not surprising in the light of the much advertised propensity of human beings for tolerating intellectual and practical inconsistencies and conflicts. We emphasize, however, that to call attention to inconsistency presupposes the pertinence of patterns of consistency and coherence. Without these we could not identify inconsistency and conflict in the first place. Our types of validation, in particular, constitute such patterns, and because several types are applicable to each case, we are able to locate the points of tension or potential tension within that tradition.

It is also worth noting that the diversity of types of practical justification within each tradition does not necessarily strengthen the case of the conceptual relativists. Our evidence, limited though it is, suggests that the range of variability in patterns of practical reasoning is determinate, not indeterminate. It further suggests that there are certain descriptive universals in matters of practical justification within which variations may be plotted and compared. Much work remains to be done in confirming and clarifying these patterns in relation to the practical experience of human beings. We hope we have contributed to the enterprise.

REFERENCES

LADD, JOHN.
    1957   *Structure of a Moral Code.* Cambridge: Harvard University
            Press.
LUKES, STEVEN.
    1970   "Some Problems About Rationality." In *Rationality,* pp. 194–
            213, Bryan R. Wilson, ed. New York: Harper & Row.
SMART, NINIAN.
    1973a   *The Phenomenon of Religion.* London: Macmillan.
    1973b   *The Science of Religion and the Sociology of Knowledge:
            Some Methodological Questions.* Princeton: Princeton Uni-
            versity Press.
WINCH, PETER.
    1970   "Understanding a Primitive Society." In *Rationality,* pp. 78–
            111, Bryan R. Wilson, ed. New York: Harper & Row.

Notable Books for the Comparative Study of Religious Ethics

Aronson, Harvey B. *Love, Compassion, Sympathetic Joy and Equanimity in Theravada Buddhism.* Ann Arbor, Mich.: University Microfilms, 1975.

Baier, Kurt. *The Moral Point of View: A Rational Basis of Ethics.* Ithaca, N.Y.: Cornell University Press, 1958.

Banton, Michael, ed. *Anthropological Approaches to the Study of Religion.* London: Tavistock Publications, 1966.

Barnsley, John H. *Social Reality of Ethics: The Comparative Analysis of Moral Codes.* London: Routledge & Kegan Paul, 1972.

Benn, S. I., and Mortimore, G. W. *Rationality and the Social Sciences.* London: Routledge & Kegan Paul, 1976.

Benn, S. I., and Peters, R. S. *The Principles of Political Thought.* 2d ed. New York: The Free Press, 1965.

Bohannan, Paul, ed. *Law and Warfare.* Garden City, N.Y.: Natural History Press, 1967.

Brandt, Richard B. *Hopi Ethics.* Chicago: University of Chicago Press, 1954.

Broad, C. D. *Five Types of Ethical Theory.* Paterson, N.J.: Littlefield, Adams & Co., 1959.

Carter, Curtis L., ed. *Skepticism and Moral Principles.* Evanston, Ill.: New University Press, 1973.

Castaneda, Hector-Neri, and Nakhnikian, George, eds. *Morality and the Language of Conduct.* Detroit: Wayne State University Press, 1963.

Christian, William A. *Meaning and Truth in Religion.* Princeton: Princeton University Press, 1964.

Danto, Arthur. *Mysticism and Morality.* New York: Basic Books, 1972.

D'Arcy, Eric. *Human Acts: An Essay in Their Moral Evaluation.* Oxford: Oxford University Press, 1963.

Durkheim, Emile. *Sociology and Philosophy.* Translated by D. F. Pocock, Glencoe, Ill.: Free Press, 1953.

Edel, May and Abraham. *Anthropology and Ethics.* Springfield, Ill.: Charles C. Thomas, 1959.

Emmet, Dorothy. *Rules, Roles and Relations.* London: Macmillan, 1966.

Frankena, William. *Ethics.* 2d ed. Englewood Cliffs, N.J.: Prentice-Hall, 1973.

Fürer-Haimendorf, Christoph von. *Morals and Merit: A Study of Values and Social Controls in South Asian Societies.* Chicago: University of Chicago Press, 1967.

Gauthier, David P. *Practical Reasoning.* Oxford: Oxford University Press, 1963.

Gluckman, Max. *Politics, Law and Ritual in Tribal Society.* New York: New American Library, 1965.

Golding, Martin P. *Philosophy of Law.* Englewood Cliffs, N.J.: Prentice-Hall, 1975.

Hare, R. M. *Freedom and Reason.* New York: Oxford University Press, 1965.

Hare, R. M. *The Language of Morals.* Oxford: Oxford University Press, 1952.

Hart, H. L. A. *The Concept of Law.* Oxford: Oxford University Press, 1961.

Hobhouse, L. T. *Morals in Evolution.* New York: Henry Holt, 1916.

Hoebel, E. Adamson. *The Law of Primitive Man: A Study in Comparative Legal Dynamics.* Cambridge, Mass.: Harvard University Press, 1954.

Hollis, Martin. *Models of Man: Philosophical Thoughts on Social Action.* Cambridge: Cambridge University Press, 1977.

Houlden, J. L. *Ethics and the New Testament.* London: Penguin Books, 1973.

Hudson, W. D. *Modern Moral Philosophy.* Garden City, N.Y.: Anchor/Doubleday, 1970.

Kant, Immanuel. *Foundations of the Metaphysics of Morals.* Translated by Lewis White Beck. Indianapolis: Bobbs-Merrill Co., 1959.

Kemp, John. *Reason, Action and Morality.* London: Routledge & Kegan Paul, 1964.

Kent, Edward A., ed. *Law and Philosophy.* New York: Appleton-Century-Crofts, 1970.

King, Winston L. *In the Hope of Nibbana.* LaSalle, Ill.: Open Court, 1964.

Kluckhohn, Clyde. *Culture and Behavior.* Glencoe, Ill.: Free Press, 1964.

Kraemer, Hendrik. *Christian Message in a Non-Christian World.* Grand Rapids, Mich.: Kregel Publications, 1956.

Ladd, John, ed. *Ethical Relativism*. Belmont, Cal.: Wadsworth, 1973.

Ladd, John. *Structure of a Moral Code: A Philosophical Analysis of Ethical Discourse Applied to the Ethics of the Navaho Indians*. Cambridge, Mass.: Harvard University Press, 1957.

Leiser, Burton M. *Custom, Law, and Morality*. Garden City, N.Y.: Anchor/Doubleday, 1969.

MacBeath, Alexander. *Experiments in Living: A Study in the Nature and Foundation of Ethics or Morals in the Light of Recent Work in Social Anthropology*. London: Macmillan, 1952.

Malinowski, Bronislaw. *Crime and Custom in Savage Society*. Totowa, N.J.: Littlefield, Adams & Co., 1967.

Malinowski, Bronislaw. *Magic, Science and Religion*. 2d ed. Garden City, N.Y.: Anchor/Doubleday, 1954.

Middleton, John, ed. *Gods and Rituals*. Garden City, N.Y.: Natural History Press, 1967.

Middleton, John, ed. *Magic, Witchcraft, and Curing*. Garden City, N.Y.: Natural History Press, 1967.

Middleton, John, ed. *Myth and Cosmos*. Garden City, N.Y.: Natural History Press, 1967.

Ossowska, Maria. *Social Determinants of Moral Ideas*. Philadelphia: University of Pennsylvania Press, 1970.

Otto, Rudolf. *The Idea of the Holy: An Inquiry into the Non-Rational Factor in the Idea of the Divine and Its Relation to the Rational*. 2d ed. Translated by John W. Harvey. New York: Oxford University Press, 1950.

Outka, Gene H., and Ramsey, Paul, eds. *Norm and Context in Christian Ethics*. New York: Charles Scribner's Sons, 1968.

Outka, Gene, and Reeder, John P. Jr., eds. *Religion and Morality*. Garden City, N.Y.: Anchor/Doubleday, 1973.

Phillips, D. Z., ed. *Religion and Understanding*. Oxford: Basil Blackwell, 1967.

Pospisil, Leopold. *Anthropology of Law*. New York: Harper & Row, 1971.

Piaget, Jean. *Moral Judgment of the Child*. Glencoe, Ill.: Free Press, 1965.

Quiniton, Anthony, ed. *Political Philosophy*. London: Oxford University Press, 1967.

Ramsey, Ian T., ed. *Christian Ethics and Contemporary Philosophy*. New York: Macmillan, 1966.

Rawls, John. *A Theory of Justice*. Cambridge, Mass.: Harvard University Press, 1971.

Reichard, Gladys A. *Navaho Religion: A Study of Symbolism*. Princeton, N.J.: Princeton University Press, 1974.

Saddhatissa, H. *Buddhist Ethics*. New York: George Braziller, 1970.

Twiss, Sumner B. *The Dialectic of Moral Communication: A Conceptual Inquiry*. Ann Arbor, Mich.: University Microfilms, 1974.

Von Wright, Georg Henrik. *The Varieties of Goodness*. London: Routledge & Kegan Paul, 1963.

Wallace, G., and Walker, A. D. M., eds. *The Definition of Morality*. London: Methuen, 1970.

Warnock, G. J. *Contemporary Moral Philosophy*. London: Macmillan, 1967.

Warnock, G. J. *The Object of Morality*. London: Methuen, 1971.

Weber, Max. *The Sociology of Religion*. 4th ed., rev. Translated by Ephraim Fischoff. Boston: Beacon Press, 1963.

Weber, Max. *From Max Weber: Essays in Sociology*. Translated and edited by H. H. Gerth and C. Wright Mills. New York: Oxford University Press, 1946.

Index